Digital
Marketing

Digital Marketing

Strategies for
Online Success

Godfrey Parkin

Published in 2009 by New Holland Publishers (UK) Ltd
London • Cape Town • Sydney • Auckland
www.newhollandpublishers.com
Garfield House, 86–88 Edgware Road, London W2 2EA, United Kingdom
80 McKenzie Street, Cape Town 8001, South Africa
Unit 1, 66 Gibbes Street, Chatswood, NSW 2067, Australia
218 Lake Road, Northcote, Auckland, New Zealand

10 9 8 7 6 5 4 3 2 1

A catalogue record for this book is available from the British Library

ISBN 978 1 84773 487 7

Publishing Director: Rosemary Wilkinson
Publisher: Aruna Vasudevan
Editor: Julia Shone
Inside design: Sarah Williams
Cover design: District-6 Design
Production: Melanie Dowland

Reproduction by Pica Digital Pte. Ltd., Singapore
Printed and bound in India by Replika Press

The paper used to produce this book is sourced from sustainable forests.

Contents

Introduction

This book is a guide to succeeding in today's business world, the marketing rules of which have been forever changed by the collective power of the online consumer.

At the end of this book you will find a guide that summarizes the action recommendations covered in this publication. It takes you through the strategy development and implementation process step by step, and poses the questions that you need to answer to build a successful emarketing approach, or an entire ebusiness. Although you will learn the essential tactics for mastering every element of the emarketing landscape, this book is about marketing strategy, not about web technology.

You can learn technical hints, tips, and website optimization secrets from my seminars or from hundreds of other sources. But there is little point in building a website or fine-tuning your emarketing tactics unless your strategy is right in the first place. To build a competitive strategy to capture the loyalty of your online consumers requires rethinking your vision for your business from the ground up. It also requires an intimate understanding of what this online environment is all about, from the perspective of your business, from your competitors' point of view, and particularly in the eyes of your target customers as individuals. Without those insights, you cannot begin to put together a digital strategy that has any hope of succeeding.

This book will provide you with the insights and inspiration, as well as the step-by-step processes, to succeed in marketing to the new consumer.

Wherever it is necessary to dip into technical detail I do so in laypersons' terms. A glossary is included at the back of the book for easy reference and for clarifying any term that is not clearly defined in the text.

Though I am a closet geek, I'm not one of those people who believe that technology in itself has any real value. There are many instances where new technology is merely a solution looking for a problem. I have been immersed in this world of the web for too many years, have linked customers, businesses and brands through too many online experiences, battled too many IT policy makers, been frustrated by too many miracle software packages, been disappointed by too many consultants, and confronted too many medieval corporate prejudices, to be anything but pragmatic about technology's role in strategic business growth.

Properly used, the internet unleashes personal communication and experience-sharing on a scale unprecedented in history.

Through that pragmatism, there's a very simple, powerful, burning light that all of us need to keep in focus: properly used, the internet frees customers and marketers from the constraints of time and space, which in turn unleashes personal communication and experience-sharing on a scale unprecedented in history.

Any online marketing model which still uses the internet as merely a cheap means to broadcast canned one-way messages is simply missing the point. All companies need their brand bibles for defining what their brands are and how they seek to be perceived. But those brand bibles need to evolve constantly to stay relevant to changing consumer environments. Marketers can actively add huge value to their brands by embracing the power of the web as a catalyst for exploration, organic growth, experience-sharing, and relationship-building – making every customer both a convincing salesperson and a compelling advertising medium.

So why are the brilliant examples of how it should be done so few and far between? Why is it that almost every digital project that I get involved in seems to be seeking to use technology to re-centralize the locus of control, to choke off collaboration and to make marketing more tightly administered than ever before?

The answer is that most businesses have an increasingly fuzzy vision of what their future should be, so their tendency is to clutch tightly to the past. As the world around them changes faster and faster, the future becomes ever more blurred and uncertain. Without a bright light to head toward, they feel safer not to move away from their fundamentals and put their efforts into shoring up their defences. Those companies that do stumble forward usually head in the general direction that they have always followed, tactically groping their way through the fog, turning to dodge obstacles, and grasping at opportunities reactively as they fly by. Without a vision, they have no idea where they are headed. Without a vision, they cannot put together an effective strategy.

> **You first need a clear idea of what you want to build before you dig the foundations.**

One of my recent clients wanted to throw out all the marketing solutions currently in play and start from scratch. Well, nothing wrong with wielding a new broom. But it is the strategy of 'starting from scratch' that I take issue with: this company wanted to get a new content management system and build a new website, then create new marketing communications activities that would run on it. The argument is that you first need a good foundation before you can build.

But surely you first need a clear idea of what you want to build before you dig the foundations?

Throughout this book I will be using the terms 'marketing', 'emarketing', 'marketer', and 'online consumers' repeatedly. Without becoming too academic about terminology, this is what these terms mean to me:

- **MARKETING** is the overall set of activities, processes and attitudes that a business applies to understanding the needs of its customers, and developing, supplying and communicating products or services that address those needs. It includes all the activities, inputs and outputs that might be classified under the traditional 'Four P's of Marketing': Product, Place, Price and Promotion. Since the web is increasingly one of the places where individuals and companies market, marketing includes what you do online.

- **EMARKETING** is the same as marketing, except that it focuses on those consumers whose attitudes and behaviours are being transformed through their online experiences. An 'online customer' is not necessarily someone who buys online or who engages with marketing experiences online. An online customer is a customer (or potential customer) whose life is influenced by digital communication, peer-to-peer collaboration and the digital revolution. Emarketing is about people who use the internet; it is not merely about the internet as an advertising medium. Emarketing is the collection of processes that seeks to understand and respond to customer needs in the online environment. It forms relationships with customers, builds brands, and drives business to online and offline channels. Emarketing drives visitors to your site or other digital experiences that have been designed to be customer-centric. It delivers a remarkably satisfying experience throughout the entire period during which the customer is in contact with your brand (from research to selection, sale to delivery, consumption and referral), and encourages the visitor to share that experience with others.

- **MARKETERS** include all the people involved in the process of marketing, both on the 'client side' (such as product managers, brand managers or marketing communications people) and on the agency side (such as account directors, creatives, media planners or market researchers). Emarketers are those marketers engaged in trying to communicate with online consumers. In many manufacturing or service companies there is no real distinction between marketing and emarketing people; in most advertising agencies the digital operations are typically kept segregated from the traditional above-the-line media operations, not because this makes marketing sense but because each requires a very different business model.

▨ ONLINE CONSUMERS are those whose lives have been influenced by digital technologies. They include people who never buy anything online, who never play online games and who don't have a Facebook page. If they use email, or own a mobile phone, or access the web for any reason, they are online consumers because their information-sharing, opinion-formation and decision-making processes are inherently influenced by the internet.

This book will help to build an understanding of how our customers – consumers and businesses – are changing the way they become informed, form opinions and make purchasing decisions. It will explain, in non-technical terms, all of the interrelated concepts, tools and processes that make up the field of customer-centric emarketing – and how to use them to best effect. Most importantly, it will lay out ways in which your business can develop a clear vision of the immediate future and build a strategy that will ensure commercial success.

Emarketing is all about building relationships with these people, getting to know them and getting them to know you, or at least your brands. In addition, while traditional marketing is neatly framed by the four P's, emarketing spills over into territory previously occupied by other corporate silos, such as sales, customer service, IT, finance and corporate strategy. A small business that is unencumbered by corporate structures can gain some benefit from the web with, for example, email marketing and a brochure-ware site, but major players need to be able to integrate all their internal processes in real time, at web speed, or else their investment in advertising, promotion or even the website itself, may be completely wasted.

Emarketers may not control those out-of-silo projects, but they do have to initiate and drive them.

I tend to use the terms 'the web' and 'the internet' interchangeably, but of course they are not the same thing – the not-so-user-friendly internet has been with us for longer than the microwave oven, while the web (the graphical, point-and-click, browser-based environment on the internet) has only been around since 1992.

Finally, this book is peppered with what my American colleagues like to call 'factoids'. Any facts mentioned in it are either derived from formal studies carried out by various research bodies, from documented case studies or from my own professional experiences or those of my colleagues. Since this is not an academic treatise, I have not annotated every statement with footnotes and reference sources.

Online in context 1

By 2008 the internet was fully validated around the world as an indispensable component of any marketing mix. Online advertising expenditure had leapt by 50 per cent on the previous year. The web was the place where creativity blossomed. Online video was ubiquitous. Despite having spawned dozens of me-too competitors, YouTube served more than 200 million videos a day. Marketers scrambled to create their own branded video channels. An online community allowing women to share videos of their shoes (called, of course, Shoetube.tv) was launched, attracted a huge following, and then within a year reinvented itself, adding designer boutiques and e-commerce. It was a breakout year for women and the 'silver-surfer' older generations, who started to dominate web usage and ecommerce. Even the Queen of England started her own YouTube channel. The Dalai Lama started to Twitter. The Vatican opted for a more conservative approach, and launched its own daily podcast.

Online experiences provided by global brands such as Coke, Wrigleys, Pampers and dozens of others all received millions of unique visitors. Consumer goods websites, microsites, nanosites and social sites proliferated. Google consolidated its position as the largest advertising agency – and advertising medium – in the world. Along with other bands, Radiohead rubbed salt in the wounds of dying business models by launching their new album online on a pay-what-you-like basis and made more money than they had on all their previous albums combined. Apple dropped 'computer' from its name, in anticipation of the mobile phone becoming the new web access device. The car industry moved billions of marketing dollars from conventional media into digital media, not as a trial, but as the result of experience. Television viewership and newspaper readership started falling around the world. Mothers in America spent seven times as long on the web as they did watching television.

Consumers are online, en masse. Digital marketing is no longer a peripheral experiment, but an essential fundamental in the strategy of every serious marketer.

Yet while the avant-garde of marketers are building online customer relationships, the majority are still building websites. A website is not enough, no matter how 'optimized' it may be. In fact, websites as you know them may be quite unnecessary if your emarketing is dynamic and focused.

> **A website is not enough, no matter how 'optimized' it may be.**

To many businesses, the website has become an end in itself, the new vehicle by which senior marketing people conspicuously wield their power and importance.

And what status symbols they have become! At a recent symposium I shared a lunch table with two rather senior marketers from different companies. One alluded, with some pride, to the fact that he had spent a small fortune on a new website. The other smugly announced that he had spent three times that, and that was before the integration costs. Not only does a new website give you something to boast about, it can give you total control over every micro-move that customers and marketers make. If you were not a bureaucrat before the emarketing revolution, it is hard to resist becoming one now.

It is not too late for marketers to back out of this pretentious, site-centric cul-de-sac and rediscover the creativity, connectivity and infinite potential of the world wide web. Social media, user-generated content, marketing 2.0, web 2.0, web 3.0 and mobile marketing are now on the agenda of every progressive marketing company. These concepts, how they are creatively interpreted and what they evolve into, are some of the building blocks of New Marketing. Customer-centric online marketing is your future, or you're history.

> If your current approach to emarketing consists of a website, a few banner advertisements, and a budget for Search Engine Optimization (SEO), you are not really taking the new consumer seriously. It is time to rethink your strategic vision.

In many respects, the future has already happened. You don't need a crystal ball to see clearly how digital lifestyles and the technologies that connect us all will fundamentally change the way companies run their businesses; you simply need to look beyond your own comfort zone at what is happening in other industries, in other countries, in other cultures, in other generations. Or, if that is asking too much, you can look at the impact of the web a little closer to home, in your consumer bases, in your families, or in your own personal behaviour. People need to accept that these influences are neither isolated, nor trivial or transient; they are all interconnected and interrelated, and collectively they are deeply disruptive.

THE ONLINE LANDSCAPE

I have been running businesses in what analysts like to call the 'digital space' since 1991, when commercial use of the internet was first permitted. While I have tried not to be cast as a zealot, I have always been an optimist. Every step of the way, I have encountered people – academics, venture capitalists, business partners, prospective customers, even technologists – who have viewed the web with a mix of scepticism, denial and fear.

The digital revolution shakes things up, and established models do not like being shaken, particularly if they are fragile.

Ask anyone to give you a few examples of what they think of as digital, and they tend to respond with a list that includes computers, cameras, iPhones, printers or cell phones. These are just 'things'. True, they all use digital technology to function, but they are still merely tools. In themselves, they are not responsible for the digital revolution. Very few people seek to own 'things' for their own sake. It is what those things can do for them that drives their desire to own them.

The true digital revolution is not in the appliances, but in the processes that they improve: designing, learning, sharing, communicating, job-searching, dating, researching, purchasing, exploring, and all the other activities that occupy your time. Digital technologies, particularly the web and the mobile phone, have enhanced the processes that you live by. Those processes have become cheaper, faster, more reliable, more convenient or more satisfying. And where digital technologies have facilitated those enhancements, people have adopted them voraciously. It took 125 years for landline telephones to reach one billion subscribers worldwide (that happened only in 2001). In 2002, the number of mobile phone users passed the 1 billion mark. It had taken 21 years. From there, the mobile phone global user base trebled to 3 billion people in a mere 5 years.

> The true digital revolution is not in the appliances, but in the processes that they improve.

Sometimes the digitally enhanced process is a simple improvement on what already exists. Sometimes it is a replacement. The former is easy for companies to invest in, since it clearly adds value. The latter usually meets with resistance, since it threatens established investments and business models. It is far easier for a new company to succeed in a new business model, than for an existing company to abandon its existing approach and start again.

A BRIEF HISTORICAL PERSPECTIVE

Because the internet keeps evolving so rapidly, people tend to think of it as a new phenomenon. In fact, the internet has been around for longer than Microsoft Windows. It started out during the Cold War. The 1960s were a time of mutually assured destruction, the Cuban missile crisis, the assassination of John F. Kennedy and the Soviet invasion of Czechoslovakia. Computers were huge mainframes, connected only by dedicated cables. The military feared that a missile strike against one computer would break the chain that connected all of them, so they asked a think-tank of scientists at the Advanced Research Projects Agency (ARPA) to come up with a fail-safe solution.

The result was the first computer network. It used revolutionary concepts that still form the basis of the internet today. At the time, if you wanted to send a file from one computer to another, you sent it as one big file along a dedicated cable. While it was being sent, you could not use the cable for anything else, and if it got corrupted along the way, it was useless at the other end.

The first innovation was to break the individual data files into thousands of smaller 'packets' and send them off. Each packet was handled like a postcard, with the address of its destination and its sender. This allowed multiple messages to use the same cable system simultaneously. When they arrived at the other end, the packets were re-assembled into the original file, and even if some packets got lost or corrupted, the result was usable.

The second innovation was to build a mesh of cables like a large fishnet across the country, with a machine at each connection point that would receive the packets and route them to the next node. If a strand or a node in the net was broken, these 'routers' would send the packets down the next most efficient path. This 'packet switching' system was tested using four academic institutions in 1969, and the resulting network, the ARPANET, was the precursor of the internet.

There is a delightful irony in the fact that a system intended to strengthen the military-industrial complex became the most massively democratising engine of global freedom since the printing press.

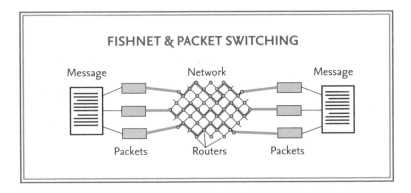

FISHNET & PACKET SWITCHING

The first email to use the '@' sign in its address was sent in 1971.

The ARPANET expanded, and other similar networks were developed. But they all used different standards, so communication between networks was problematic. By 1983 a common communication technology called TCP/IP, for Transmission Control Protocol/Internet Protocol, became the only standard communication protocol for computer networks. Still used today, TCP/IP allowed all the diverse networks around the world to talk to each other, and the internet was born.

An internet is a network of networks, and for many years 'the Internet' was spelt with a capital 'I' to differentiate it. In the 21st century, the internet has become such a household term that most sources have abandoned capitalization of the term.

The internet remained a closed shop for many years, with only scientists, governments and academic institutions having access. It was controlled by the United States National Science Foundation, and commercial or personal use was banned. All of that changed in 1991, when the ban was lifted and the internet was opened up to anyone who wanted to use it.

A remarkable thing happened. A point-and-click interface was developed at the University of Wisconsin, which made it simple for non-programmers to use the internet. This was a potentially very valuable piece of software, yet it was made available for free. The software, called Gopher, was downloaded by thousands of people, and it fuelled an explosion in usage of the internet.

The following year, in 1992, the internet evolved from simply a way to move files around into a way to tap directly into the contents of those files. Tim Berners-Lee, an English scientist working at CERN, the particle accelerator institute in Geneva, invented a way to 'link' from within the text of one document to within another document at the click of a mouse. He called this system 'hypertext'. He created a software package that allowed anyone to use hypertext to build what is called a website today, and he released that incredibly powerful tool for free. It was immediately downloaded and used by thousands of people. The name of the software was 'World Wide Web' and the web was born.

Hypertext is not a programming language, but a means of 'marking up' a document so that 'web browsers' such as Internet Explorer or Firefox know how to display it, and so that any system searching for the document can identify what it is and what it is about. This Hypertext Mark-up Language, or HTML, is still the basis of most websites on the internet today.

The first graphical user interface to take full advantage of HTML was released in 1993. In a business model that continues to make developers wealthy, it was released for free. Developed by a team led by Marc Andreessen at the University of Illinois, it was called 'Mosaic' and similarly to earlier free releases, it was downloaded by millions of people. Mosaic became the de facto web browser standard, and turned the internet into a marketing medium.

After graduating, Marc Andreessen evolved Mosaic into Netscape Navigator, and with Netscape's IPO, he became a millionaire in his early 20s and the poster-boy for the dot-com pre-bubble-burst era. A few years later, America Online acquired his company for more than US$4 billion. (In the meantime, Microsoft had licensed Mosaic from the University of Illinois, and developed from it its own browser, called Internet Explorer, which would rapidly send Netscape into obscurity, before it rose again in the form of Firefox.)

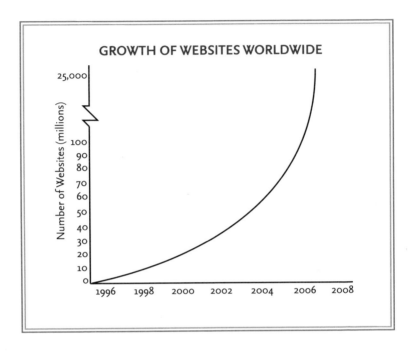

While this short history of the origins of the web may be interesting, what happened after the release of Mosaic is nothing short of astonishing. By the end of 1993 there were 50 websites on what had become known as the world wide web. Six years later there were 17 million. By the end of 2006, there were more than 100 million websites. By 2008 there were an estimated 25 billion web pages, and one sixth of the world's population (1.4 billion people) had internet access. Global business-to-consumer (B2C) ecommerce amounted to $517 billion in 2008. Business-to-business (B2B) ecommerce was $5.2 trillion. That makes business on the internet larger than the GDP of Japan, the world's second largest economy. The growth is exponential, and by 2012 B2C will double, with $1.2 trillion changing hands online, and B2B transactions soaring to $12.4 trillion. (I am using the American billion, which is a thousand million, and the American trillion, which is a thousand billion).

Far from slowing down, the web is growing at an exponential rate. Even though countries such as the United States, Japan, South Korea and the Scandinavian countries are virtually saturated, the number of internet users in the rest of the world keeps climbing, as does the volume of ecommerce. At the same time, the bandwidths available to the general public keeps getting faster, while costs keep on falling.

The bandwidth capacity of a dial-up modem is usually 56 Kbps. In reality, you never get that speed because any connection is as slow as the slowest piece of line through which your signal must pass. At dial-up speeds it would take you over 20 hours to download a music CD. With early-stage broadband, you get around one megabit per second. At this bandwidth you can download a CD in 45 minutes. With more advanced broadband speeds, which are available in Europe and Asia, you would get anything from 40 Mbps to 90 Mbps, and that same CD downloads in less than a minute. Finally, at the 4.2 Gbps bandwidths that are currently being tested for Internet2, you could

@ Bandwidth is the speed at which data travels. The higher your bandwidth, the less time you have to wait for web pages or files to download. It is measured in kilobits per second (Kbps), or megabits per second (Mbps). (A megabit is a thousand kilobits.) Really high-speed bandwidths are measured in gigabits per second (Gbps). Bandwidth is always measured in bits, whereas file size is usually measured in bytes. A byte is approximately eight bits. The industry standard is to abbreviate bytes with a capital B and bits with a lower-case b to distinguish the two. It is not unusual for internet service providers to use these terms in a misleading fashion, particularly in their marketing material. A one megabit per second (1 Mbps) connection cannot download a one megabyte (1 MB) file in one second – it will actually take eight seconds.

download the CD in less than a second while watching a full-screen high-definition streaming video at the same time.

Of course, this is not as fast as it gets. Most broadband still uses existing copper cable infrastructure or a wireless signal. Fibre optic cable holds the promise of truly amazing speeds. Recent tests have demonstrated the potential to move the equivalent of 1,900 music CDs across a single strand of fibre in less than a second! But then, who listens to CDs these days?

THE IMMEDIATE FUTURE

Because of its organic nature, there will, without doubt, be surprises in the future of the web. But some trends are unmistakable. Ten characteristics will define the nature of the web in the immediate future. The web will be:

- fast
- disruptive
- global
- social
- virtual

- mobile
- ubiquitous
- local
- disintermediating
- contextual.

- FAST: The speeds at which you can access the internet are becoming faster. While there are significant inequalities among and within countries, the fastest data transmission speeds that are available to the general public from commercial providers have rocketed upwards over the past year or two. For many web users, flipping through pages on a website is already as fast as changing television channels. There is simply no download wait. Over the next year or two, internet users will be able to watch hi-definition videos, run web-based applications and engage in 3-D virtual worlds without annoying delays or interruptions. The implication for marketers is that online communication will be less constrained. There will be more creative freedom within existing frameworks such as websites, rich media banners or video overlays, as well as the potential for entirely new forms of marketing engagement.

▨ MOBILE: The web has gone mobile, and the mobile phone is the new computer. People can increasingly access the internet while on the move through a number of technologies. Most laptops are equipped with wireless cards that will allow them to connect through local WiFi 'hotspots' that are virtually everywhere – in airports, hotels, conference centres, on university campuses, in coffee shops and in bookstores. In addition, higher-end mobile phones come equipped with 3G, HSDPA, or HSUPA technology. This allows the phone to be used as a web browser, or as a broadband modem that will connect a computer to the web from anywhere through the mobile phone network. HSDPA cards that plug into a laptop do the same thing.

Over the past few years there has been a concerted move by cities and towns across the globe to make high-speed broadband access available to their entire populations. Enlightened city governments realize that access to the web is a utility much like electricity. They realize that providing it to everyone can give a significant boost to education and commerce in the city, and can be a boon to smaller businesses and lower-income families. A technology known as Wi-Max can enable a city to become a vast wide-area hotspot, serving up internet access at speeds that outpace mobile-phone or landline solutions. Typically, this municipal Wi-Fi access (known as muni-WiFi) is either free, or is supported by advertising. While it is relatively inexpensive to set it up (the city of Philadelphia spent nearly US$17 million), the political opposition from telecommunications companies and the ability of service providers to retain customers presents major obstacles. Many over-ambitious city-wide projects have stumbled as a result of poor consumer up-take, but smaller projects with a more focused purpose have been very successful.

▨ DISRUPTIVE: The internet is not something that is ever going to mature. It has always been a disruptive technology, and it becomes more disruptive every day. The easier it becomes for ordinary people to create and share content and applications, the more potential there is for overnight viral outbreaks of culture-changing behaviour. The impact of this on business, and on marketing in particular, is most keenly felt in the unpredictability of consumer trends and the rapidly diminishing life-spans of products. The nature of change is itself changing – change is no longer linear. You can no longer approximate the future by plotting on a graph where you were in each of the past five years and then simply extrapolating forward. You can no longer rely on annual planning and budgeting cycles, and you have to be prepared to take risks, to abandon projects mid-stream, and to make tactical leaps of faith. The internet is an inescapable agent of change – understand it, work with it, or be marginalized by it.

Europeans spend as much time online as watching television.

■ UBIQUITOUS: The web will become ubiquitous. It will be seamlessly integrated into the lives of every person who has access to it, and into the processes and planning of all marketing organizations. Already, Europeans spend as much time online as watching television, with those aged 16 to 24 spending 10 percent more time online than they do watching TV. In Britain, over-65s are spending more time online than any other age group. However, ubiquity does not mean that everyone will have access. The so-called 'digital divide' will still be around. But within major target consumer sectors, the web will become even more of a mainstream means of communication, and the place where consumers go to access all their media: movies, television programmes, music, news, sports, magazines, photography, phone calls and correspondence. With the amount of online content formatted for mobile use growing every day, the web is now on the verge of being available anytime and anywhere.

🕅 GLOBAL: One of the biggest advantages of the web for small to medium businesses is the ready access it provides to remote markets, nationally and internationally. This advantage of the web is often dismissed as irrelevant by large businesses, whose vision does not extend beyond their core strength: geographic proximity to their local markets. Before the internet, while the need for widespread physical presence was a massive barrier to entry for small businesses, it was a bankable asset for large businesses. Today, the reverse is true. As consumers move their interactions with vendors online, a company that insists that its customers physically come to its premises to do business can easily be outflanked by a smaller competitor who provides a more satisfying online experience. Perhaps the most successful companies today are those who have managed to integrate their online and brick-and-mortar operations in a way that provides an optimal service to their customers.

The downside of global ecommerce is that local businesses now face competition from foreign companies they may never

---

@ Global markets, too, are today only a click away. If you are selling gold-plated garden gnomes from your road-side farm stall, your business depends on the hundred or so cars that pass by every day. On the internet, your market expands exponentially. You can now sell your gnomes to people in Korea, Russia or Brazil. No longer do you need to spend a fortune on placing newspaper or television advertisements in multiple countries; an ad on Google that costs you 20 cents every time a potential customer clicks on it to get to your website will do just fine. You don't need to rent and fit out physical stores around the globe. You simply need a search-optimized, commerce-optimized website, and an arrangement with a shipping company.

have heard of. National retail chains selling, for instance, HDTV television sets, face the prospect of their local target market buying the same models from online suppliers on the other side of the globe at half the price, even after shipping, duties and taxes. I know someone who did an overland motorcycle trip from London to Cape Town, and instead of equipping herself through the motorcycle shop across the street, she sourced everything from online suppliers in China at a third of the cost. The local store never knew how much business it had lost.

You can, of course, try to compete on price, but it is usually a strategic mistake to allow yourself to be commoditized. Your best defence is to change your business vision: instead of seeing yourself as a reseller of 'stuff' you need to focus on becoming a provider of a superior experience that is engaging, compelling and trustworthy, and adds value to your customer's buying process.

▨   LOCAL: In the same way as local radio has experienced a renaissance round the world, local web usage is a growing phenomenon. Local businesses and organizations are increasingly using the web to find local customers, and vice versa. Whether you are a restaurant, a panel beater, a dry cleaner, a church or a school, you primarily service a small neighbourhood. Marketing to your target audience through the local newspaper, or by stuffing flyers into neighbourhood post-boxes is one way to go. But there are other approaches that leverage the fact that consumers use the web to find, and share, solutions. These approaches include, for example, providing an easily found location-specific website; collecting and using email addresses from physical visitors; identifying your premises on Google Maps; running geo-targeted advertisements on search engines; advertising on local Wi-Fi hotspots or on municipal Wi-Fi when it arrives in your area; engaging with local online communities and having members recommend you.

▨   SOCIAL: The web is becoming increasingly social, with users wanting to use it more and more as a medium for publishing and exchanging information, rather than as a medium for simply absorbing information. The trend towards consumer-generated media (CGM) is causing many marketers to re-evaluate their brand-centric approach to communicating on the web, and to encourage consumers to contribute content such as product reviews, photographs or videos. This boom in what is known as 'social media' is providing fertile ground for entirely new marketing approaches, which will be explored later in the book.

DISINTERMEDIATING: Traditional business models simply couldn't work without a chain of intermediaries that ultimately connect manufacturers or service creators with the consumer. These intermediaries might include wholesalers, distributors, retailers, value-added resellers, brokers or agents, depending on the industry. In some industries, business partners such as the media or advertising and public relations agencies act as communication intermediaries. All of these entities are, in one way or another, under threat of disintermediation by the web. Once a company is able to transact with and talk with its customers directly, many of the previously important intermediaries may become redundant. This potential causes at least two strategic upheavals: companies have to struggle their way through the politics and logistics of reformulating long-standing business relationships, and intermediaries have to seek out better ways of making themselves an essential part of the value chain. Both of these require rethinking of a company's business model and strategy.

VIRTUAL: Social networks have stormed into the consciousness of journalists and marketers in recent years, although they have been a significant factor in the appeal of the internet for decades. In fact, social networks have been around since the dawn of humanity. As the web evolves in different directions, increasing bandwidth and the desire to socialize online have stimulated the growth of virtual 3-D worlds. At the moment, your primary interface with the web's content is through Google's two-dimensional text-only listings. In the near future, your interface with web content will probably be through 3-D environments.

The king of the massively multiplayer online 3-D worlds (MMOs) is usually thought to be World of Warcraft, which is game-based, and has a population of around 12 million. But there is a bigger world, occupied by teenagers in Japan, China and Korea: Fantasy Westward Journey, which has a population of more than 80 million. At peak times, the game clocks up 2 million concurrent users. Because video game consoles are still officially banned in China, PC gaming has massive appeal. At $2.5 billion in 2008, China is now the world's largest market for online role-playing games, with an estimated 147 million players playing for 14 hours a week on average.

Online places such as Second Life have captured the imagination of western media and marketers. With a registered virtual population in excess of 15 million, it is only the 10th largest virtual world. In fact the number of active members (around 68 thousand users online at any point in time) is a lot lower than the media buzz would suggest. You can join, for free, and acquire a 3-D character or avatar to represent you in the world. The avatar can be personalized in shape, appearance and clothing. For a small subscription, those avatars can acquire the virtual cash that allows them to buy property, build homes and decorate them. There is a Swedish Embassy, and Reuters has a full-time correspondent filing reports from Second Life. You can also attend virtual classes at virtual versions of Yale and Harvard. Your avatar can go on virtual shopping sprees for new clothes or hairstyles, which you buy from shops run by other virtual residents.

You can purchase virtual representations of real-world branded goods. Second Life's Adidas store will sell your avatar the latest running shoes, often before they are available in real-world stores. Toyota, Ford, or any other car manufacturer will sell you virtual versions of the latest-model cars. You can buy books from online bookstores run by most of the real world's large publishing houses. And if you really want to get away from it all, Starwood Hotels has built a fully functional Second-Life version of its latest Caribbean resort hotel. It may seem high-tech, but if you wanted to open a store in Second Life, you could do so with a lot less than 10 thousand dollars. For all the hype, though, there is currently considerable doubt about the real business impact of the marketing effort. See it as an investment in getting a little real-world publicity, and in acquiring experience in operating in a virtual mode. Remember that it will not be long before your primary interface with the web is in a 3-D environment.

> **Technology is not a prerequisite for social marketing, and never has been.**

There are other online worlds with much larger active populations, of which you may never have heard. Habbo Hotel is aimed at teenagers, as is Gaia Online. Then there are Entropia Universe, There, Active Worlds, Kaneva, and the Red Light Center.

Club Penguin, a Canadian start-up now owned by Disney, has more than 12 million members. Its target market is 6-to-10-year-olds. This social network allows members to take on avatars that look like penguins, and they hang around an ice-floe, playing games and catching fish. Parents love the fact that their kids can learn to communicate with others from different cultures in a very safe environment. The world also exposes members to issues of social responsibility: the recipients of Club Penguin's million-dollar annual charity donation are determined by children, who vote online with the club's virtual currency. Club Penguin gives large sums to charities like War Child and Free The Children, to help AIDS orphans in Ethiopia and children affected by war in Georgia, Afghanistan and Northern Uganda; to care for children in Haiti and Rwanda; and to build schools in India,

Ecuador and rural China. Far from being a trivial environment, Club Penguin will have a massive impact on the next generation of teenagers, and on the future of the web.

Facebook, a social network in a mere two dimensions, had 220 million active members in early 2009, each spending an average of 20 minutes a day immersed in the environment.

🔲 CONTEXTUAL: Though its unfortunate label gives web 2.0 the impression that it is all about bleeding-edge technology, technology is not a prerequisite for social marketing, and never has been. The networking tools certainly help and have projected the notion of social networks onto marketing radar screens, but hasn't marketing always been marketing 2.0? Even way back when the secrets of hunting mammoths or making fire were being bartered by one social cluster to the next, the informal, spontaneous networks of shared experience and wisdom enabled such transfer. Palaeolithic marketers just didn't have the mobile web.

All societies need labels to make the world an easier place to live in. People buy into categorizations, stereotypes and generalizations to help take some of the complexity out of the true diversity of their surroundings. People do it to people ('She's an ENFJ'); people do it to companies ('They are an innovative organization') and people do it to systems and processes ('We are using emarketing for that'). There is nothing wrong with labels of convenience, as long as they are accurate and as long as people acknowledge that there are many other perhaps more important dimensions to the object or process thus labelled. Attila the Hun was an ENTJ, but his Myers-Briggs classification is hardly the aspect of his character that one would choose to describe him. You also need to be sure that everyone else shares the same understanding of what those labels imply.

As the complexity of information gets more baffling, it is becoming increasingly necessary to label, or 'tag', objects or processes. The volume of 'new digital data' produced in the world in 2007 was three million times all the knowledge in all the books ever written. To deal with it people need to have a way of classifying it so we can store and retrieve what we need. Not too long ago, there was the Yahoo! directory system on the web, where a web page would get placed under one, and only one, subdirectory in a vast tree of classifications. Then search engines started reading the hidden headers on a page and letting you look for those. Later on, Google started reading the actual words on the page and recording the number and importance of other pages that linked to each page, so you could get a pretty solid listing of important sources for any word or phrase of interest.

> The volume of 'new digital data' produced in the world in 2007 was 3 million times all the knowledge in all the books ever written.

But even the best search engines can't make value judgments about how 'good' a piece is: how well written or authoritative it is, or how well it fits the context of your query. For that, you need to go back in time to the directory approach, where human eyes and human judgement can make those hard-to-programme qualitative decisions. When even the best search engines today encounter, for example, the word 'rose' on a web page, they have difficulty knowing whether it is in the context of a poem, a metaphor, a woman's name, a botanical treatise, a gardening guide, or the past tense of rise. Google is primitive compared with the intuitive data retrieval system that your own brain uses to tell you what you know when you need it. As web 3.0 (what is known as the semantic web) starts to creep into being, context will become a more important guide than content itself, just as it is in your own thinking processes.

A similar phenomenon that lets you access what others in your immediate and more distant networks know, think or have experienced is what makes 'marketing 2.0' (another expedient label) so compelling. This is where web 2.0 social phenomena such as wikis, Del.icio.us (an unstructured support network where people voluntarily share their experience and wisdom) and Digg are starting to make inroads – places where individuals en masse can add contextual tags and commentary to anything that they find on the web, can supplement the content where it is deficient, and where searchers can tap into that collective wisdom to find the really pertinent diamonds in the coal dust.

Corporate marketing is often still a formal, centrally controlled, structured megaphone into which carefully crafted branding messages are shouted repeatedly. It is all about limiting perceptions, focusing context, even manipulation. But the communication that is most frequently used by individuals for forming opinions and making decisions is informal, more peer-enabled and organic. The communication that shapes brands today has more in common with Del.icio.us, than with the pre-determined frameworks and limiting dogma of the 20th-century brand bible.

While online tools help to facilitate informal sharing, they are not essential to it. In trying to understand how best to apply the tools or encourage their use, people need to understand why and how informal peer-to-peer communication processes flourish in technology-free environments. You need to be careful that, in your passion to explore and understand corporate marketing, you do not get all tangled up in the technology at the expense of understanding the root human processes that make the technology usable and useful. If the processes you are nurturing would work in a Palaeolithic society, you can assume they would work extremely well in a tech-savvy one. After all, the internet is not a network of computers, it is a network of people. And collectively they have launched a new economy.

THE WEB WORLD BEYOND AMERICA

Consumers have adopted the internet faster than any other technology in history. The pace at which the cycle of innovation, acceptance and re-innovation takes place is breathtaking. While nobody can deny that the web has fundamentally changed the way business is done around the world, the nature of its impact is by no means universal.

It is not unusual, even today, to hear sceptics assert that the web will never really be a significant force in commerce or education anywhere outside of developed nations, because developing nations are not suited to it. The availability of basic telecommunications access, computer hardware, affordable bandwidth or even basic literacy are often cited as reasons why the web won't matter much in Africa or parts of Asia.

It is true that vast chunks of the population of the world will never own a conventional computer or a landline with which to connect to the web, even if they could afford the access. But 8 out of 10 urban Africans have access to a mobile phone, which requires neither a landline nor even a power point on the electricity grid. In the marketplaces of the poorest parts of the planet you will find entrepreneurs selling phone charge-ups from car batteries or crank-handles.

Most of the customers of the majority of marketing-driven businesses in countries such as Nigeria or Indonesia are already online. Marketers need to focus not on the universe, but on their own target markets and the communications and supply chains that are necessary to reach them. For some industries the web may be irrelevant, at least for now. But for most industries that think of themselves as sophisticated marketing entities, the web is already vital. Whether a business is marketing cars, machinery, jewellery, raw materials, clothing, insurance, travel, restaurants or professional services, its customers are using the web to help them make informed buying decisions.

All of this is happening despite the fact that much of the world's web environment is relatively underdeveloped, at least for now.

Guess which country matches the following description:

- Only a small percentage of the population has web access.
- Less than 10 percent of these people have broadband access.
- Broadband access is very expensive and typically only 2Mbps.
- Buyers and sellers fear ecommerce fraud and data security.
- Most people believe that the 'real world' is a more satisfying place to do business.
- Where ecommerce is available, it is dominated by major offline companies with established brands – and even they are losing money online.
- Most businesses (including those currently engaged in ecommerce and their advertising agencies) do not know much about emarketing.

This was China in 2006. It was the UK in 2004. It was the United States in 2000. From the late 1990s I ran an elearning business out of Washington DC, the central hub of world internet technology. Until the turn of the century, my personal web access was through a dial-up modem, as was the access of thousands of my corporate elearning customers. In fact, American consumers only started moving en masse to broadband in 2001. Before that it was too slow, too expensive or simply unavailable. Ecommerce was hamstrung by fears of fraud and identity theft, and there was a widespread belief that, except for books, videos and air tickets, nobody would ever buy goods online. Despite this unpromising start, web commerce has become an indispensable part of the global economy, and it only took a couple of years.

For latecomers to the web, such as South Africa, the evolution from geeky novelty to indispensible utility is increasingly compressed into months rather than years. Both the UK and China are now way ahead of the US, in technology, bandwidth and application. Already, more people in China are accessing the internet than in the US and Canada combined. At least a dozen other countries such as South Korea, Japan, Australia, Finland and most European countries have leapfrogged the US, and their populations have access to very high-speed, very low-cost internet that is fully integrated into their everyday lives. The populations of these countries are already abandoning landline phones in favour of mobiles.

The US usually pays the price for being a pioneer, leaving a beaten path that allows those who follow to do so rapidly, inexpensively and without the legacy baggage that makes it so hard for pioneers to surge ahead. In two years or less, the digital economies of most developing nations will catch up with the rest of the world, and they will do so despite the obstacles unenlightened governments and self-serving national telecommunications monopolies will leave in the road. Consumers will drive the evolution, and companies, academic institutions and governments will either embrace the new culture or be dragged reluctantly into engaging with it.

Many people who think of the internet as an American phenomenon might be surprised to know that only 1 in 6 internet users are in the United States and Canada, while 27 percent come from Europe.

Asia already accounts for 4 out of 10 people on the web, despite only 15 percent of its population being online.

Growth of internet penetration has slowed in America, as 74 percent of the population is already online. There is still growth ahead for Europe, where only 48 percent of the population has web access.

@ Asia has 480 million internet users

@ Europe has 384 million

@ North America has 248 million

@ Latin America and the Caribbean have 139 million

@ Africa has 51 million

By contrast, figures are only beginning to pick up pace in Asia. The Chinese middle class is already bigger than the American middle class, and by 2010, Chinese will be the dominant language of the web.

As countries start to adopt the web, there is a pattern. At first, the overwhelming majority of users are technology-savvy geeks. They are rapidly joined by young urban professionals who have the money and time to afford early-stage web access. Soon after, women come to outnumber men, and more senior age groups become significant users. Then, once major mass-market retailers (such as Wal-Mart and Sears in the US) go online, lower-income users started to flood the web, attracted by its convenience and comparison-shopping advantages.

> The web has revolutionized commerce because it has empowered customers through allowing them to network their knowledge.

Often holding down two or more jobs, and having neither the time nor the transportation to shop around, lower-income consumers find the web a very helpful tool. In a similar vein, small businesses are able to use the web not only to grow a larger customer base, but also to source better suppliers from across the globe.

Online markets are wide open to competition, and present huge opportunities for any innovative business with a professional approach to user experience and a commitment to real customer engagement. If you are running a large established business, the web can be a wake-up call. Unless the loyalty of your customer base is fuelled by something more significant than geographic proximity, you can rapidly lose those customers to a world of new alternatives.

The kind of widespread competition that is enabled by the internet is healthy for any industry, particularly those dominated by a few big players that have become complacent about responding to customer needs. If you form real relationships with customers you create a sustainable differential advantage that does not rely on artificial crutches such as protectionism, regulation, or collusion.

Nor, it turns out, is it a necessary precondition of customer satisfaction that they be kept ignorant. Knowledge-sharing is what fuels revolutions. The web has revolutionized commerce not because it has allowed companies to become more efficient (though it has), but because it has empowered customers through allowing them to network their knowledge.

Many commercial giants in developing nations manage to stay stuck in the paternalistic business practices of the mid-20th century. Despite being treated dismissively, their customers have not yet started abandoning them because competition is thin on the ground.

The internet is changing that. And it will rapidly revolutionize business practices around the world. Those businesses that understand web culture and embrace it will continue to thrive; those who do not will go the way of the dinosaurs – not gradually, with many second chances to evolve, but suddenly, as in the impact of a comet.

This prognosis is not hype. It was clear right from the beginning 15 years ago that web adoption would be a powerful democratizing force. The web allows consumers to communicate with each other to share experiences, information and opinions. It also allows organizations to communicate with their customers, not in the unsolicited mass-market broadcasts of conventional marketing-speak, but in an intimate and personal two-way conversation. The web brings transparency to relationships and makes it very hard for organizations to hide behind advertising, PR spin or policy small-print.

However it is not in the nature of large powerful corporations to show much concern for what consumers are saying. Small businesses change when they smell opportunity for growth; large businesses often only start to change when they feel pain, and they only feel pain when either their profits or their share price start falling. That happens when competitors come out of nowhere and do what marketing was always intended to do: understand and respond to real consumer needs.

A slow or expensive internet service infrastructure is an albatross around the neck of economic and educational progress in any nation, and is a major handicap to the growth of an entrepreneurial class and the small to medium businesses that it spawns.

Small business generally receives little respect or attention from the media, the financial community or politicians. The focus, particularly among policy makers, is on a few hundred corporations listed on the stock markets. Yet looking to such organizations for solutions to unemployment or economic instability is ridiculous – you could double the number of employees in each of the listed companies, and it would barely make a dent on the wellbeing of the economy. Any nation, especially a developing nation, has to focus on growing – not crushing – the smaller businesses that should make up the backbone of the economy.

In most countries in the world, small companies account for more than 8 out of 10 businesses. In the United States, where the Fortune 500 employ less than nine percent of the workforce, small businesses account for more than 99 percent of all employers – as do they in the UK. The SME sector in most nations accounts for half of the GDP and creates most of the new jobs. Small businesses are also overwhelmingly more creative and innovative than mega-corporations – in the US for example, the SME sector files 15 times more patents per employee than large companies do.

Throughout the world, the web and ecommerce have been a major boon to small businesses. The web lets small companies compete in global markets and allows them to market themselves locally for a fraction of the cost of conventional marketing. It permits them to function virtually, without the overheads of a physical business, and gives them access to support networks that can help them learn, manage and grow.

New marketing | 2

The late 20th-century marketing model is broken. The first time someone such as the Global Marketing Officer of Procter and Gamble asserts something like this, you wait for the punch-line, an anticipatory smile on your face. But it is not a joke, it is a fact, and an increasingly large number of marketers are being forced to respond to it.

The term 'new marketing' seems to rear its head every time a new medium comes along. In the past, it has described emerging advertising opportunities, additional channels with which to reinforce brand messaging and fresh challenges for agency creatives and media buyers. I can remember people talking about the new marketing decades ago, when local radio started coming into vogue.

What is different about the 'new' new marketing, also known as marketing 2.0, is that it is not about the internet as an advertising medium. It is about 1) consumers who have suddenly developed minds and muscles and the will to use them and 2) the competitive environment in which geography has become irrelevant, barriers to entry have disappeared, and traditional media have lost their audiences.

Irreversible changes in the balance of power in every market, facilitated by the internet, are making many of the practices of traditional marketing increasingly obsolete or irrelevant. At the same time, new opportunities are emerging that, if exploited, can massively improve the effectiveness of today's marketing strategies.

Before marketing came along, there was advertising. Advertising was originally about announcing your product to the world. From advertising, the broader field of marketing management gradually emerged, which was eventually codified by Phil Kotler in the 1970s. In its most respectable incarnation, marketing was about understanding your consumer, identifying unsatisfied needs, and then devising products to satisfy these needs. Selling was said to be all about getting rid of what you have, while marketing was all about having what you can get rid of.

In the 1970s, marketing focused on understanding and responding to authentic consumer needs. By the 1990s it was all about manipulating consumers' perceptions of their needs. Somewhere along the way marketing became a euphemism for hard-sell practices. The mantra of 'reach and frequency' ruled, and advertising became more interruptive and repetitive. Creativity was the primary tool for trying to get increasingly resentful consumers to pay attention to the message. By shouting at consumers loudly enough and often enough, it was hoped that they would eventually absorb the message, believe it and act on it.

When the web came along, early-days emarketing (what might be called emarketing 1.0) was a natural evolution from this approach. Back then it was called new marketing, too. The web was a billboard on which businesses placed banners, and, as with outdoor advertising, they wanted their banners in high-traffic locations. The comfortable model of reach and frequency seemed to fit rather snugly.

Emarketing, as it exists in the mainstream today, is still emarketing 1.0. It is emarketing at the Model-T stage. You can have any colour you want as long as it blinks. It is mass-market, brand-focused and centralized. Essentially, it is marketing as usual, but at a distance, with a little digital convenience thrown in for both customers and producers. While mainstream emarketing exploits some of the capability of the web, it rarely leverages the power of interpersonal networking – and it certainly has not allowed the nature of the web to influence the essential characteristics of 20th-century marketing. Those characteristics (architected, structured, hierarchical, linear, centralized, copy-written, non-customized, driven by corporate needs, one-way and controlled) are simply no longer relevant in the chaotically evolving business culture of today.

This would not really matter, if it were not for two things: the norms, expectations and behaviours of online consumers are changing the way companies think and act from the bottom up; and more agile marketing companies are already evolving away from the formal, centralized, slow-changing habits of the previous century. Traditional marketers are in the uncomfortable position of being held back by the weight of traditional processes, practices and dogma, while having to respond to the expectations of consumers who are already ahead of them on the learning curve.

THE NEW ONLINE CONSUMER

The way people use the web today is significantly different from the way they used it 10 years ago. The term 'web 2.0' is used to describe this shift away from centralization and hierarchy towards distributed knowledge, collaborative online communities and personal social networks. Most importantly, web 2.0 represents the massive empowerment of individual consumers that results from collaborative knowledge sharing.

> Web 2.0 represents the massive empowerment of individual consumers that results from collaborative knowledge sharing.

Web 2.0 can work for you or against you. Viral marketing or consumer brand endorsements could not happen without the spontaneous word-of-mouth sharing that takes place in web 2.0. But in the same way as your customer base can now grow exponentially overnight, established brands can lose their customers in no time at all. I will revisit web 2.0 and the information-empowered new consumer in Chapter 6, because it is absolutely core to online marketing success.

Applications and interfaces are changing the way you access, and perceive, information. Take the evolution of mapping, for example. Google Maps and Yahoo! Maps were so different from Map Quest's static product as to barely compete in the same marketplace. You could not only zoom in and out and drag around the maps, you could overlay them on aerial photos, and search them for points of interest such as hotels or restaurants, and click to make reservations. Then, with connections to blogging and image-storage sites such as Flickr, you could click a map to link to photos of a specific location that were taken by people who have been there, and you could read their comments. With another click you could call a comment author anywhere in the world, and talk to him or her for free using voice over internet protocol (VoIP). Provide all this on a mobile phone, and maps jump into a totally new dimension of usability. Now, because nothing stands still for long anymore, layer into your phone-based maps the convenience of mobile location-based services, which will show you not only where you are, but also the current whereabouts of all your friends and how to get to them.

What started out as a static graphical representation of the landscape, printed on paper, has evolved into an always-available dynamic tool, personally customized to your own particular needs. I said in an earlier chapter that digital tools become enthusiastically adopted only if they add value to your processes. Think about the processes you go through to get from one place to another across unfamiliar terrain, and consider what value mobile location-based services have added.

There's a new seamlessness to data flows that allows you to approach knowledge acquisition from multiple perspectives – without having any technical expertise whatsoever.

The implications for marketers are profound. The brand-centric paradigms of the 1990s led to the proliferation of mundane marketing websites and all the expediencies that they spawned. Corporations now have a hefty investment (in both cash and credibility) in such sites, so they continue to dominate strategic thinking. The problem is that insistence on one particular web strategy can shut companies off from other more relevant, flexible and effective applications of ubiquitous networking. Those website-constrained strategies are now making it much harder for marketing departments to make the conceptual changes that would allow them to embrace the chaotic flux of the web 2.0 world.

Marketing today should not be conceived as a series of online campaigns; it should be an evolving capacity enabled by social networks that are characterized by user-created content, contextualized search and retrieval and personal interaction. To stay relevant, marketers and marketing departments need to evolve into catalysers rather than controllers, facilitators rather than directors, and synthesizers rather than copywriters.

As digital communication permeates the lives of more and more of target consumers, the 'e' in emarketing and the '2.0' in marketing 2.0 become increasingly redundant, and the lessons that you learn about communicating while in web mode simply migrate into marketing itself. Eventually (in internet time that means about three years) the segregation of emarketing from mainstream marketing will seem foolhardy and dangerous, because

> **Currently the life expectancy of any new brand is rapidly shrinking at the same time as the costs of creating it are growing.**

consumers segregate neither their life experiences nor their decision making into 'online' and 'offline'. The web will be ubiquitous and integrated into their daily lives, as unremarkable as electricity, and only brought to mind when it is unexpectedly not available.

One of the reasons why it is important for corporations to embrace informal marketing and distributed experience-sharing is the inherent adaptability that it provides. The traditional marketing approach was defining needs and related market performance objectives for a target group and then designing, building and deploying a 'campaign'; this is too slow and expensive to be viable when needs change daily, or when only one person has a need.

Currently the life expectancy of any new brand is rapidly shrinking at the same time as the costs of creating it are growing. For example, to conceive, create and launch a major fragrance brand worldwide can cost 100 million euros; yet its typical life expectancy is less than 2 years.

Leveraging the informality of social networks may allow you to guide consumers to the virtual places or processes where their needs can be met most cost-effectively. If you have done your job right, the consumers who frequent those places will provide a credible endorsement of your brand. You should be doing everything you can to make available the tools and policies that encourage the development of social networks and to stimulate or support informal experience sharing.

Consumers now have the ability – and the will – to control the messages and the media with which they engage.

This is something that sends a chill down the spine of every old-school marketer. How can you possibly yield control over how your brand is described? Fortunes have been invested in tightly constraining the language used to represent your brands, the colours that you associate with them, the features and benefits that you ascribe to them, the personality or character that the brands exude, and the values they espouse. You have wrapped your brands in layers of bubble-wrap and preciously protected them from outside tampering. Surely it is a mistake to liberate them and let them go out into the world to engage with consumers where they might get corrupted? But do you risk over-protecting your brands to the point where they become weak and vulnerable, unable to stand on their own feet, or, even worse, simply become boring?

Whether you like it or not, consumers now have the ability – and the will – to control the messages and the media with which they engage. They have developed a distrust of communication from traditional marketers and prefer to use the opinions, experiences and advocacy of fellow consumers to help them form their own judgments about companies and products. They expect more from the brands that they use and the companies behind them: transparency, honesty, generosity, eco-friendliness and engagement. Largely as a result of digital communication, purchasing decisions are more communal, collaborative and informed than they have ever been.

Online consumers are taking control over how brands are perceived and positioned. Television and print were once the most influential media. Now the online consumer is the medium that marketers must master.

If you don't help online consumers to do things their way, you will be bypassed or ignored, becoming increasingly irrelevant to those individuals and to the decisions they make. For many online consumers, the brand is the buzz and formal marketing messaging is merely static in the background.

The implications of online consumers' new power go much deeper than mere brand marketing. The attitudes of companies to their customers, and their behaviour, are being forced to change. The ability to hide dismissive service and abusive customer policies behind layers of bureaucracy and obfuscation is disappearing, as online consumers share their experiences and collectively impose a new transparency on corporate customer relations.

No business, no matter where it is based in the world, can afford to ignore the internet's impact on markets and marketing. Senior executives in countries such as South Africa, where the web is a relatively recent phenomenon, find it hard to give online marketing the balanced attention it deserves. If your personal experience of the internet is limited, it is easy to see it as black or white: either as an annoying over-hyped medium or as an exciting means to revolutionize your business. Though superficial, each of these perceptions is correct. Yet neither comes close to adequately describing the complex and profound implications that the web holds for the immediate future of every business. There is no escaping the changes that the web continues to impose on businesses in every industry, but you can use those changes to your own competitive advantage.

The new consumer is one key aspect of new marketing. The other, which is as devastating for tradition-bound companies, is the new competitive landscape.

THE NEW COMPETITIVE LANDSCAPE

There was a time, less than a decade ago, when companies could rely on their customers to behave in a more or less predictable way. Most markets had crystallized into clearly defined territories, and you knew who your competitors were. As a marketer, your differential advantages were defined by the neat but superficial dimensions of geography and price positioning, refined a little by brand promise and values. Barriers to competitive entry were high, especially for small start-ups who could not afford the marketing or shop-fitting costs of local, let alone national, launches. Faced with the limited choices that mass marketing imposed, consumers were content to make compromises. Life was good.

Then the web opened the gates to competitors of all sizes from all over the globe. Not only were those competitors able, with a little design and a lot of customer focus, to be much more professional than established big businesses, they were able to do it without having to make massive strategic investments. Moreover, because many of them were start-ups with no legacy baggage, they could target very specific needs of individual customers, providing products and services that were more relevant than those on offer by mass marketers. Because such targeted businesses have relatively low overheads and as they are able to sell to customers around the world, non-viable local niches collectively become very attractive global markets.

The phenomenon of exploiting the web to offer highly targeted products and services to niche markets was best described by *Wired* magazine's Chris Anderson in his best-selling book *The Long Tail*, an essential read for anyone in marketing. When plotted on a graph that has the number of buyers on the vertical axis and specific products or solutions on the horizontal axis, most markets produce an exponential curve that tends to infinity at each end. The vast majority of purchases come from a very small range of products that make up the 'head' of the demand curve. There is nothing new about this curve – economists have talked about it since they first asserted that market prices are set by supply and demand. But most businesses have historically focused on the mass-consumption 'head' of the curve, leaving the 'tail' to specialist niche suppliers.

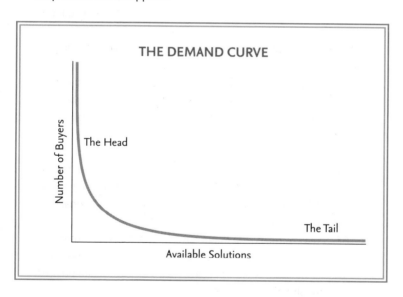

Large companies inhabit the head of the demand curve, providing a limited number of products that broadly address the needs of large market segments. A Mercedes comes in a handful of standard colours because the market for neon pink is not large enough to be interesting; Marks & Spencer and Wal-Mart choose to market a limited range of relatively generic clothing because neither haute couture nor Jermyn Street tailoring can attract the volumes of consumers that large corporations are structured to require.

The 'tail' of the demand curve represents many different products, none of which achieve much volume compared to those in the head. The closer to the long end of the tail, the smaller the niche. But these 'long-tail' products, when magnified by the low-cost global-access lens of ecommerce, become rich hunting grounds for entrepreneurial businesses. On the web, the gold-plated garden gnomes I referred to in Chapter 1 move from the road-side farm stall into Korea or Russia, without any major marketing expenditure. Conversely, the dominant life assurance company in South Africa can now lose its customers in droves to competitors from Canada or Australia.

The aspect of the 'long tail' that should give marketing strategists in most big corporations sleepless nights is this: consumers who take advantage of long-tail products and services do not appear from nowhere – they come out of the head of the curve, effectively causing those mass-market sectors to shrink. The implications are simple:

- To maintain volumes, mass marketers have to compete ever more vigorously for a larger slice of a declining pie. Costs of marketing go up, prices may go down, and return on investment declines.
- Alternatively, mass marketers have to adopt a more customer-centric approach and start competing for niches further down the tail. Ironically, while small businesses can compete here with little investment, big businesses face significant barriers to entry: not only can it be very costly to reconfigure legacy systems and processes, their established branding can get in the way too.

Appealing as the long tail may be, you don't have to pursue a niche need to take a big online bite out of a major player in any industry. You can tackle the market head-on by doing a better job of addressing the mass-market needs about which big companies have become complacent. Often, those needs are simply in the area of receiving respect and consideration.

Customer-focus, not programming skill or artistic talent, is what brings about enduring business success online. The better you know your target market as individuals, not as a mass, the better you are able to identify and exploit those niches that offer the best potential. It is a rare thing indeed to come across a web developer who understands anything about marketing, let alone has any insights into your specific business or customer base. Anyone in business who wants to succeed online should know enough about the technology and design to manage and direct the work of coders and artists, but should never simply hand over all decision-making to them. In emarketing, abdication is death.

However, with a clear vision of what you want to achieve and how you are going to achieve it, a marketer can focus the efforts of all those involved in a web project and create the vehicles that will deliver real business results.

It is easy to think of the web as a new frontier that you cannot master without huge budgets and a degree in rocket science. Yet it is surprising how small businesses, or brands with small marketing budgets, have exploited the web with tremendous success. In the United States, 4 out of every 10 small businesses receive more than 75 percent of their income from the web. Small businesses account for more than 99 percent of US companies, so the web has proven to be massively important to the US economy at grassroots level. In fact, half of all US companies (and 40 percent of UK businesses) are home-based, so the web is also fundamentally changing the dynamics of industries such as real-estate and transportation.

Online business has moved far beyond the basic ecommerce concepts of a decade ago, when everyone was focused on selling physical products via a web store. Today, the internet is a marketing channel promoting products and services of which you take delivery offline: nail salons, restaurants, tax consultants, doctors, hotels, lawyers, plumbers, architects, panel beaters – even retailers with no ecommerce facility – all promote their businesses on the web.

Of all consumers with internet access, more than 6 out of 10 use the web as their dominant source of product information and for window shopping – 10 times more than those who use television as an information source. The new consumer turns to the web to research solutions to particular needs, and if you do not have an effective web presence, you simply do not exist.

The elements of emarketing 3

Since the web is a crowded place, simply having a website is not enough to bring you business. Whatever the business purpose of your online presence may be, getting people to want to use it requires a sustained marketing investment. You have to have a strategy to make your target market aware of your site, to stimulate their interest in it, to make them want to experience it, and to get them to actually visit it. This follows the classic Attention, Interest, Desire, Action (AIDA) marketing communication model.

THE WEB 1.0 MARKETING COMMUNICATION MODEL

Attention ➭ Interest ➭ Desire ➭ Action

In a web 2.0 world, AIDA doesn't go far enough. Before the first phase of the model, before people become aware of you, they are searching for information. At the end of the model, after they have taken the desired action to visit your site, you want to take your customers through an experience that is so remarkably satisfying that they will want to recommend it to their friends. If you add Research at the beginning and Recommendation at the end, the web 2.0 version of AIDA becomes RAIDAR. Search marketing and SEO are targeting

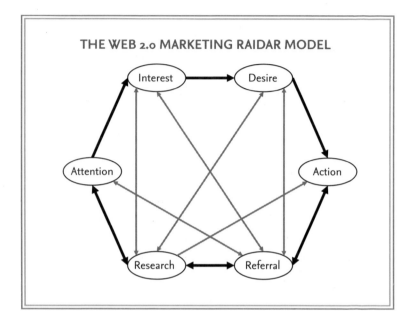

the Research component; and usability, social networking and user generated content (UGC) are being applied to the Recommendation component. If you get a good volume of sustained recommendations online, it boosts your search ranking, closing the circle and starting a viral spiral.

The new communications model is rather complex. It is not the simplistic linear model of the days before web 2.0. Attention triggers a desire for both more research and referral from actual users before a real interest is formed. Interest can pass through cycles of additional research and referral before it becomes desire, which in turn may go through several iterations of research and reference-checking before any action to purchase takes place. Research can lead to instant action, the result, say, of clicking on a search-engine listing. Attention, stimulated by an online or offline advertisement, or as a result of hearing some PR buzz, typically leads to research – going to 'Google it' is the next step for many in the protracted path to purchasing.

You want to use all of the marketing approaches available to you to support and relate to the people in your target market at every step of the process. Yet almost without exception, whether they are stock-market listed household names or one-woman start-ups, the companies I have worked with have initially seen building a website as both the starting point and the end goal of their emarketing initiative. Most have soon regretted being so limited in their thinking.

Since a website is the most visible and most familiar aspect of online marketing, it is not surprising that people assume that emarketing is all about building websites. Important as a website is, it is only one component in the more complex set of tools and processes that drives your web presence. Unless you have limited business goals for your online presence, a website is in itself rarely sufficient. It may not even be essential. Indeed, the term 'web presence' is dangerously misleading, because it suggests a passive role, as if you simply want to be a wallflower at the web party. Marketers who want a more proactive engagement with the online consumer, and have meaningful business goals that they expect this engagement to achieve, need to put their website into a broader more dynamic context.

WHAT IS ECOMMERCE?

It is important to step back and look at the business as a whole, and work out how all of the different aspects of the internet can enhance it.

So what are the elements of emarketing? Assume, for now, that you have a website. For the sake of example, assume that it is an ecommerce site to which you want visitors to come and buy whatever it is you are selling. The first three elements are your website (the 'front end' to your store), your target consumers, and your ebusiness 'back end' (which takes care of operational things such as payments and inventory).

If you are selling anything online, an important component of your site is the ecommerce engine that links your front-end website with your back-end order processing systems and allows you to take

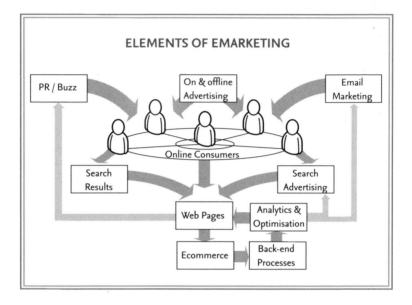

real-time payments online. Before looking at the other elements of emarketing, let's consider some issues associated with ecommerce.

Ecommerce is not the same as ebusiness. Ebusiness is the real-time integration of internet activities throughout the supply chain and throughout all of your company's processes. It integrates the customer's front-end experience into all of the company's back-end systems and processes that make the promise of complete customer satisfaction a reality.

Ecommerce is merely an online cash register. It processes orders and payments in real time. Put simply, ecommerce is the interface between your shop and your back-end operations.

The ease with which you can integrate ecommerce into a website is what has allowed small businesses around the world to thrive. But ecommerce is a significant step up from simply having a website. The cost of technical development is greater, and the scale of online transactions fees can be prohibitive.

Development and hosting costs rise once you move from a

passive website into one that requires a database or secure transactions processing. Many web developers are people with basic skills in HTML coding, which is adequate for a good-looking non-interactive site. The programming skills required for ecommerce are more sophisticated, and development time can escalate. Small businesses that are new to the internet have the perception that they have to do business with someone they can get face-to-face with, and they feel that working with someone on the other side of the planet is risky. As the web gold-rush accelerates in early-stage internet economies, many local developers exploit this angst and get away with gouging their local clients. But you don't need to work with a local company. Service providers such as Yahoo! allow you to set up a competent template-based website and host it with full ecommerce functionality for a net outlay of $40 (28 Euro) per month. Or, if you want to do something a lot more customized, you can find thousands of talented and experienced web developers online in the United States, India or Australia who may charge far less per hour than their counterparts down the street, and take a lot fewer hours to complete the project. As I mentioned earlier, the web is a two-edged sword.

Then there is the transaction-cost problem. The catalyst that allowed ecommerce to proliferate around the world was PayPal. Owned by eBay and now registered as a European bank, PayPal acts as an intermediary that links credit card companies, online buyers and online businesses.

@ When I opened my first PayPal account in 2000, it was to take online payments from people who did not have a credit card or did not want to use it online. At the time there was a lot of debate about whether or not putting PayPal on an ebusiness site targeted mainly at corporate customers made you look somehow amateurish or downmarket. Not any more.

As the de-facto banker of the world wide web, PayPal has become a vast financial institution with 170 million accounts, processing more than US$60 billion (42 billion Euro) in transactions per year. PayPal now owns Verisign, the web's largest provider of secure transaction services. People living in 190 countries, including Peru, Indonesia, Croatia and Fiji, use PayPal to send money via the web, though less than two dozen currencies are accommodated. In nations whose currencies are unstable or whose foreign exchange processes are still so bureaucratically baroque as to be unmanageable in an online marketplace, local businesses can't deal directly through PayPal in the local currency.

In those countries (for example, Bolivia, Papua New Guinea or South Africa), if you want to sell in local currency to local customers, you need to work with one of a handful of often appallingly designed local payment gateways, which in turn interface between the credit card companies and your merchant account at your bank. Each of these parties typically gets away with taking a large chunk of each transaction, sometimes totalling 15 to 20 percent. Compare this figure with 2 to 3 percent charged by PayPal or its competitor Google Checkout, and you realize why online businesses outside of the developed nations have difficulty being competitive.

Until the costs of credit card ecommerce drop, which happens very rapidly, online SMEs in developing nations have to muddle through with internet banking options, higher consumer prices or lower margins. Large companies do not have those barriers since they act as their own payment gateway and have the kind of commercial clout that allows them to negotiate really low transaction rates with their banking partners. But, despite higher prices, small companies can compete successfully with the big guys by hitting them where they are weakest. As ebusinesses the world over have discovered, if you provide customer-centric online experiences, which result more from attitude than from investment, you can sustain premium prices.

Now, let's put all of this back into the context of emarketing.

EMARKETING STRATEGY AND TOOLS

In an ideal world, you would build a website and your target consumers would stampede to it like bargain hunters to the January sales. Once there, they would enthusiastically buy from you, sending bucket-loads of cash into your ebusiness 24 hours a day, while you laze by the pool sipping mojitos and waiting for the buy-out call from Google.

Sadly, the real world just doesn't cooperate like that. An ebusiness is a business. It takes vision, strategy, investment, hard work, creativity and attention to detail, in perpetuity.

Your website needs to have a business purpose, unless you build it purely as an ego exercise. Its design, information flows, functionality and usability have to be conceived and executed to deliver on those business goals. Above all, it should be customer-centric and deliver a remarkably satisfying experience. I shall return to all these points and more in Chapter 7 (Website design).

Your target consumers will not stampede to your website, because they do not know that it exists.

Your ebusiness back-end must work. Customers must be able to do whatever it is you expect them to do, quickly, intuitively and painlessly. This includes processing a credit card payment so that data security is taken care of, executing an order so that the right product is shipped in the right way, managing your inventories so that your site does not sell items that you no longer have, making customer service impeccable, and all the other tasks that make a business run smoothly. It is relatively easy and inexpensive to build a website. It can be vastly more expensive than building the site itself to get your back-end IT systems to synchronize with your site and work in real time.

Your target consumers will not stampede to your website, because they do not know that it exists. The internet is a very crowded and confusing place these days. Your site has to stand out. Even those who know that your site is there may see no reason to visit. Your site has to be compelling. The better you understand your target customers, the more likely it is that they will find your site relevant and useful.

There are two approaches to driving traffic to your site. The first is using advertising and PR. The second is using search engines.

Advertising and PR covers an huge territory. Advertising takes various forms including off-line advertising in traditional media, online advertising and email marketing. Several are really good at getting potential customers to visit your website, although they can be expensive. Thanks to digital communication, PR is enjoying a major renaissance and is no longer the poor cousin to advertising. The primary aim of PR is to get people, and the media, talking about your brand. It includes traditional publicity activities and emerging online PR techniques, which have collectively become known as buzz marketing. It also includes word of mouth (WOM) and social media optimization. Social media optimization is a convoluted term that covers all the activities a marketer might use to get individual online consumers and online communities to talk about their brand. All these elements will be revisited in Chapter 6 and Chapter 11.

Search engines have, not surprisingly, become an absolutely vital element of emarketing and account for more than half of the visitors to fast-growing sites. With more than 20 billion pages on the web, consumers use search engines such as Google, Yahoo! Search and MSN Live to help them find solutions to their problems. Unfortunately, online consumers have little patience and they rarely glance beyond the top three or four results returned in response to their search query. The page on your site that addresses the need expressed in the search query has to rank right at the top of the thousands listed, or it may as well not exist.

The field of search engine optimization (SEO) covers all the aspects of your website that ensure that Google not only understands what each page is about, but considers it to be better than all the other pages out there on the same subject. This gives your page the top spot in what are known as the 'natural' or 'organic' search results.

Not everyone can get to the top of the natural rankings, so search engines provide the ability to advertise contextually. When someone searches using a term that you have nominated, your advertisement appears alongside the natural results. Typically these advertisements appear on a pay-per-click (PPC) basis – you pay a small fee, typically a few cents, every time someone clicks on the advertisement to visit your page. For many small businesses with limited marketing budgets, PPC advertising is the most cost-effective way to connect with online consumers.

The last and possibly most important element of any emarketing strategy is performance management, which requires web analytics and a commitment to performance improvement.

Web analytics is a relatively new field that deals with measuring the activity generated by your emarketing initiatives, monitoring precisely where site visitors come from and what they do, and evaluating the commercial impact of your online investments. One of the most significant advantages that emarketing has over traditional marketing is your ability to measure the behaviour of online consumers, at a very granular level of detail, and to link that behaviour to marketing causes and effects.

Performance improvement is the ongoing process of interpreting the analytics and making decisions that will fine-tune or optimize relevant areas of your emarketing. The ability to measure the performance of your emarketing is pointless if the measurement does not result in taking action to improve that performance continuously. You can tune up your email campaigns to get better click-through rates, your website to get lower bounce rates, your pay-per-click advertising to get better conversion rates, or your rich-media banner advertisements to get longer immersion times. The web allows you to test alternatives, such as two

If you increase your conversion rate from 0.2 to 2 percent, you achieve a tenfold growth in your revenues.

different calls to action, and can give you instant real-time feedback on those tests.

Why does it matter? If you can increase your conversion rate (the proportion of visitors who actually become customers) from 0.2 to 2 percent, you have achieved a tenfold growth in your revenues. Emarketing in itself is cost effective; optimized emarketing can dramatically maximize that effectiveness.

THE EIGHT STAGES OF EMARKETING EVOLUTION

Not everybody needs or wants to be an Amazon.com. In fact, although Amazon.com is normally seen to be the epitome of personalized ecommerce, its model of customer interaction is rapidly becoming old-fashioned. On the web, what was leading-edge five minutes ago is, well, so five minutes ago. Businesses are now scrambling to find ways to exploit the messaging synergies inherent to online communities, something which Amazon.com has yet to do. Amazon's focus is both mass-market and individual. It has arguably

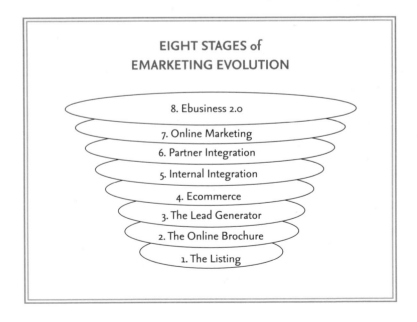

EIGHT STAGES of EMARKETING EVOLUTION

8. Ebusiness 2.0

7. Online Marketing

6. Partner Integration

5. Internal Integration

4. Ecommerce

3. The Lead Generator

2. The Online Brochure

1. The Listing

the most sophisticated tools in the world to personalize the user experience and optimize the user's view of the Amazon catalogue. It uses product-focused community features such as reader reviews, information about what others bought, and shared wish lists.

But while Amazon has very granular information about each individual shopper, it has yet to combine those individuals into communities of shared interest at a higher, more mutually interactive level. There are no John Grisham discussion forums, no blues-music fan groups and no Italian-cookery-enthusiast communities. Amazon's focus remains retailing: It engages with each consumer to promote relevant, sharply defined products, pulling in insights about the behaviour of other shoppers as sales collateral. Amazon has not yet become a catalyst that uses its consumers as a marketing medium in their own right. But that can change overnight, and probably will.

Businesses online tend to move through a number of stages of emarketing evolution before they get even close to the sophistication of Amazon.com, eBay, CB2.com or Dove. Let's look more closely at each of the eight stages of emarketing evolution, as shown in the diagram opposite.

STAGE 1: THE LISTING

The most elementary level at which a company can have a web presence is a listing in one or more online business directories or portals. Think of this as an online business card or a web-based Yellow-Pages entry. This is fast and inexpensive to do and does not require a website or even an email address. The directory simply lists your company name, specialization, physical address and contact details. There are dozens of directories, some mass-market (for example, yell.com) and some niched (for example, dotukdirectory.co.uk).

A directory with a niche focus, such as accommodation or restaurants, is referred to as a portal. Portals tend to proliferate in the early days of ecommerce, since they offer what small businesses perceive as a quick and easy web presence. They are inexpensive to set up and generate fast subscription revenues. Those portals that re-invest in their sites and work hard at keeping them high-profile, well branded and well trafficked can survive a long time. But most portals are set up as get-rich-quick cash-cows, and accordingly have limited lives. Subscribers quickly learn that they get little real benefit from being an undifferentiated name buried in a long list of their competitors. They abandon their commoditized listings and move on to a more customized web presence.

STAGE 2: THE ONLINE BROCHURE

When most businesses, even large corporations, put together their first website, it is nothing more than a basic brochure. Small businesses are product-centric, and 'our website' is nearly always 'all about us'. Large corporations follow the same focus; their first sites are often no more than an abbreviated annual report. None of this is remotely interesting to online consumers, whose primary interest lies in solving their own problems. If someone is looking for a little black dress for the company cocktail party, do they really care about your share price or who your chairman is? If they want to find the best HDTV for their budget, how useful is a list of the brands you stock in your physical stores with no model numbers, technical specs, prices, or reviews?

There is nothing wrong with a brochure-ware website, as long as your emarketing goals are restricted to what a brochure can do for you.

These so-called 'brochure-ware' sites dominate the web. They are the quick-and-dirty solutions that most website developers offer to clients who have little understanding of emarketing. They are frequently based on pre-existing templates, require little in the way of coding or design expertize and contain only 5 to 10 pages. Because they can often be knocked together in an afternoon and can be charged for as if real time and talent went into them, they are the profitability sweet-spot of the SME web development industry. There is nothing wrong with having such a website, as long as your emarketing goals are restricted to what a brochure can do for you (which, online, is not much), and as long as the cost-benefit equation works in your favour.

Brochure-ware sites are priced across a broad spectrum, and any business that wants one should shop around, locally and internationally. You can download templates from the web that are documented well enough for people with limited computing ability to modify. You can simply cut and paste your own text and replace the images, and you can have a reasonably professional-looking site for anything from free to 100 dollars. At the other extreme, developers can charge you up to $50,000 for a 10-page brochure-ware website with no back-end functionality. Shop the same project around online and you might be able to knock a zero or two off the price.

STAGE 3: THE LEAD GENERATOR

Brochure-ware sites serve a purpose as an entry-level web presence, but it is not long before their owners want to get more out of their site. The next step is to try to capture sales prospects. Instead of being 'all about us', the site is modified to encourage visitors to provide their contact details, to contact the company, or to enquire about its products or services. In some instances, visitors may even be encouraged to make a purchase, although there is no ecommerce payment processing system in place.

It is at this stage that many companies start to run into trouble. Usually, the site uses a simple web form that the visitor fills in and submits, its content going into a database or spreadsheet, or to an email.

The technology that is used to capture visitor information should be secure, but typically it is not. Secure data is encrypted before being submitted by the visitor's computer to yours, and is decrypted at the other end. This prevents sensitive information from being intercepted in transit by the army of malicious programmes or hacker-bots called packet sniffers. A bot is a robot, a small piece of code that travels the internet looking for whatever it is that it has been programmed to seek out. The internet is infested with them, and they come knocking on your computer's door constantly looking for a way in, or cruise around the web looking for potentially useful information: passwords, names, birth dates, credit card numbers, addresses or ID numbers. Naïve web users will send this kind of information via unsecured web forms or even in emails, but the more experienced your visitors are, the more rightfully paranoid they will be. A small business such as a local bed-and-breakfast will lose many potential customers simply because its booking systems don't match the security needs of the site visitor.

Security aside, successful ebusinesses exploit immediacy. Very few people are willing to engage in the delays inherent to email-based correspondence in order to make a simple purchase. They would rather move on to your competitor who can tell them directly what is available at what price and can take an instant payment online. This level of service requires an ecommerce engine.

STAGE 4: THE ECOMMERCE SITE

Ecommerce lets your site visitors transact in real time, instead of having to undertake the turn-based communication of stage-3 sites. You simply need to provide secure ecommerce transactions abilities if you wish to take payments online. If you cannot take payments online, you can never be competitive as an online seller.

Many SMEs don't make the leap into ecommerce because of the increased cost of doing so: it requires database programming, the monthly overhead of a secure site and often unacceptably high transactions processing fees.

A secure site is one where any input from a visitor can be encrypted before it leaves their computer, so it traverses the internet in a form that cannot be read. It uses a technology known as secure socket layer (SSL), and any business can set up such a site through the services of third parties such as Verisign or Thawte, by paying a small monthly fee. Alternatively, a business can opt to direct its visitors to a secure page owned by a payments processing service such as

PayPal. That service accepts all the confidential data securely, then returns the visitor to the original website.

While you can minimize payments processing burdens by working with a packaged ecommerce service from providers like PayPal or Yahoo!, such services don't readily help you to differentiate yourself as a competent independent business. Without a great deal of customization work, such template-based solutions typically look less in harmony with the desired perception of your brand, and feel less supportive of your desired shopping experience, than you would like.

STAGE 5: INTERNAL INTEGRATION

You can have ecommerce without integrating your back-end systems. Many businesses can do this because their volume of transactions is small or they find that response times are not too demanding. In fact, many SMEs don't have any back-end systems that they could integrate and are rather set up to process everything manually.

However, if you want to grow, or if you want to stay competitive, you have to automate and integrate wherever possible. There are three reasons for this:

- First, automation cuts overheads.
- Second, it makes your business scalable.
- Third, it gives your customers instant information, which pumps up your credibility and vastly improves the online experience.

The most critical processes to integrate with your website front-end are those that touch the consumer. The consumer does not care whether you have 100 people scurrying around in your offices pushing bits of paper from one tray to the next. What is important to the customer is that they can immediately see online whether an item is in stock, or check the status of an order.

Complete integration, at web speed, of all of your relevant back-end systems is a prerequisite for any professional emarketing business. It typically involves re-configuring or totally replacing large legacy inventory, finance and production systems, and can cause the overall cost and timeframe of a website project to be many times larger than the cost of the front-end website. It is for this reason that many IT managers groan when a marketing manager approaches them to help with an online strategy.

STAGE 6: PARTNER INTEGRATION

Apart from its capacity to get really close to customers, one of the appeals of online business is its efficiency. You can set up a company with limited overheads and integrate all your automated internal processes in such a way as to run a lean and cost-effective business. Once you do this, you discover that your business partners can get in the way. Very few businesses exist in isolation. They are all part of a set of intersecting systems, processes and supply chains. Any system is as inefficient as its least streamlined part, and getting the business partners on whom you depend to operate as effectively as you can become a significant strategic hurdle. Leaping that hurdle moves you onto a whole new level of performance.

In an ideal world, your suppliers are linked into your systems, so that an order placed online is communicated to them instantly. At the same time, your shipping company is automatically informed of the need to pick up a package for delivery, and the details of that package and its addressee are seamlessly communicated to their systems. Any other players in your supply chain know instantly what is required of them, because their systems and your systems talk to each other in real time.

Once you and your business partners all share the same nervous system, delays and inefficiencies drop away, and you are able to provide superb service to your online customers, often at a significantly lower cost than brick-and-mortar businesses.

STAGE 7: ONLINE MARKETING

While emarketing is something that should be inherent to everything you do, no matter what your stage of online evolution, this is sadly not the case. Typically, online business struggles through the evolution process and gets to a stage where it has a wonderfully smooth-running set of systems and processes, and a website that can handle ecommerce. Then, having built the machine, you start to wonder how you can create more business with it.

Businesses at this stage have a marketing strategy and a substantial budget for implementing it. They advertise online and offline, use all of the PR and social networking opportunities available to them, invest in securing the loyalty and advocacy of their customers and make extensive use of both email marketing and search-engine marketing.

This is the stage at which you may begin to regret having built your current website in the way that you did. The more you look at the needs of your customers and what your site visitors are actually doing, the more you realize that the inherent structure, content and focus of your site needs to change. There are three primary drivers for change:

- First, your online advertising or PR activities should be driving customers to landing pages or guiding visitors through conversion funnels (structured page by page processes that progressively 'convert' a site visitor into a customer), and your site may not be structured to accommodate the smoothest, most effective flows.
- Second, as you start trying to optimize your site for search engines, you realize that your information architecture and the themes of your pages are not really suited to getting good natural rankings.
- Third, your site has to become totally customer-centric, so as to make the experience of your visitors as usable, enjoyable, relevant, rewarding and remarkable as possible. Most ecommerce sites start out extremely product-centric, are built around a catalogue of items for sale, and seek to close sales. Stage-seven emarketing companies have sites that are built around customer

needs and their solutions, while also seeking to provide an experience that customers will want to repeat and recommend.

It is not unusual to get as far as this stage and then abandon your site and start over. Even the largest of companies have done it. You can avoid some of this waste of time and money by working with sound emarketing principles right from the outset. But you also have to accept that every serious online business must continuously upgrade its site, and every three to five years must produce an altogether renovated version.

STAGE 8: EBUSINESS 2.0

You don't get to the pinnacle of online business without being a marketing organization with a sound grasp of emarketing principles and a strategy that implements them. At this stage, the online business is customer-centric and search-optimized. It is using online marketing wisely and has fully integrated real-time back-end and supply-chain processes. It also has a commitment to customer service that goes beyond lip service and exploits social networks extensively as a significant complement to its more traditional online advertising. It is search-engine friendly and uses search marketing appropriately. Its marketing and customer contact processes are intimate, respectful, in tune and dynamic. The business is built and managed in such a way that it can maintain the integrity of its branding, but be flexible and fluid in the way in which it responds to rapidly changing market circumstances. Its brands are generous, sincere and engaging. Above all, it is forward-looking, willing to take risks and resourced to move quickly.

There are not many online businesses that manage to get high scores on all of these criteria. But those are the targets worth aiming for as you put together your emarketing strategy.

Your emarketing strategy 4

The major cause of fatalities among online marketing operations is not technical failure, it is process failure flowing from a failure in vision. Short-sightedness, tunnel vision and a focus on brands or technology can leave a company very exposed.

So how do you find your way through the techno-hype to make sound strategic emarketing decisions? The first step is to understand that your emarketing strategy is part of your marketing strategy, and not something separate. In the same way as the rest of your marketing strategy, your emarketing strategy is designed to support your endeavour to achieve your business objectives. What makes it complicated is the fact that your emarketing activities may require quite different operational resources, business processes and infrastructures than your traditional activities.

As most companies have found out by now, marketing online involves more than simply building a website, hiring someone 'to search-optimize' it, and posting banner advertisements. Among the major processes you will have to deal with are:

- designing your 'brand experiences' (the words 'site' or 'advertising' are too limiting)
- coding those experiences for web, mobile or other access
- deploying them in a dynamic, trackable, maintainable emarketing environment
- hosting the digital marketing experiences and any related systems
- building resources, in terms of both people and technology

- ⚡ tracking, measuring and analysing consumer engagement with and effectiveness of the emarketing activity
- ⚡ supporting and building relationships with customers
- ⚡ upgrading technology, design, content and consumer experience over time.

Whatever you do, don't simply jump into action. Your first step in emarketing is not to build a website. Before you even think about technology, get a good grasp of your corporate business goals. Define the vision, business and operational strategy for the brand or product group. Then, making use of whatever gap analyses, marketing needs analyses or competency tools you may have, define your marketing objectives by brand and by customer. Once you have established a clear picture of your available technology resources and your target customer platforms, decide on the optimal modes and media for each experience. Next, examine your existing business processes, and decide how they need to change to support your vision.

While formulating your strategy, revisit your competencies. If you are an 'offline' company, you probably define your competencies by your internal processes, that is, the things that you know you do well. But online companies need to define their competencies by the unique value they add to their customers' processes. Think about what this means to you as a marketer. What value are

@ If you live at web-speed, you can die at web-speed if you do not function like a well-integrated customer-centric ebusiness. This means, above all, that your information flows must be real-time, not batch-time. You are looking to create an intimate relationship with each customer, not treat customers like herds of sheep. You want to be more efficient than offline companies and provide a higher quality of customer service.

you going to add to your customers' knowledge-seeking and decision-making processes?

Part of any emarketing strategy is to look at costs and competitive advantages. Don't look for savings (if at all) only in emarketing itself, look for the savings that an emarketing process can bring to your overall business processes. A competitive edge based on internal processes is more sustainable than one based on innovative products or business models.

It is easy to get lost in the details, but emarketing strategy is no different from any business strategy in one important respect: wherever possible you must focus on growing your business in those areas where your competitors are weak and your customers' need is strong. Going head-on against competitors in the areas where you all share similar capabilities calls for sustained heavy investment in branding to create the impression of differentiation; or if this is not possible your only option is to compete on price. Too many products are commoditized and fight only on price, not because they are

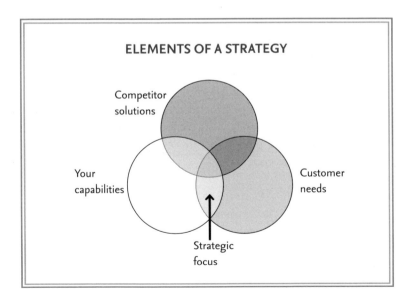

ELEMENTS OF A STRATEGY

Competitor solutions

Your capabilities

Customer needs

Strategic focus

identical to their competitors in all other respects, but because their managers have not identified and protected the relevant differences.

A sound emarketing strategy is built on sound business goals, not on ebusiness aspirations. It is driven by business opportunities, not by the availability of technology. It brings efficiencies to internal and shared processes. And it exploits opportunities for market growth and competitive advantage. Your strategy should tell you how you will:

- build an online presence and a community of customers
- treat customers as networked individuals
- retain and grow those customers
- deliver services faster and faster (not in terms of bandwidth, but responsiveness)
- continually improve the cost-effectiveness of creation, delivery and support
- position your business
- evolve

In the early days of ecommerce, customer service was second only to price in vendor selection. Most recently, as companies like Amazon.com have demonstrated, excellent customer service (the whole online experience) can now make pricing a secondary issue. In many markets, consumers have always been willing to pay a premium for excellence, and, unless you have allowed your brand to be commoditized, the product you are selling is only one aspect of the purchasing experience.

THE EIGHT STEPS TO AN EMARKETING STRATEGY

There are eight steps to developing and implementing an emarketing strategy. These steps are generic to any strategic process. They would be suited to implementing a corporate digital strategy, a brand-specific communication strategy, a new product launch strategy or an overall business strategy.

Whether you spend 10 days on each step or 10 seconds will depend on the context and scale of the project, but the steps are not optional. Each step is an essential part of the process.

The web is packed with examples of good ideas that are implemented badly. It is equally heavily populated with proficient implementations of bad ideas.

It is not unusual for a company to use the web inappropriately. The web is evolving rapidly as a medium, as are the consumers who access it. Your first online attempts may be perfectly in synch with the times, but they date rapidly. Often companies have to face the expense of abandoning an existing web investment and starting all over again.

Without a strategy, you simply cannot plan. Nobody enjoys planning, because planning is boring. It takes time, feels bureaucratic, makes you commit yourself and forces you to justify your decisions. It is true of businesses generally, that they never have the time to formulate plans properly in the first place, yet always have the time – and the money – to rework everything when the first endeavour fails. In large corporations, this failure costs millions in unnecessary expenditure. In opportunity cost terms, the impact is immeasurable.

Even a well designed website is not a magic wand.

For smaller companies, though the actual amount of money involved is a lot less, the waste can be crippling. Since they have no in-house web expertise, small businesses fall victim to unscrupulous vendors all the time. In the early years of a web boom, every programmer and graphic designer is attracted to the easy money to be made as a web developer. Almost without exception, these web developers are clueless about business in general and marketing in particular, yet they happily take large fees from clients who, because of their own lack of experience, simply abdicate all decision-making to them. The result is a proliferation of over-priced cloned brochure-ware that cannot serve as a business tool. (What is worse, when the business owners eventually realize that their site is doing nothing for them, they frequently face extortion from their developers who demand a ransom to release the site code or even the site's domain address).

To be fair, many web developers are savvy and competent, but they struggle to get clients engaged in the design process at the level required for their site to become a sound business tool. And few first-time online businesspeople want to understand that even a well designed website is not a magic wand.

A clearly thought-through strategy can help you avoid these problems and their consequences. It can save you time and investment, and can accelerate your development of a relevant, powerful, effective and flexible web presence. It will also help you to communicate within the organization and with vendors, and it will simplify the process of budget negotiation.

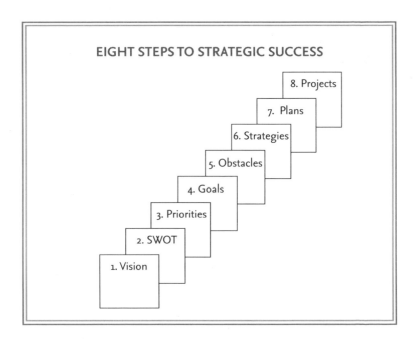

EIGHT STEPS TO STRATEGIC SUCCESS

8. Projects
7. Plans
6. Strategies
5. Obstacles
4. Goals
3. Priorities
2. SWOT
1. Vision

The eight steps to developing and implementing an emarketing strategy are:

1. Clarify your mission and vision
2. Scan your environment
3. Set your priorities
4. Set your objectives
5. Identify your obstacles
6. Create your strategies
7. Define your operational plans and budgets
8. Develop and manage your project plans

You will notice that nowhere in these steps do I say anything about building a website. I shall talk about website design and development later in the book, in Chapter 7. If, in fact, your strategy tells you that building a website is a necessary project to undertake, the specification of that project would take place in steps seven and eight, and not any sooner. It is a classic error for a business to decide that it needs to be 'on the web' and then to immediately build a website. If you don't do the strategic thinking first, you will end up with a site that you don't need or that has none of the functionality or effectiveness you require.

The eight steps are not a one-way street. In fact, it makes a lot of sense to develop your strategy iteratively – to go through the process several times, further refining your ideas each time. What you discover in one step may make you want to go back and rethink an earlier step. Most typically, after doing the scan of your environment, you will need to go back and take a closer look at your vision. Initial visions are sometimes too linear, or too idealistic, and they really need to be tweaked until they are practical and realistic.

Let's look at each of the eight steps in turn.

1. CLARIFY YOUR MISSION AND VISION

To anyone who has spent any time working in large organizations, the mention of missions and visions is enough to induce rolling eyes and heartfelt sighs. We have all endured interminable meetings in rooms covered in flipchart paper containing countless variations of words and phrases. When, eventually, you emerge into the daylight, the final wording of those missions and visions has been so negotiated and polished that it is utterly generic, totally devoid of passion and of no real value to anyone.

Don't make that mistake with the web.

Yes, your mission and vision have to be simple, and relatively comprehensive. But they must also have passion.

Your mission is a statement of your reason for being – what you exist for, why it matters, and your overarching goals. In the context of emarketing, for instance, you want to define what it is you do online and why – what customer problems your online presence seeks to solve, and how your online activities or facilities will add value to your customers' processes. If you cannot describe all of this in a couple of sentences without sounding trite or precious, then you probably need to rethink your reason for being.

If you are having difficulty expressing the essence of your mission, think of it through the eyes of your customers and what it is that they are hoping to do. Traditional businesses tend to focus on what they believe they are good at doing, that is, what used to be called their 'core competencies'. Online, what you are good at doing matters less than what unique value you can add to your customers' processes.

What is vision about? A vision is not a set of goals. It is not a fantasy or woolly wishful thinking, but a clear, specific model of what it is you intend to build. A vision is a description of what your business looks like at a specified time in the future. For emarketing, it is best to craft two visions, one for 18 months away and another for 3 years away. It is best to write this down, in the present tense, as if you are an objective observer in the future describing what you see. Talk about the things that matter most, particularly how you interact with your customers and what they think of you and your products relative to your competitors. And think – a great deal – about what kind of company culture you want to have. Defining your vision is something that you should not take lightly.

If the difference between vision and hallucination is the number of people who can share it, a tragically large number of emarketing efforts have been built on a series of misaligned hallucinations. It is absolutely imperative that you formulate a vision that is clear, unambiguous and communicable.

The bigger the project, the more people will be involved in executing it, and the more scope there is for different people to work at cross purposes. Time spent on this step can save a huge waste of time further down the path. It does not help your business if you move into an emarketing project, and after 6 months, as often happens, find that the different parts are not coming together because everyone was working to a different understanding of the end-point.

If you are unable to articulate what your desired future looks like, then how can anyone else contribute to achieving it?

2. SCAN YOUR ENVIRONMENT

It is important to understand exactly where you are today. List all the factors working for you and against you in the context of achieving your vision. The easiest way to do this is through a traditional SWOT analysis, where you brainstorm and write down all your Strengths, Weaknesses, Opportunities and Threats.

The reason why you need to scan your environment before you decide on your strategy is to make sure that you do not miss anything, positive or negative, that might influence your choice of goals and strategies. By comparing your current situation with your vision for the future, you can identify all the gaps that your strategies will need to address.

In addition to helping you look at your own situation, the SWOT process helps you to look at your competitors and identify what their weaknesses may be. Online marketing is still new, and there are no experts. Even large corporates make mistakes, get it wrong and become vulnerable. The size of their online budget is no measure of their emarketing competence.

In your environment scan, you should consider all the dimensions that are relevant to your project or your business. Many of these dimensions are obvious:

- financial
- processes
- markets
- brands
- personnel
- competencies
- technology

While a SWOT analysis tends to prompt you to look from the inside of your business outwards, you should also try to look from the outside in. Consider dimensions such as:

- competition
- barriers to entry
- changes in consumer power
- evolutions among the companies in your supply chain

Think also about alternatives that are opening up to your consumers: other ways in which they can spend their time or their money, and opportunities and threats from beyond your normal geographic frame of reference. If you are Waterstones.com, you are competing not only with Amazon.co.uk and other local online bookstores, but with Canada's Chapters.indigo.ca or America's Borders.com. You are also competing with long-tail specialist bookstores around the world, such as scifibookstore.net (science fiction), cookbooks.com.au (discount cookery books) and travelbookstore.com (travel books).

The digital market presents some unique challenges, especially for companies to whom the web is new territory. It is difficult to scan an environment that is unfamiliar without succumbing to the myths and the hype surrounding it. Hopefully, this book will fill in some of the gaps, but there is no adequate substitute for first-hand experience. Before you get stuck into an environment scan, it is advisable that those doing the work spend as much time as possible immersing themselves in the digital environment.

This means exploring, through a consumer's eyes, the online environments of your local and global competitors, reading the journals, blogs and newsfeeds that are relevant to your market, and experiencing all of the aspects of the digital world with which your consumers are already familiar. Download podcasts and videos; set up a Facebook page; get a smart phone and a Kindle; upload some photos to Flickr and some videos to YouTube; explore Second Life; research products; buy things online; get accounts at Whrrl and Twitter; play Grand Theft Auto. In an initiative called 'Consumer Nation,' Unilever in the United States encourages (actually requires) this kind of digital immersion for all of its managers, not only those in marketing.

Finally, consider your business culture. In an environment where disruptive change has become a cliché, success depends on your adaptability, which, in turn, hinges on your willingness and ability to take risks. Risk aversion is one of the biggest risks that marketers have to become averse to, no matter how large or small their business may be. The larger the corporation, the more institutionalized its risk aversion tends to be. Such businesses are run by annual planning cycles that produce annual budgets, and often those institutions make it very difficult to change course mid-year, or to exploit transient opportunities. So changing the culture of your organization, while hard to do, may become one of the first things your strategy will have to address.

> **Risk aversion is one of the biggest risks to which marketers must become averse.**

3. SET YOUR PRIORITIES
You will find that the environment scan produces so much data that it

gets a little overwhelming. The web offers so many opportunities that anyone with an entrepreneurial streak has to fight the urge to pursue them all. This is why you set your vision first, and why you look at the strengths, weaknesses and threats as well as the opportunities.

In sifting through your environment scan to establish the priorities, ask yourself, 'What are the most attractive emarketing opportunities to pursue?' It is tempting to try to do too much: build a dozen search-optimized microsites, run a series of web 2.0 viral competitions for user-generated content, deploy a bunch of rich-media advertisements, start a social network for each of your brands, get your executives to blog (or even podcast), seek distributors in China and Brazil, start your own online video channel, move the major part of your budget into contextual ads, recast your brands as consumer-centric digital brands, and build neat stuff for mobile phones. Consider, though, what is going to provide the biggest bang for your buck where your brands are concerned, and what is going to help you develop the most enduring relationships with your customers. Much of the exciting, creative activity in the digital space is just that: activity. The web is awash with gratuitous self-indulgent activity that may never contribute anything to the development of customer engagement.

Be smart about which opportunities are going to play to your strengths and deliver real business value. Remember also that emarketing is a part of a bigger marketing picture, so look for synergies where your offline work supports your online work and vice versa.

What strengths should you leverage most? Identify the strengths which give you the greatest ability to differentiate yourself uniquely. Just because you have strengths in many areas does not mean that you have to exploit them all. Some of your strengths will give you greater advantages than others.

What threats do you absolutely have to deal with? You cannot deal with all of the threats that are out there. Some of them you simply need to keep an eye on, while others must be tackled immediately.

What weaknesses must you cure, or decide to live with? As with threats, it is unlikely that you will ever overcome every one of your weaknesses, nor do you need to. Plan to live with many of them, but prioritize for action those weaknesses that are likely to get in the way of achieving your vision. Any weaknesses that seem both significant and impossible to deal with are obstacles. Park them off to one side temporarily, until you get to step 5.

4. SET YOUR OBJECTIVES

Now you need to take a look at your vision, SWOT analysis and priorities, and distil from them what your strategic emarketing objectives should be. Your ultimate goal in this process is usually to lock in customer loyalty and, through this, to generate profitable sales and market share. But in the context of your particular project, how is this expressed in manageable, measurable objectives? Make sure that your objectives are not overly brand-centric; that you are rather trying to address customer problems or desires. So your focus should be on how you will make the consumer's experience more rewarding and satisfying, not merely on how you will convey brand attributes.

As with any business objectives, of course, you should specify the dimensions and time frames by which you will measure success. An objective is not an objective if you are never able to measure that you achieved it. This means that your objectives need to be specific, observable and quantifiable. To say that you want your customers to talk about you more positively is not a helpful goal. It is far better to say that you want to increase the positive online consumer references to your brand by 60 percent and reduce negative references by 20 percent, by year-end, as measured by Nielsen BuzzMetrics. Or that you want 40 percent of the traffic to your website to come from search engines by the end of July, and that 5 percent of those visitors become online customers on their first visit.

It is not easy to set objectives. In fact, it is terribly difficult, especially if it is new territory and you have no historical experience or industry norms to use as a benchmark. Sadly, industry data available in emarketing is often a little pointless. Things change so rapidly, the spread around the average is so great, and the universe is so difficult to encompass, that the available studies, while interesting, are often dangerously misleading.

For planning purposes, some of the best data are your own. Before embarking on any emarketing initiative, always benchmark your own performance so that you can see what impact you are having. This does not help you in terms of relative competitive performance, but it may be time to start letting go of old-marketing performance criteria such as market share.

5. IDENTIFY YOUR OBSTACLES

An obstacle is something, either internal or external, that will prevent you from achieving your objectives. It may seem strange to start looking at obstacles only at this stage of the process, but there is a compelling reason for this. Most informal planning is shaped by obstacles. Particularly when innovation is in the air, it seems to be human nature to focus on the reasons why something will not work. As a result, your perception of obstacles causes you to set objectives that are sub-optimal or easy to achieve. We simply move the goal posts. If you set objectives first and only then consider the obstacles, you create a different perspective. Obstacles now become things that you have to remove, overcome or bypass, and your strategy has to address them accordingly.

> A strategy is simply a broad-brush description of the approach you intend to take to achieve your goals.

There are many potential obstacles. It is common for finance or technological expertise to be major issues. In the case of ecommerce businesses, logistics – finding reliable fulfilment houses or shipping companies – might get in the way. Sometimes legal or regulatory requirements present significant problems. Whatever the source, it is important to identify the obstacles clearly, not as reasons why goalposts must be moved, but as an input to your strategy.

6. CREATE YOUR STRATEGIES

A strategy is simply a broad-brush description of the approach you intend to take to achieve your goals. It usually includes some of the 'big-picture' decisions that sometimes effectively shut out potential alternative approaches. For example, if you aim to become the dominant online destination for airline bookings, your strategy will define whether you do in-house development or outsource it, whether you provide a luxurious service-rich environment or a bare-bones cut-price site, whether you create your own content or exploit content provided by others. Every aspect of how you move forward requires a strategic decision, without which you have no context for making detailed tactical decisions.

There are always a number of alternative approaches that will take you from where you are today past your obstacles, to the achievement of your vision. You need to identify and explore these alternatives before selecting the one that will work to your best advantage.

Everybody in business knows that it is a mistake to select strategies based only on their likely cost. Yet many strategic emarketing decisions are made this way because often there is no precedent for this kind of marketing investment. You get stuck in a Catch-22 situation, in which you have to make a case for a particular investment but you require the experience that will result from that investment in order to justify your case in the first place. Because emarketing is often automatically dismissed as hype by financial people, you end up investing inadequately and produce results that do little to change their opinions.

Cost is frequently an obstacle. There is never enough money to do what needs to be done in the time available. Your strategy may be able to deal with the obstacle. For example, you may put together a strategy to pitch for the needed budget, pull the money across from other budgets, enter a joint venture, or get venture capital involved. If the obstacle is genuinely insurmountable, you have to scale back your ambitions in a way that will rapidly demonstrate a good return on investment.

7. DEFINE YOUR OPERATIONAL PLANS AND BUDGETS

The last two steps in building and implementing an emarketing strategy are relatively simple, although they involve a great deal of hard work. If you have done a good job of defining your strategy, your operational plans should flow from the strategy without any complications.

Whereas a strategy deals with general approaches without too many specifics, operational plans are detailed. It is here that you lay out who will do what, by when and at what cost. You put flesh on the bones of the strategy and make it workable by allocating resources and making specific decisions.

8. DEVELOP AND MANAGE YOUR PROJECT PLANS

Finally, and this is a rule that should never be broken, always use the tools, disciplines and methodologies of project management to ensure that the project comes in on time, within budget, and to specification. There is nothing as prone to scope-creep as a web project. Project management will break down the work to be done into packages of specific deliverables with specific time frames and allocated resources. The project plan will allow all the people who are involved in the project to know exactly what has to happen by when, who is accountable for it and what the dependencies are. If you neglect to use project management, your project will probably fail.

Craft a project plan, then manage it ruthlessly but creatively. The plan is not a tool that will break if things go wrong or if, as often happens, priorities change mid-project. It acts as a powerful tool for decision-making. A well managed project plan evolves with the project, accommodates changes and keeps everyone informed of their impact.

If you are in an organization of any size and you are embarking on emarketing, one resource that is worth its weight in gold is a good project manager.

A WORD ON TECHNOLOGY

Acknowledge that your first efforts will not be perfect (truth is, no matter how big your budget or how much time you spend on it, no emarketing is ever perfect out of the box). As long as you stay true to your integrity and focus your work on attaining the marketing objectives, you will do fine.

Use guerrilla development. Spend little, abandon easily, keep moving on, keep innovating, keep diversifying. Staying close to the edge is not about taking big expensive risks with unproven technology; it's about committing to perpetual prototyping. I have heard senior people in large corporations say they are waiting till emarketing models stabilize before defining their strategy. Stabilize? The real world is evolving exponentially, and you want your approach to helping customers deal with it to be stable and formulaic? I don't think so.

Waiting till you have some major technology platform in place, say your latest website or a high-end content management system, is the biggest mistake that companies have made in getting an emarketing initiative off the ground. It leads to technology-driven strategies and reactive development models. Worse, it can seriously limit a company's flexibility and ability to evolve dynamically.

The content management system (CMS) phenomenon is a case in point. Here's how the thinking goes: you need to get into emarketing; you need a CMS; you put out a request for proposal (RFP) that you modified from one copied from the web because you don't really understand what you want or why you want it and your IT folks don't know what your marketing needs are well enough to help you; you go with a recognizable name-brand vendor that fits your budget because you are seriously risk-averse and you're spending more money on technology than you have ever spent in one pop; you insist that all emarketing is conformant to the constraints of your CMS because otherwise your CMS choice seems inadequate and because you believe that's the only way your CMS is actually going to work, even though it means excluding much of the dynamic less-canned approaches to emarketing that are gaining traction; you reject any notion of using emarketing models that are not plug-n-play with your CMS environment, and you accept the dumbing down of your marketing outcomes, because that way 'things always work' and you avoid having to confront technology challenges.

Far from liberating your marketing, your expensive technology foundation has become a ball-and-chain.

Technology-enhanced marketing is a steep and perpetual learning curve, and it is understandable that people want to tackle it in a series of small steps. But often you get to the top of the first step and find that you are comfortable where you are, and moving on up seems like an unnecessary effort. And there you are, stuck in a website-and-SEO mode of emarketing communication.

This is the internet age, in its web 2.0 era – not the age of computers but the age of communication, collaboration and creativity. Things change constantly. Wait till a technology foundation is selected, implemented, and tested, and you risk being committed to a direction that is no longer where you want to go. Often, evolving is not about building on the base in which you have invested so much time, money and reputation. It may require you to abandon that base completely and start over – or to build multiple bases in parallel that may never converge. The more you have invested in your base technology, the less willing you are to abandon it, so companies keep relying on far-from-optimal outdated emarketing, for years. They believe their customers don't notice, and many don't because their expectations are conditioned by their past experience. But savvy consumers find more appropriate solutions to their needs, and ways that bypass the formal systems put in place by marketing departments. They use online communities, social networks, informal learning, comparison and review sites or social search to form opinions and make decisions. And you never know it is happening.

Assume that 'a technology' is all that you need, and you shut the door to all the other emergent opportunities. Assume you need to implement the technology before you start putting brand experiences online, and you risk becoming a captive of your own solution.

Best and worst practices 5

I am a little hesitant to use the consultant-speak term 'best practices' in the context of emarketing, because, where change is so rapid, yesterday's best practices can easily become today's worst practices. For example, for many years emarketing was all about a single website and banner advertising; over the past couple of years marketers have focused on multiple websites and SEO. In their time, these strategies represented the perceived best practices for emarketing, but today they seem quaint and inadequate. Now there is a rush to experiment with online video, mobile access, and social networking. But to many global corporations, social networking is already being labelled 'social not working'. As we learn more about how online consumers seek solutions, discover and evaluate brands, and make buying decisions, emarketing will continue to evolve. It will become more sophisticated, with all of the ingredients integrated into a dynamic but holistic strategy, which in turn is integrated into an overall marketing strategy. But while the way in which they are most effectively implemented changes constantly, the universal principles do not change.

SOME GENERAL POINTERS

Here are 12 cardinal rules that apply no matter what the size, scale or stage of your emarketing initiative may be.

1. DO NOT START UNTIL YOU HAVE A CLEAR VISION AND A DEFINED BUSINESS PURPOSE

The money that companies have wasted by prematurely embarking on poorly conceived emarketing initiatives would probably buy Google 10 times over. Resist the urge to leap into action until you know what success will look like, why you are doing something, and the strategy to achieve it.

2. BE CUSTOMER-CENTRIC

View everything you do through the eyes of your customers. Focus on improving the processes that occupy their time, and on helping them to achieve whatever it is they need to do, instead of focusing only on what it is you want them to do. Never compromise on usability. Regard usability as a non-negotiable essential characteristic of the design of your user experiences, always.

3. DO NOT RADICALLY RESTRUCTURE YOUR OLD MARKETING APPROACH

If you are an existing business with legacy systems in place, trying to do any kind of radical restructuring is fraught with obstacles. Not only is it slow and expensive to dismantle existing processes, personal attitudes and passive resistance to change will always get in the way. It is better to introduce new approaches in parallel with existing approaches and cut across gradually once those new approaches have proven themselves.

4. DO NOT PLUG IN AN E-MARKETING APPROACH WITHOUT INTEGRATING IT WITH EXISTING MARKETING PROCESSES

Introducing new approaches in parallel does not mean introducing them in isolation. It is important that marketing presents a unified face to the world. It is not uncommon, especially in large organizations, for an ecommerce unit to operate almost independently of the marketing department, and for initiatives invested in by one to not have a parallel in the other. For example, one major clothing retail chain recently ran a major television, print and outdoor campaign, investing millions in double-page advertisements and prime-time slots to promote its summer collection. Yet none of those advertisements carried the retailer's website address and the website itself did not reflect the imagery of the campaign. Not only does this risk undermining the brand, it wastes great opportunities for reinforcement.

5. USE PROJECT MANAGEMENT DISCIPLINES AND TOOLS

Nothing is more prone to scope-creep, fuzzy vision and budget bloat than a web project. No matter how small the project, it is essential to use the disciplines and methodologies of project management to ensure that it comes in on time and within budget, and that the end product delivers in line with the initial vision. Project management does not force you to stay on track – in fact doing so in a fast-changing environment is frequently not in the best interests of the project – but it does help you to quantify the implications of proposed changes and to make informed decisions.

6. DO NOT LET TECHNOLOGY DICTATE MARKETING STRATEGY

It is easy for marketers to abdicate decision-making to IT people or web developers, particularly if they feel a little unsure of their own technical expertise. This situation is aggravated when a company has already invested heavily in a technology base, such as a content management system or a legacy order-processing system. The capabilities of the technology should not be allowed to define the customer processes or limit the functionality that the site provides. Rather, marketers should define what it is they wish to accomplish and then have their technical partners seek the technology that can support the need.

> Marketers should define what it is they wish to accomplish and then have their technical partners seek the technology that can support the need – not the other way round.

Should you build your site in Flash? If your business objective is simply to look cool and have lots of animation, Flash is an option. But what about the desired user experience? Do users want to come to your site and be blown away by your creativity, or do they want to know more about your products and make a purchase? Do they typically have the bandwidth for your site to be usable, or will they be waiting 45 seconds for every page to load? How easy is it going to be for you to maintain the site and update its content? Will the technology help you achieve your goal of top search rankings, or will it be a hindrance? Be sure to examine all of your business objectives and requirements before opting for a technical solution.

7. MATCH THE CUSTOMERS' PREFERRED WAYS OF INTERACTING WITH YOU

This flows from point 6. If you want to be customer-centric, you need to find out how your customers would like to interact with you and structure your processes accordingly. Too often companies dictate to their customers how they should do things because the company is too inwardly focused or too lazy to change. If the online experience you provide is slow, turgid, unnecessarily confusing or insulting, your visitors will not come back.

8. DO NOT TREAT A WEBSITE LIKE A ONE-TIME INVESTMENT

One of the saddest fantasies of emarketing is the notion that a website is a once-off investment. The truth is that you can expect to spend at least as much as the initial development cost every year thereafter on maintenance, upgrades, updates, content management and tactical activity. If your site is a publishing site, or a retail site with continual inventory or pricing changes, expect to spend more. If you do not budget your website and its associated emarketing as an ongoing investment, you might as well not build it in the first place. It is a business, not a work of art.

9. EXPLORE NEW POTENTIAL CUSTOMERS AND MARKETS

An online business can bring the world to your door. Geographic and demographic market sectors that you previously ignored can suddenly become viable. Even though your primary purpose in online marketing may be to succeed with your established markets, you need to expand your horizons and try to see where else you can find new business.

10. BOOST YOUR COMPETITOR RADAR

Just as you might use your online presence to venture into new markets, other businesses around the world are already competing for your online customers – and you may not even be aware of it. Invest in refreshing your understanding of who your competitors really are. One of the easiest ways to do this is to search on Google, Yahoo! or the Chinese search engine Baidu, using the kinds of search terms you would expect your target audience to use when looking for solutions that you provide. It can be a sobering experience.

11. DO NOT EXPECT SUCCESS TO BE FAST, EASY AND DRAMATIC

Not everyone gets to be a YouTube, where a two-person college-dorm project becomes a multi-billion-dollar business within two years. It is important to be realistic about any emarketing initiative and to understand that, with the possible exception of campaigns that go viral, success usually takes a little time.

12. PLAN FOR SUCCESS TO BE FAST, EASY, AND DRAMATIC

Success is your second-worst nightmare in online business. Dramatic success can close you down if you have not done your planning correctly, and have not designed your site infrastructure, back-end systems, customer service or supply chain to be rapidly scalable. Unplanned success can waste a massive launch marketing effort, lose a huge amount of business and badly damage your credibility as an ecommerce company. At best, you suffer a little embarrassment, annoy your

potential customers and give your competitors something to
smile about; at worst you do serious damage to the brand, and
cost the business a fortune.

Some of these principles may seem like no-brainers, but
implementing them is never trivial. Any organization that is marketing
its products or services in a brick-and-mortar or face-to-face mode has
problems migrating into the online space. The web is disruptive,
forcing you to embrace risk, and any move into web-based business
invariably meets with resistance. The hardest resistance to overcome
is locked into the mind-set of your management, your staff and your
external marketing agencies.

You may at first get overt opposition ('That's not going to work,
because …'), which is best overcome right at the outset by engaging
key stakeholders in a process of vision building or scenario
development. This process should then be reiterated down into the
organization. This is not as trivial as it sounds, particularly in large,
established businesses whose forward momentum makes
directional shifts difficult to achieve. However, it is an essential step
in managing change.

Once key personnel are overtly on board and focused on
achieving the same end result, your biggest drag on progress is often
a lack of understanding of the online environment. This translates
itself into uncertainty, hesitation about making decisions and
a reluctance to move too far from the familiar. If your people
view the online environment with the same limited perspective
as package-tourists on a bus tour through Belgium, your emarketing
initiative is unlikely to produce a satisfying customer-centric
online experience.

Sometimes the people who need to change most are those at
the top. People at grass-roots level are frequently more aware of the
changes necessary than the leaders of an organization. If senior
managers do not do a regular reality check to stay up to date with the
future, they risk creating an ever-widening credibility gap.

This lack of insight handicaps your marketing and can result in the kind of grotesque ecommerce web experiences that companies like Selfridges, Accessorize, Next or PCMall provide, or the lovely-but-lacking sites provided by companies like Habitat Shoes (see later in chapter).

ORGANIZATIONAL STRATEGY

It is essential when staffing your emarketing initiatives to hire people who 'get' the web – not as coders, but as users. This is not as simple as making sure your recruits are all under 25 years old. A surprisingly large number of new entrants into the job market are not web-savvy at all; and even if they are, they may not have the marketing skills that you need. Remember, the web has been around since 1992. You might be better off hiring experienced marketing people who have been using the web for a decade or so, if you can find them.

If staffing is a problem, and it usually is, you have to turn to training and outsourcing. It is perfectly possible to change the knowledge-base and even the culture of an organization through intensive training and organizational development.

Outsourcing, particularly of those functions that do not require local knowledge, can be fast, uncomplicated and inexpensive. You should focus on your core competencies, and outsource everything else – at least initially. It is quite unlikely that you will have existing in-house competencies in areas such as search engine optimization, search marketing, online advertising, buzz marketing or email marketing. Your IT group may have some competencies in back-end systems, but this does not mean they can build effective websites, so you should consider outsourcing many aspects of website design, including information architecture, usability, look and feel, and web analytics. If you wish to get your website up and running quickly and effectively, don't try to take on board new competencies unless they are strategically vital to your future competitiveness. In fact, the web is an opportunity to shed a few.

With any strategic shift, it is a challenge to identify what your core competencies are. Competencies are contextual. They are relative to the scenario in which you need to apply them. The world in which you engage the online consumer is different from the earlier world in which online consumers did not exist. Offline businesses think of their core competencies as simply those things that they do really well. But online consumers only use the web in so far as it enhances their day-to-day processes, making the things they do easier, faster, less expensive or more rewarding. So an online business has to look at its competencies as those things that it can do to add value to its customers' processes. Figure out what those are, and leverage them. Once again, unless you have a deep understanding of your customers, you cannot identify the core competencies that you need to leverage or acquire.

Many companies in the United Kingdom, United States and Canada that have gone through the digital-strategy process have found that the best way to jump-start an ebusiness initiative is to form a separate department or division, or even a new company, instead of trying to transform their existing operations. This unit acts as a hot-house, a separate profit centre and 'centre of excellence', where the digital business has no choice but to prove itself.

Free from the legacy baggage of the existing offline business, the hot-house can rapidly create its own culture, policies and processes. It has more freedom to innovate and a strong incentive to succeed. In most cases, this separation is not intended to be permanent, and the unit will be merged into the existing business infrastructure after a few years.

If such a unit does not form a separate company, a large business will typically create an ecommerce department. This group is in partnership with the established marketing department and draws on the IT and financial resources of the rest of the company. But its goal is to generate revenue online. The offline marketers, IT people and financial people learn from their involvement with the ecommerce department, developing their own knowledge and skills over time. Eventually, the ecommerce department is disbanded, its web coders are assimilated into IT and its designers, writers, marketing people and project managers are assimilated into the marketing department.

BUDGETING

A business that wants to create an effective web presence has to budget accordingly. Not surprisingly, the larger the company and the bigger the vision, the more this initiative will cost. You require a development budget that is appropriate to the scale of the project. If a web development organization, internal or external, is willing to quote you a ballpark figure for building your site without first clearly detailing its scope and schedule in a project plan, find another developer.

It can cost you anywhere from a few thousand euros or dollars to many millions, though these price points are extremes. Think of development budgets as a bell curve. For half of large businesses, the initial costs of website development, including basic back-end ecommerce, might fall somewhere between 50 thousand and 200 thousand dollars (40 thousand to a 150 thousand euros). For the other half of large businesses, it could be considerably higher or considerably lower. Similarly, half of SMEs might find that their website development costs are about a quarter of those of large businesses, falling into a similar broad spread. With spectrums as wide as this, you have to make sure that your developers are planning to build exactly what it is that you have in mind. The importance of the initial visualization step cannot be overstated.

If you are determined to build your site entirely in Flash, expect huge ongoing costs compared with what it would cost to take care of the same site built in HTML.

You also require a maintenance budget, since sites do not take care of themselves. There are ongoing costs for technical maintenance and enhancement, design upgrades, content management and ongoing performance improvement. These costs can be as high per year as your initial development cost. Maintenance for sites with particularly changeable content or leading-edge looks can set you back a great deal more than development costs. If you are determined to build your site entirely in Flash, expect huge ongoing costs compared with what it would cost to take care of the same site built in HTML.

In addition, you need to factor in budgets for IT, connectivity and bandwidth. It is typically many orders of magnitude more costly, and far slower, to re-engineer all your internal systems and processes than simply to build the front-end website.

Since a web project is primarily a marketing initiative, you will also need the staff and budgets to cover marketing, PR, creative, information architecture, databases, search and metrics. And it is absolutely imperative to allocate resources to project management.

For a business of any size, emarketing is not a Skunk Works project – one that you run informally without any real mandate, budget, vision, or methodology. You cannot entrust it to Joe in the photocopy room who appears to be terminally addicted to Facebook, Nicky in IT because she spends her life playing World of Warcraft, or Jamil in the finance department who has a cousin with a blog.

The same applies to SMEs. Since they usually have to be extremely careful with their every cent, it is even more vital for them not to launch into an emarketing endeavour without a carefully crafted strategy. Small businesses have the advantage of spontaneity and flexibility, but must take care that this does not make them impulsive or reckless. Without the checks and balances of a larger company, a small business can rush headlong into building a website or outsourcing search marketing, only to regret not having taken the time to clarify its vision, decide what its commercial objectives are and ask the right questions before selecting an outsource partner.

The more vulnerable your business is, the more cautious you have to be in selecting your development partners. Since they have no real understanding of emarketing or the internet, small businesses in particular can fall victim to service companies that are predatory or incompetent. I have worked in more than three dozen countries around the world, right from the very beginnings of the web and it is almost universally true that web developers and other emarketing service providers abuse their perceived authority when dealing with small businesses. There is hardly a single small business that has not had a major issue with its developer.

It is not only back-bedroom developers who are at fault. Some surprisingly large companies, be they website developers, email marketing companies, SEO service providers and even advertising agencies, can fleece their customers through a combination of overcharging, hidden fees, incompetence and carefully crafted legal small-print.

Any high-profile new industry is characterized by naïve customers and inexperienced suppliers. Small businesses should not hesitate to exploit all the business opportunities that emarketing offers. But you have to be cautious about who you do business with. Above all else, know your business objectives and have a clearly communicable viable vision. Understand as much as you can about what can and cannot be done in online marketing. Then take time to shop around,

---

@ One company wanted to move its site from its developer because they were tired of having to accept slow responses and high fees for every content change. They were told that they did not own the code and would have to pay a large sum for receiving it. Another business, in a similar situation, had its web address held to ransom – the developer refused to give them the name they thought they had paid for unless they paid over another fee. And one small business was forced to sue two web developers in succession, the first having taken his fees and never produced anything, the second having built, for an absurdly high fee, what is arguably the world's worst website. Countless other SMEs have recounted similar tales.

talk to references, look at samples of work done, and make sure you sign a contract that protects your interests.

That said, here is why start-ups are attracted to the web, and why large companies can never be complacent again: anyone who knows what they are doing can get a professional-looking ebusiness up and running in a few weeks for only a few thousand dollars or euros.

> **Anyone who knows what they are doing can get a professional-looking ebusiness up and running in a few weeks for only a few thousand dollars or euros.**

A small business, unencumbered by existing systems, can build a site for nothing other than the time that it takes to download a free template and tweak it. Or, for less than they would spend on lunch, they can use a hosted service that gives them free access to all of the more or less idiot-proof tools to build an ecommerce site. Ongoing costs are mainly related to hosting – the amount you pay to have your website on a computer that is linked to the internet. Today, this is pocket change. Other than the overhead of a basic computer and internet access, your biggest costs are your time and your ecommerce transaction fees. Beyond that, if you know how to use the web and can leverage social networks into creating some buzz, you can get by with no cash marketing outlay at all – unless of course you are launching a new brand into a major market! Wherever you are, the time is now and the opportunities are unlimited. Though it has been around for more than a decade, and despite the millions of websites already out there, there are very few ecommerce sites that do a good job. Most of them are outdated or amateurish, and cater rather poorly to an increasingly discerning online population hungry for satisfying shopping experiences. With customer insight, a clear vision and a well-conceived strategy, you can do real damage to established market leaders.

EMARKETING OPPORTUNITIES

Let's look at a couple of sites that belong to relatively big-name companies to see exactly how much opportunity there is to do better. Everything in this section relates to sites in existence in January 2009. If the companies concerned were paying any attention to customer needs in the online market, their sites would be radically different.

CLOTHING RETAIL

Around the world, clothing, shoes and accessories are the biggest selling category of goods purchased online. Ten percent of clothing in the United States are bought online. Online shopping is a natural evolution from paper-catalogue mail-order businesses. Clothing companies discovered decades ago that if you make it easy for people to order on impulse, and simple for them to return stuff that doesn't fit when they try it on at home, you can move tons of product every day. This is especially true in places where it just takes too much time to get to a physical store.

Whether you are in central London, where trying to squeeze clothes shopping into a busy schedule is impossible, or in a far-flung village in Mexico, where the nearest store is half a day's drive away, you are delighted to give your business to a clothing firm who lets you buy your way.

As one of the dominant clothing retailers in the UK, apparently targeting a web-savvy demographic, you would expect a clothing retailer such as Next to have done everything possible to capture the online market. Yet their website is a badly executed online version of their catalogue. Almost entirely image-driven, the only option to find products by text description is to use the site search box. Obviously well designed, this returns not a list of options but yet another page of pictures.

The use of images is competent (it should be, given the company's print catalogue origins), and the now ubiquitous ability to pass a magnifying frame over images to see a zoomed detail is there. But what is lacking is the ability to see anything but the single shot chosen by the photographer. Details are mostly absent too – it's as if the customer should not care about anything other than what the picture reveals. Where is it made? Is it a house label or some other tag? Are those buttons plastic or bone? What is the stitching quality like? And the sunglasses the model is wearing, it would be nice to know more about them other than that they are 'Medium Plastic Sunglasses; filter category 3; dark tint; for sunny conditions'. There is a massive opportunity here to make the products sound interesting and desirable, not merely generic. All of the things that you would look at in-store, that are important parts of the customer's decision-making process, are treated with disdain by the website.

A site like Accessorize, part of the Monsoon family, has its problems too. It appears to have been designed for Internet Explorer (IE) and some of its important functionality doesn't work in Firefox, the web browser now being used by one person in four. For example, when you click on an image labelled as 'zoomable' another window pops up. In IE, this eventually loads a Flash image that you can zoom into or spin on its head (but not rotate, so you can't see the back or sides of the item). In Firefox, the pop-up window doesn't find Flash, so you get taken to the website's home page. On the positive side, the site has 'tell a friend' links on every item, but it is far from clear what Accessorize will do with your friend's contact details once you have sent a notification. Will you be inadvertently adding your friend to a mailing list? If you look for guidance, you find there is no easy link to a privacy policy – an inexcusable failing on any e-commerce site. The policy is included in the terms of use, and is effectively a disclaimer, asserting the rights of the company rather than clarifying the rights of the customer.

Finally, the site of Selfridges, an eminent London department store, leaves so much to be desired. Again, there is no obvious privacy policy. Another site that appears to not have been tested in Firefox, its home page has chunks of site code displayed where the headlines should be. '@TEXT_CATEGORY_TITLE_H1@' shouts out at you in 25 point font. Elsewhere on the page, instead of headlines you get things like '@TEXT_COL_RIGHT_H2@'. If you find yourself on the specials page, which pitches food hampers, there is no way to escape. For some reason, all of the links back to the home page, or to any other page, keep bringing you back to the specials page. How can anyone – let alone a major retail institution – allow a website to go live without even the most superficial testing?

It gets worse. Though there are menu links to sections such as 'Mens', 'Womens', 'Kids' and so on, they lead to articles, not to products. Other than gift cards, and a few oddities like food hampers, you can't actually buy anything on the site, nor can you window shop. The Selfridges site does not help you to do anything, really. It's a stage two brochureware site without the brochure. If you are looking online for information that will help you to plan a clothes shopping trip, you will bypass Selfridges completely and move on to the sites of retailers who care about the online consumer.

Visit selfridges.com, accessorize.co.uk and next.co.uk, and then contrast them with endless.com, gap.com, macys.com or bebe.com.

ELECTRONICS

Electronics runs a close second to clothing as a massive global online seller. Although three out of four electronics buyers ultimately make their purchase in a physical store, most of them first use the web to do their research. The web is a perfect environment for electronics shoppers who are trying to make purchasing decisions. Items are expensive, complicated and confusing. The difference between the TH-42PH9WK and the TH-42PS9WK television sets is hard to figure out in a bustling retail store where salespeople are hustling you every couple of minutes and few details are available.

You need time to comparison-shop, and you want as much relevant, credible information as possible to help you shorten your list. The web helps you to decide what to buy and where to buy it. You want to read reviews by professional journalists, compare specifications, and hear what fellow consumers think, especially those who have already been through the buying process. And you want to know about the stores and their service reputations. You can do all of that on the web in a few minutes. Anyone wanting to sell electronics absolutely has to have a data-rich, compelling and customer-focused website.

The same weaknesses in Next's clothing site are true of the Next electrical catalogue. A small photo of a Panasonic 42 inch plasma TV with only eight bullet points about its specifications, no model number, no links to either user reviews or professional reviews, and no ability to compare similar products side by side, is hardly enough to get you to part with the asking price.

In the US, PCMall.com is one of the big players in computers and accessories. This is despite the fact that the site fails many of the most basic usability and customer-centricity tests. The site provides good product information for each item stocked, but the ability to compare products side by side is missing. It allows customers to upload reviews of products, but provides no links to professional reviews. The site is missing an essential ingredient: usability. It is crowded and claustrophobic, allowing ill-formatted chunks of text to stretch right across windows, making reading difficult, and making any extended research really tiring. Each page is crammed with content, in a layout that shows no concern for clarity. The information architecture is not intuitive and it is really difficult, once you move away from a page, to find your way back to it again. The site-search function delivers results in a seemingly random list. The interface is ugly and unwelcoming, clearly designed by a database programmer rather than an information architect, and would not encourage anyone to spend any time on the site. Finally, because the site is not user-friendly, it is also not search-engine friendly.

Why does the PCMall.com site still do well? It is probably because its target users know exactly what they are looking for, and are not shopping around.

I have picked on these companies to illustrate how much opportunity there is for anyone to make an emarketing impact in this market. These are big players, and they have left the goals wide open. Without doubt, they will improve and, if they take online consumers seriously, they will improve continuously, not in giant steps every couple of years. In the meantime, they are totally vulnerable to any mass-market or niche supplier who wants to capture the online consumer.

Contrast these utilitarian sites with bestbuy.com, circuitcity.com, and, for a brilliant example of online retail customer-centric usability, though not in the electronics field but in homeware, cb2.com.

BEST PRACTICES IN ONLINE RETAIL

An online retail site should be designed to maximize sales, but at the same time be usable, relevant and useful. Here are some of the ways in which these characteristics are implemented in practice.

- **COLLECT EMAIL ADDRESSES:** Do whatever you can, without being intrusive, to gather the email address of your visitor. At the same time, use a double opt-in process to get their express permission to send specific content to them. (Double opt-in entails sending visitors an email confirming that they have subscribed to your list. They then have to click a link in this email to reaffirm their decision.) Ideally, you should do this on the home page before they dig deeper into the site, but you can also do it at appropriate places within the site. Provide visitors with a compelling reason for giving you their information, such as subscription to a newsletter or monthly specials, membership of a community of interest, or a coupon that is redeemable online or in-store.
- **MAKE ORDER-TRACKING EASY:** Customers should be able to track online exactly what the status of an order is and see when they can expect it to arrive.
- **PROVIDE ASSISTANCE:** This is different from help, which is typically a generic list of bits of useful information. Assistance is personalized. Customers should be able to contact you and receive an immediate answer to their question. Ideally, you

should provide multiple ways for customers to do this: email, live chat, voice-over IP and telephone. This assistance should be available 24 hours a day, 7 days a week. If you cannot manage to staff this economically, outsource it to a call centre in India. That's what everyone else does.

- **ENCOURAGE FEEDBACK:** Make it easy for online visitors to tell you what they think. Let them do so anonymously if they so choose. If they give you their contact details, always respond, if only to thank them for taking the time to communicate. Have a policy of feedback review so that any input you get is incorporated in your continuous improvement process.

- **ADOPT A PRIVACY POLICY:** Provide a privacy policy that is explicit and clear, and adhere to it. Tell people what information you are collecting, what you will and will not do with it, how you will secure it, and how they can access and modify that information.

- **MAKE FINDING STUFF EASY:** Provide multiple ways for visitors to find what they are looking for, or to make a purchasing decision. Monitor what people are looking at, what they are searching for, and what they are buying. Provide links to well-designed sub-catalogues that short-list categories that are meaningful to the visitor. For example, gifts for the host, the geek or the chef; or gifts for different budgets, different occasions, or favourite gifts. Provide a good site-search tool that presents results in a user-friendly way – do not rely on your navigation buttons, which few site visitors use these days. And then run a usability test on your navigation to make sure it does what visitors expect it to do.

- **PROVIDE VALUE-ADDED SERVICES:** Allow customers to request and select gift-wrapping, order online and pick up in-store, pre-order soon-to-be available items, or to run a wish list or wedding registry.

- **SHOW THE PRODUCT:** Provide multiple views of products, from different angles. Give customers the ability to zoom in (Ajax makes this really fast and bandwidth-friendly). Where relevant, show the product in isolation and in context. Hi-fi speakers all look the same size until you see them in a room. Clothing and accessories look different when worn as an outfit.

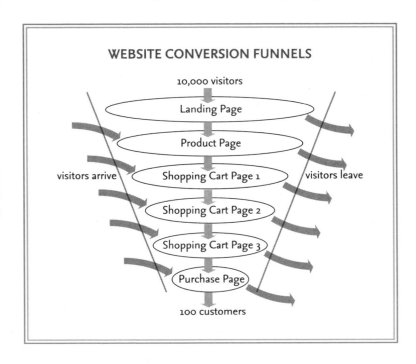 **PROVIDE PRODUCT DETAILS:** Do not skimp on information, but make it easy for visitors to skip the details. The more purchase-support information you can provide, the better. Provide a link to reviews on other sites (always let these sites open in a new window so that visitors don't leave your site), and provide reviews on your own site – by both experts and customers. Allow side-by-side comparisons of all major features, and even downloads of product brochures, spec sheets and user manuals. You don't need to do this yourself, as there are online sites to which you can link.

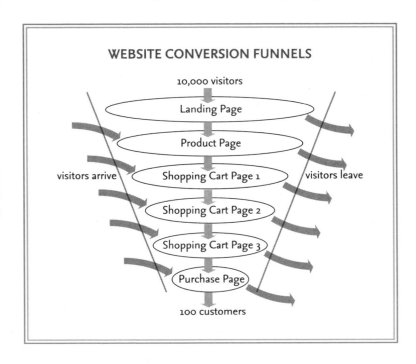 **ENCOURAGE USER-GENERATED CONTENT:** Do not be afraid of what visitors might say. Provide a compelling facility for

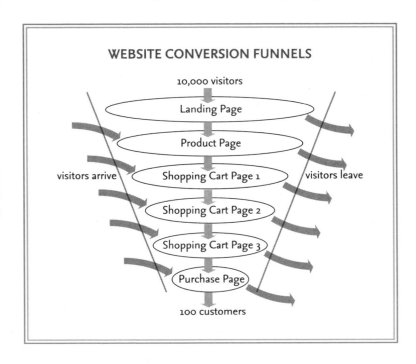

WEBSITE CONVERSION FUNNELS

10,000 visitors

Landing Page

Product Page

visitors arrive — Shopping Cart Page 1 — visitors leave

Shopping Cart Page 2

Shopping Cart Page 3

Purchase Page

100 customers

comments or reviews. Whenever you do, provide a credibility system, such as asking people who read these reviews to vote on how useful they are. That way, good content floats to the top and encourages more good contributions.

☒ **MAKE SHIPPING COSTS TRANSPARENT:** Let visitors know what the costs are at any stage in their decision-making. Do not make them wait till they get to the check-out, or you risk one of the main causes of shopping cart abandonment – surprise costs. Provide as many shipping options as possible, from express overnight to slow conventional post.

☒ **UP-SELL AND CROSS-SELL:** Take advantage of opportunities to up-sell and cross-sell. The web is a great place to stimulate impulse purchases and make your visitors happy that you made a suggestion. If they add a blender to their shopping cart, suggest some margarita glasses to go with it; if they choose a shirt, suggest a tie; if they buy a television set, suggest a DVD player. Make these suggestions informative by showing what other people bought when they bought the product. If your systems are up to it, offer a bundled discount.

☒ **WORK IN CONVERSION FUNNELS:** A purchase decision is like a funnel. You might have a thousand people look at a product page. Of these, a hundred move on to the purchase form, and only five actually buy. Identify your funnels, monitor where you are losing people, and tweak those areas to keep as many people moving through as possible. Constantly shorten the funnels, reduce the number of required clicks, and reinforce reasons-to-buy assurances, until you are happy that each funnel is optimized. Then start over again.

☒ **OPTIMIZE CHECKOUT PROCESSES:** Once visitors want to check out, make this process as rapid as possible. Never force them to open an account. Allow them to simply provide credit card details and a delivery address if that is all they want to do. If they already have an account, allow them to do a one-click checkout, with payment going to their default card and delivery to their default address. If they choose to open an account, keep the questions relevant to the process. Do not ask for their income, date of birth, passport number, golf handicap or the name of their cat. They simply want to be able to buy stuff from you – they are not applying for a job, looking for a loan or asking to marry you. Many would-be customers will simply abandon you forever if your questions are intrusive. Once they become customers, you can start developing the relationship and populating the fields on your database. It comes across as abusive to force an interrogation at the beginning of the customer relationship.

If you are a wholesaler, a retailer or a service provider and for some strategic reason you do not want to provide your target customers with the ability to transact online, your web presence should still serve a clearly defined marketing purpose. A restaurant, for example, may want its site to drive visitors to phone in to make a reservation. A tax consultant may want site visitors to sign up for a newsletter. A department store may want to ensure that anyone planning a shopping trip includes a visit to their store. None of these goals can be achieved with a website that lacks focus or is poorly conceived or badly executed.

Ten years ago it was thought that you could sell only books, CDs and videotapes online. CDs and videotapes have since gone the way of the dinosaurs, and Amazon's digital book service, the Kindle, is even threatening paper-based books. The products are gone, and digital retail remains.

Is there anything that consumers will not buy online? Not really.

How about cars? In the United States and many countries in Europe, cars are the third largest category of online sales by value. Once a place where geeks sold old stuff, eBay is now America's largest car dealer. In fact, one car is sold every minute via the site. If you are in Chicago and want to buy a previously loved Porsche, you can search the country on eBay. If you find one of the right age and mileage in Miami, the 'long tail' kicks into gear: you will find, also through eBay, all the different niche businesses that will test drive it for you, do a mechanical check, fix the bullet holes, finance the purchase, insure it, and transport it across the country to your doorstep. You no longer need to spend your weekends slogging around used-car dealerships in your area, because eBay has found ways to add value to your purchasing processes.

Online real-estate and property sales are huge. I recently had a South African at one of my seminars who lives in Spain and sells Turkish real estate to Irish investors via his website. Another client sells properties for millions to buyers around the world who purchase them off-plan, without ever seeing them, to hold as investments.

> No matter how big and established you are, and no matter what industry you are in, you are vulnerable if you do not take the new consumer seriously.

Would you ever buy a diamond ring online? Many people do. One of my favourite businesses is called Blue Nile. The company has no physical jewellery stores at all. It is the third largest buyer of wholesale diamonds on the planet and is second only to Tiffany in retail diamond-ring sales – and it is all done on the web out of a warehouse in Seattle.

The price of the average ring that Blue Nile sells is double that of the industry, so like many of the web's more successful companies it is competing on value, not price. Blue Nile grew to market dominance by being one of the first emarketers to leverage three vital components of online loyalty: information-richness, word of mouth and trust.

In 1996 a one-man jewellery store built the Blue Nile website for US$2,000. The site was populated with educational information, telling its visitors everything they ever needed to know about diamonds. Very soon, without any marketing, Blue Nile was taking a quarter of a million dollars per month.

Three years later, 29-year-old Mark Vadon, newly graduated from business school, went looking for an engagement ring. This is a traumatic process for most men, to whom all diamonds appear identical yet represent a major expense. The sales person in the Tiffany store was unhelpful when he asked how to decide which diamond to buy, telling him somewhat archly to buy the stone that spoke to him. Angry and a little humiliated at this dismissive treatment, he went online to try to learn more about diamonds, and he found Blue Nile, which makes that traumatic purchasing process so much more easy and reassuring.

> **Blue Nile has no physical jewellery stores at all. It is second only to Tiffany in retail diamond-ring sales – and it is all done on the web out of a warehouse in Seattle.**

He bought a ring. Then he bought the company, using 5 million dollars in venture capital. Applying his recently acquired MBA expertise, he borrowed more money and blew it on advertising, rapidly losing 30 million dollars without seeing any impact on sales. Then he got smart, abandoned advertising, and focused on generating word of mouth. From then on, his sales grew by 50 percent per year.

Mark Vadon invested in making his site the best place on the web to learn about diamonds. You can build your own ring online, and search for stones by colour, cut, clarity, size or budget. There is a thirty-day returns, no-questions-asked policy, and free courier delivery anywhere in the world. If your purchase warrants it, you get free armoured car delivery. There are 'forward-to-a-friend' links on the site, and endorsements from happy customers. Major financial publications write glowing articles about the company, further pumping up the perception of trustworthiness already created by the transparency, tone and usability of the site.

Today Blue Nile has massive buying power, so its diamond costs are low. Its overheads are low too, because there are no luxurious physical retail outlets occupying expensive mall space. Blue Nile's overheads are only 13 percent of its revenue, which is one-third of what a traditional jeweller has to carry. The web-based cost structure allows it to sell at cost plus 20 percent, while retail jewellers add on 50 to 100 percent. Tiffany is no longer smug and comfortable, nor are any of the independent jewellers in malls around the world.

The lesson for large companies in the Blue Nile story is that no business is safe from a smart emarketer focused on customer processes. No matter how big and established you are, and no matter what industry you are in, you are vulnerable if you do not take the new consumer seriously. The more competition-proof an industry may seem to be, the more complacent it tends to become. For innovative SMEs, there are online opportunities everywhere.

New consumers and web 2.0 | 6

The terms 'new consumer' and 'web 2.0' have been so overused in the past few years that it has become fashionable among digerati to be disdainful of them. But, while you can dismiss the labels themselves, the phenomena that they describe are vitally important to any marketer. 'New consumer' and 'web 2.0' are not ephemeral marketing buzzwords; they represent fundamental ongoing shifts in the structure of the marketing landscape.

The 'web 2.0' phenomenon has turned the world of marketing on its head. Consumers have finally found their voice, and they demand to talk back. They have started sharing their brand experiences with each other without any corporate filters. Over the past five years the web has become an uncontrolled multi-way conversation instead of a controllable one-way medium. Marketing models will never be stable or comfortable or predictable again. The evolution is explosive – a Big Bang rather than a linear progression. Multiple approaches evolve simultaneously. Many die rapidly, others mutate and spawn new approaches. Diverse as they are, the surviving models all have this in common: they provide targeted solutions to specific consumer problems and they show the same old-fashioned respect for the individual that the village grocer showed a century ago.

MARKETING TO NEW CONSUMERS

There is much talk these days about marketing to the 'new consumer' – that individual who has been so information-empowered by digital technologies that he or she is far less influenced by the blunt instruments of traditional marketing. This new consumer requires a different approach, a different set of tools, a refinement that has become known in the press as new marketing (or marketing 2.0). The 'marketing 2.0' name is an unfortunate label that comes directly from the equally inappropriate term 'web 2.0'. It is inappropriate because it suggests a finite release of a technology upgrade, which is the opposite of what is really happening.

It is hard to see renewed freedom, informality, creativity, transparency and revolutionary chaos in the label it has been given. It is the Big Bang of new approaches to finding, building, sharing and applying knowledge and it is a renaissance in consumer culture – not something as trivial as a software release.

> To earn customer loyalty, businesses must provide honest, complete, useful information, instead of merely finely crafted marketing spin.

In 1999, long before web 2.0 entered people's vocabulary, Christopher Locke, Rick Levine, Doc Searls and David Weinberger wrote a brilliant book called *The Cluetrain Manifesto*. An essential guide to the demands of the new consumer, it rapidly worked its way into the nightmares of every CEO in America. It attacked the business norms that had progressively relegated the customer to the status of a necessary evil, and it asserted, quite presciently, that the web is liberating consumers from this subservient role. Companies now have to learn to communicate with their customers in a two-way conversation that requires listening and talking and pays appropriate homage to the people whose business can never again be taken for granted.

The book's central thesis is best encapsulated in the idea that customers are human beings, not target segments, and that their power is now greater than that of any company. Because of the connective power of the internet, there are no more secrets. Consumers have the power to find out everything about companies and their products and services, and, thanks to the web, they tell everyone what they know. To earn customer loyalty, businesses must provide honest, complete, useful information, instead of merely finely crafted marketing spin. And, to stay competitive, companies need to make an effort to form human relationships with their customers, which requires them to stop putting all the usual bureaucratic barriers in the way of real contact.

One of the best things about *The Cluetrain Manifesto* is that it is true to its online roots – you can download it from the web for free. Its assertions have been validated over and over again, and, as the new consumer continues to gain power, smart companies are responding, reinventing themselves and their marketing strategies to synchronize with the web 2.0 Zeitgeist.

Of course, much as Pulitzer prize-winning author Thomas Friedman would like us to believe that digital technologies have made the world flat, the world of marketing is more like an iceberg, with 80 percent of it lurking below the surface. Only about 1 in 5 businesses around the world are exploring at the digital edge of marketing. They cover the spectrum, from small start-ups, through SMEs to global organizations with household brands.

ONLINE MARKETING AND WEB 2.0

Marketing giants such as Procter & Gamble, Nike and Volkswagen are all moving their marketing budgets online and are exploiting the potential of social networking. While established brands seek new ways to get closer to the consumer, much of the pioneering conceptual work in this field is being done by new companies seeking to dominate long-tail niches such as organic sugar-free chocolate bars for diabetic eco-warriors, 'babymoon' holidays for couples about to have their first child, insurance products for micro-occasion risks, or matchmaking services that connect scientists to research projects.

Whatever their business models, web 2.0 sites have many characteristics in common. They are loaded with customer engagement – not the trivial mouse-clicking interaction of days gone by, but immersive mental and emotional involvement. They are designed to pull you in and make you want to stay, and to tell your friends to stop by too. They make extensive use of consumer-generated content. In fact, many web 2.0 sites are simply targeted venues that encourage you to hang out and contribute. They foster communities and facilitate social networking among their visitors, and they show respect for their visitors in every detail of their design.

WEB 2.0 AND ITS CHARACTERISTICS

Web 2.0 sites are usually informal and distinctly un-corporate in their tone. They load fast, and don't waste user time on gratuitous gimmickry. Wherever possible, visitors are not taken away from the page they are on, but can access layers of detail, which loads within the page, using programming techniques such as Ajax. Often, these sites make extensive use of mash-ups, in which content from different sites is pulled in and 'mashed' together. For example, they might overlay Google Earth images with a tool for labelling points of interest, which in turn may have a discussion forum or a photo upload tool merged into it.

> A site built 3 years ago looks like it is 10 years out of date, and the immediate presumption is that its content is not current or the company behind it is out of touch.

Despite their desire to be unique, all of these new ebusinesses have adopted a similar look and style, which has almost become a cliché. Traditional marketers who have not yet joined the customer-centric revolution, but are smart enough to know that packaging is a vital part of perception, are cosmetically updating their sites so that, at least on the surface, they appear to be current. It is this tendency that causes some people to mistakenly dismiss web 2.0 as merely another gimmick.

In the same way as hairstyles and book covers, websites go through fashion phases. The look of a website conveys as much about the site to a first-time visitor as your choice of clothing or the car you drive conveys about you to a total stranger. Based on appearances, people rapidly come to conclusions about whether or not they are interested in finding out more. A site built 3 years ago looks like it is 10 years out of date, and the immediate presumption is that its content is not current or the company behind it is out of touch. Online, those judgments are made in a fraction of a second.

The sites of the web 2.0 businesses of 2009 are all pretty much alike. At the core is simplicity, with no crowding on the page and a great deal of white space. By comparison, the websites of 2003 look like pages torn from a phone book. Current sites all use a central layout, not the left-aligned look of years gone by. They also frequently make use of only one or two columns. Their navigation is bold and simple, and often eschews the old-fashioned categories of about/products/services in favour of customer-centric tabs such as play/live/eat. Gone are the little horizontal bars, squeezed in at the top of the page, which contained logos and other office-era letter-head emulations. Instead, large loud mastheads proliferate, using strong colours, typically with some kind of rich texture or graduation in them. Icons are fun and young, not corporate and dull, and they are always designed to have intuitive meanings.

The pervasive trademark of a 2008 site with web 2.0 leanings was the illusion of shiny, reflective surfaces. For some examples of early web 2.0 sites, go to Jambo.net, Gather, PodZinger, JotSpot, Writely, Yedda, Trulia, 9Rules, 37Signals, LinkedIn, Twitter and CafePress.

The look in 2009, though it has much in common with earlier sites, has shifted to a more architected style. Earlier sites all used a similar palette of colours – avocado greens, light blues, oranges and greys. This palette has shifted to pinks, earthier greens, charcoals, cyan and beige. Page areas that appear to be reflective, typically making text look like it is standing on a glass surface, are disappearing, giving way to a look that has a distressed, grungy, hand-crafted appearance. Layouts now have a substantial link-laden footer, commonly occupying the lower third of the page. Navigation has become a lot more complex, allowing you to get to about any significant page without needing to go through a series of intermediate pages. Moreover, large panoramic photos and streaming video are now commonplace. This will, doubtless, yield to another design trend within a year or less.

One of the best examples of the power and simplicity of web 2.0 is Last.fm, an online radio station that plays a personalized selection of music. Last.fm epitomizes the benefits of sharing. You simply enter a list of the artists whose music you like, and the site will play you your kind of music all day. It looks at the music that other members who share your preferences want to listen to, and lets you discover new performers who were not on your list. You can allocate a score to anything that is playing, and the system updates your music programming accordingly.

Web 2.0 businesses are springing up to target all kinds of niche interest groups. InnoCentive is a social network for scientists, designed to match researchers to projects around the world. LinkedIn targets business professionals who seek to make connections with others in their field. A site named Eventful allows anyone to list, and comment about, any kind of event, from a church picnic or school football game, to a global convention of dental technicians.

These are all new business ideas, built around the sharing of knowledge. But how do big-brand marketers in established business sectors interpret and invoke web 2.0?

Amazon.com has a site dedicated exclusively to handbags and shoes. It is called Endless. The idea is that they carry pretty much every make and model of footwear and handbag. The site uses the wide open spaces and gorgeous big images that today's web makes possible. Despite its vast catalogue, you can find anything easily, because the system allows you to search according to all kinds of criteria: you can find a pair of shoes by size, colour, brand, fabric, gender, age, style or price. In a world-first, you can even search for shoes by heel height. Once you have short-listed your options, which appear in an easy-to-read custom catalogue, you can pass a virtual magnifying glass over each shoe and spin it around in 360 degrees, all instantly, without waiting for downloads and without being sent to a new page.

The international clothing retailer Gap updated its ecommerce site to not only look more modern (shades of orange and grey, with loads of white space), but to provide a much more usable service to its customers. With older sites you need to leave the page that you are on in order to see what is in your shopping cart – and finding your way back again is never easy. On Gap's site, there is an in-line shopping bag, and its content opens up within the page that you are on. You can hover over any item to see its photos and details, and to make changes. If the black skirt doesn't work with the other items you subsequently selected, you can exchange it for another colour from within the shopping bag. And you can check out from within the bag at any time, with one click. On the site, you can leave comments or reviews in context against any item, and see the comments others have left. Finally, so that you don't have to search around the site to see what is new, you can subscribe to changes in the catalogue by RSS (technically standing for rich site summary, but more commonly referred to as really simple syndication) feed. This means that any time a new item is listed or a price changes, you are notified, and, if you are interested, you simply click on the link to be taken directly to the relevant item.

> **The Gap site adds great value to the customer's shopping process, without allowing preciousness about branding to get in the way.**

A year later, Gap's parent company updated the site again, and, in a fairly controversial strategic move, made the site a portal that houses the sites of their other clothing retail brands Banana Republic, Old Navy and Piperlime. Brand purists find this hard to accept. Why would you risk undermining a high-end brand like Banana Republic by associating it so intimately with a low-end brand like Old Navy? Perhaps if you view it through the eyes of the customer's processes it makes a lot more sense. A woman going to a shopping mall might go into Banana Republic to get something for herself, then go to Gap for accessories and stop in at Old Navy to get something for a teenage daughter. Online, this would involve visiting multiple websites, putting items in multiple shopping carts, and filling in multiple purchase forms. But now you can do all of this shopping with a single cart and a single checkout. The site adds great value to the customer's shopping process, without allowing preciousness about branding to get in the way.

These examples illustrate how widely new marketing to the new consumer differs from what marketing became in the 1990s. If you compare this shopping experience with the tedious processes on the majority of ecommerce sites, you will see that the difference is not minor – it is massive. In a market still characterized by product-centric online catalogues and needlessly baroque shopping processes, there are wide-open opportunities for domination of entire market sectors or highly-focused niches.

SOCIAL MEDIA OPTIMISATION: THE NEW PR

Important as they are, websites are only one vehicle for building brand awareness or facilitating sales. As marketers the world over start to move substantial chunks of their advertising budgets to digital media, much of it is going into online PR rather than into what we conventionally think of as advertising. This is because the web is such a natural environment for PR, the essence of which is generating buzz – getting consumers and the media talking about your brand.

Collectively, all the approaches that are used to generate buzz and leverage online consumer opinion have become known as social media optimization.

Individuals have always used the web primarily as a means to connect with other individuals. Initially, people connected through email and internet relay chat (IRC), then chatrooms, instant messages, SMS, MySpace, Facebook and Twitter. As social networking applications are becoming both easier to use and more sophisticated, this connectedness is becoming richer and more rewarding. Any vehicle that provides people with a valid pretext for connecting with other people is warmly embraced. This is the driving rationale behind viral marketing. People engage with viral media because these media allow them to bond with other people; they don't bond with other people in order to engage with viral media.

Today, every company I talk to wants to include 'viral campaigns' in their communication strategy. They do not like being told that you cannot create a viral campaign, you can only optimize the potential for a campaign to go viral. As with anything in emarketing, an intimate understanding of your target consumer base is an absolutely essential starting point. If you do not know what is likely to grab their attention and make them think that fellow members of that target population will thank them for sharing, you may as well stick to a blinking banner on a news site.

> **If you want to maximize the lifetime value of a customer, get to them early.**

But if you get it right, the results can be absolutely astounding.

CASE STUDIES

Honda was one of the very first companies to explore social marketing. The best-selling car in the United States is Ford's F150 pick-up truck, and it has been in the top slot for more than 30 years. At number 2 is another truck, the Chevrolet Silverado. The Toyota Camry occupies the third slot, and the Honda Accord is in hot pursuit at fourth. Car companies believe in capturing the hearts and minds of consumers at an early age, because the first car you own will very likely establish you as brand loyal for at least another couple of purchases in your lifetime. So if you want to maximize the lifetime value of a customer, get to them early.

All car manufacturers want to get teenagers to desire their entry-level vehicles – those cars targeted at first-time buyers, which are frequently paid for by parents. Honda's problem was that there was little awareness of its entry-level vehicle, the CR-V, among the target population, and no cachet among those who did know of it.

The first thing Honda did was to examine the things that mattered to the targeted mid-to-late-teen population, how they communicated, and what they shared. (As an aside, you can gain some great market insights by monitoring MySpace, Facebook and discussion forums that are currently popular with this fickle group). Then they decided to change the pronunciation of the CR-V to 'crave'.

They built a microsite to host a competition, and challenged people to upload a photo of their 'favourite crave' to the site, along with a few lines about why they craved it. In the process, they captured names and contact details. The top half of the branded competition page contained dozens of thumb-nails of the images submitted. If you moused over an image, it expanded, and also provided the name of its submitter and his or her comments about the image. Visitors could, with one click, vote on how well they liked each entry. The competition board was covered in images of dogs, food, girlfriends, boyfriends, exotic destinations, sports teams and cars of all makes. Every entry was available in the depths of the site. Visitors could click a button to see a screen filled with the most recent entries, but only the most popular stayed on the home-page leader board.

Something remarkable happened. Those who had uploaded an image told friends and family to go and look at it and vote for it. When they did so, they were inspired to upload their own image and tell their friends about it too. So they wrote about it in their blogs and on their MySpace pages. They provided links to the competition microsite, and they tagged it in social bookmarking sites like del.icio.us and Digg. The microsite started getting top rankings on Google. The traditional media found the story fascinating, and the competition featured on radio and television talk-shows and news broadcasts, locally and internationally. Virtually every major newspaper in the country wrote articles about it.

The microsite cost Honda a few thousand dollars, yet it generated the CR-V free publicity worth tens of millions of dollars. It captured hundreds of thousands of potential sales leads, and it boosted brand awareness among the target population to levels never dreamed of. In 2007, from out of nowhere, the tenth best-selling car in the United States was the Honda CR-V.

Honda did not need to offer a car as an incentive to enter its competition. The reward was participation, and the ego satisfaction of having your creation on the leader-board. Emarketers should never underestimate the power of the promise of 15 seconds of fame.

In a similar vein, Jeep was looking to pump up brand awareness for its small entry-level vehicle, the Jeep Patriot. Most people who buy SUVs imagine themselves intrepidly hurtling across open terrain, even though, in reality, they would never leave a paved road. The young male target group for the Jeep Patriot were those who led a particularly vivid fantasy life, had a tendency to geekiness, and adored comic books and graphic novels.

Jeep ran an online competition that would get these young guys deeply immersed in the brand for a protracted period of time. A partnership was formed with Marvel Comics, of Spiderman and X-Men fame, and the first four pages of a comic were created and published on a competition microsite. To win the competition, you had to write a story that completed the comic, and it had to star four friends and their Jeep Patriot. Visitors could read the entries and vote for them. The real prize? Not a car, but fame. The 12 winning stories would all go into production at Marvel, and be published with the writer credited on the cover.

> **The microsite cost Honda a few thousand dollars, yet it generated free publicity worth tens of millions of dollars, captured hundreds of thousands of potential sales leads, and boosted brand awareness among the target population to levels never dreamed of.**

This had huge geek appeal. Participants, determined to win, spent hours immersed in the technical specifications and features of the car, so that they could represent it accurately in their stories. They asked their friends to read their entries online. They linked to the competition from blogs and social networks. The media became interested. The consequences were very similar to the CR-V campaign: intimate brand awareness, millions in free publicity, great search-engine rankings, and thousands of sales leads. And, once a month for a year, a comic book that promoted the virtues of the Jeep Patriot to the target market.

Pepsi ran a series of competitions for user-generated content, also producing huge traffic numbers. Again, the most successful prizes were the chance of getting your name in lights. In one online campaign, entrants could design a Pepsi billboard using a series of tools and templates. The winning entry would become the Times Square billboard for a week. In another, entrants were asked to customize the paintwork of a Subaru Imprezza, again using Pepsi colours and iconography. The winner received the car, complete with the winning paint-job. The advantage to Pepsi was that their prizes, once awarded, continued to promote the brand to a wider off-line audience.

@ Competitions for user-generated content are inexpensive to run and, if they go viral, can produce the kind of results that no conventional advertising campaign could hope for. Unfortunately, they require innovation and sharp customer insight. There have been many lazy 'me-too' online competitions that have tried to emulate the success of earlier campaigns, but the models become old and, as they proliferate, they lose their appeal. If you really want to succeed in web 2.0 PR, you have to be willing to take a few risks with new concepts.

Another social media optimization approach that is gaining traction is the creation of brand pages on networks such as MySpace and Facebook. Typically, real people will sign up and create their own 'all about me' pages as touch-points for connecting with friends online and keeping them informed about the day-to-day trivia of their lives. Instead of signing up as a person, marketers can create a page for a brand. That branded social page can be customized and benefit from its own network of fans.

For example, Herbal Essences shampoos created a MySpace page targeting teenage girls. On their page they hosted videos that showed how to create different hair-styles, along with a mini-competition where people could upload pictures of their favourite hairstyles. Comments were encouraged, either via the competition or on the associated discussion forum. Most compelling of all, at least to the target group, was the ability to upload home-made videos in which you could show off and talk about your hair. Targeting a more sophisticated and affluent market, Cartier created a beautifully customized MySpace page for its Love collection, combining nostalgic video clips and the music of Lou Reed with enthusiastic endorsements of fans of the brand. The page has not attracted a mass market following, but Cartier has always been a long tail brand.

These social networks can be quite effective, but, as with online competitions, the use thereof requires care and creativity. Because the use of these sites is effectively free, the temptation is to regard them as quick-and-dirty marketing, and to simply throw something together. But since you are saving so much by using pre-existing functionality, perhaps you should take the medium seriously and invest in designing an innovative, creative application.

As with other online marketing initiatives, the objective is to immerse potential customers in a branded community environment for as long as possible, and get them to invite their friends to share that environment. Building positive brand awareness, rather than directly selling products, is the primary goal.

Online PR is not suited only to consumer brands. The strengths that offline PR traditionally brings to service and non-profit organizations, can be magnified online. Indeed, since many service brands or charities have much less tangible differentiators than their physical counterparts, mobilising real people to enthuse about them to their social networks is often the best possible way of standing out from the crowd. In any given star-range, there is nothing more generic than a hotel. Yet encouraging guests to upload reviews and photographs of their experience of a hotel gives the property a human dimension that no amount of marketing spin could ever replicate.

BLOGS

A blog (short for 'web log') is a personal website with a specific function. It is a type of public journal or diary that someone keeps on the web. If, instead of publishing text, a blogger uploads an audio file to which subscribers can then listen on their computers or via an MP3 player such as an iPod, it is known as a podcast.

In business-to-business situations, corporate blogging and podcasting has become almost a mainstream tool for communicating regularly with a community of subscribers, who may include customers, business partners, investors, analysts and the press. Before blogging, the only ways for outsiders to gain any insight into a business were its published financials and official press releases. Today, senior managers can publish a journal on a daily or weekly basis, allowing interested parties to access information live and unedited directly from the source. The added appeal to blog readers is that they can ask questions and post comments, thereby engaging in a dialogue at a distance.

At first, corporate blogging was viewed with alarm by senior managers and their corporate communications spin meisters. How could you trust someone with inside knowledge not to corrupt the carefully-crafted official line on any issue? Some companies even got their PR agencies to write blog entries that pretended to come from the keyboard of senior executives. These blogs were short-lived and the public unravelling of these rather obvious misrepresentations did nothing but humiliate the companies concerned and the senior executives who supposedly authored these blogs.

Today, many high-profile people in business and government write blogs that have achieved massive audiences. The chief software architect of Adobe, the marketing vice-president of Boeing and the CEOs of Sun Microsystems and Garmin all provide remarkably candid insights into their companies' strategies, and into themselves as people.

Corporate blogs do not need to have only one author. Companies such as Southwest Airlines and Google have corporate blogs to which a diverse group of senior executives contribute. Because they are monitored closely by journalists, and by financial analysts, blogs offer a rapid and reasonably credible low-profile way to get information out to a wider audience. Far from posing a threat to company security, such blogs act as an important communication channel and are sometimes used as a way to defuse issues, or to start viral discussions that benefit the business.

If you do not yet have a blog, go to blogger.com, create a name, pick a template, and write a few lines. From start to finish, your thoughts can be published online in less than five minutes.

RSS is a tool that in concept has been around for a long time, but only came into its own as a result of the popularity of blogging. RSS allows you to nominate which content on your website is available as a subscription. When a visitor subscribes to what is called your 'RSS feed' any changes that you make to that content on your site are automatically fed to the subscribers 'feed reader'. A feed reader is similar to an email application, such as Outlook, except that, instead of receiving emails, it receives the updates to all of the sites you have subscribed to.

So if you subscribe to the blog of best-selling author Seth Godin, every time he posts a new entry to the web, it is pulled into your feed reader. You do not need to visit his site to find out if anything is new. In itself, this may seem a little pointless, but if you monitor a large number of sites, the value of RSS is immense. It would take you hours every day to visit each of the sites that you have an interest in, yet it will take you less than 15 minutes to scan all the new entries via your feed reader, neatly laid out chronologically, using text-only. You may then select the few entries you wish to view, click on them, and get taken to the original. Where bandwidth and time are an issue, and they always are, RSS is a boon.

The nature of your market may make it ideal for a creative approach to using blogs, newsfeeds or social networks, or perhaps the relevance is not so obvious. These are simply tools that have evolved, often with a different original purpose from that which made them popular. You can craft many new relationship-building processes with these tools. Getting those processes right requires a commitment to gaining and maintaining a deep insight into your online consumers. It also requires the will to take risks. In the fast-paced fickle world of the new consumer, you cannot dress up imitation as innovation, and if you play it safe, you may find yourself playing alone. But if you step off the beaten path, and allow your consumer insights to inspire truly innovative approaches to communicating your message, you can move your marketing to a new level of engagement that gives you a huge sustainable advantage over your competitors.

Website design 7

I t is easy to say that in order to be successful in ebusiness, you have
to be customer-centric, but it is not very useful. A deep insight into
online consumers is the foundation of online business. But that
insight alone does not help you to create a clear vision and structure a
strategy to form lasting relationships with online consumers. Before
you can apply the eight-step strategy building approach described in
Chapter 4, you need to get really comfortable with the other elements
of emarketing. The next five chapters examine each of these elements
from a commercial perspective. They will provide a series of practical
guidelines on how best to succeed in website design, search engine
marketing, advertising, email marketing, and social media marketing
(most often referred to as buzz marketing).

In studies of websites that are experiencing high growth in their
visitor volumes, search engines dominate as the source of visitors.
One-third of your visitors should come from 'paid search' which is
also known as pay-per-click, PPC or sponsored links. A further one
visitor in five will come via natural search results. Think about that for a
second: just over half of all your site visitors should be arriving from
search engines, which effectively means Google. These visitors are
much more pre-qualified and valuable to you than those who come
to your site after clicking a banner, since they are in solution-seeking
mode – they have actively sought out content that matches what your
page is offering.

Another 20 percent of your visitors will come to your site as
a result of email marketing, and a further 20 percent as a result
of online advertising. The relative cost of these two activities is

usually the reason why companies on a limited budget will emphasize email marketing.

But there is another more compelling reason. Usually, email goes to an individual with whom you have already had some contact, and you are able to leverage that relationship and customize the messaging. Advertising, by contrast, is usually broadcast out to an anonymous flow of broadly segmented traffic, and almost by definition has to have generic messaging.

It is tempting to say that, because online advertising is relatively expensive and produces relatively little site traffic, it can be discarded from the emarketing mix. But this would be akin to suggesting that you build a house without bothering to dig any foundations. Branding is everything in crowded global marketplaces, and advertising is an important driver of branding. Despite what YouTube, Google, The Body Shop, Starbucks and others have achieved without conventional off-line advertising, they could not have made it online without online advertising.

> **Branding is everything in crowded global marketplaces, and advertising is an important driver of branding.**

All of these emarketing vehicles serve their own specific purposes. Collectively they address a number of vital emarketing needs: building brands, generating response, solving customer problems and building customer relationships.

There is no point in driving traffic to your site, microsite, blog or product page unless, once there, the site delivers what the customer needs and, at the same time, achieves your business goals. It is critically important to the success of your emarketing initiatives that you design your website correctly.

DEFINING YOUR WEBSITE DESIGN

Website design is not just about the coding of the site, nor is it about its visual appearance. These are two essential components, requiring skill and talent. But unless they take place within a carefully defined marketing brief, they can be utterly pointless.

Every site, whether it is a one-page blog, a small ecommerce store, a brand microsite, or a hundred-thousand page repository of technical information, must be architected with a clear understanding of the needs, problems and expectations of its visitors. It must be crafted to deliver remarkably satisfying experiences, and to develop positive and lasting relationships with the users of the site.

You don't achieve this by handing a brochure to a developer and asking for a five-page site that contains 'about us', 'our products' and 'contact us' pages. You have to have a vision, and that vision must be clearly communicated and shared with everyone involved with the project. It must be a business vision that puts the site into the context of your ongoing marketing goals. The vision should describe, for a given point in the future, how your customers and your business will interact, do business together and value each other.

A vision is not a vague fantasy; it takes hard work to achieve a precise definition of where you want to be. I have talked about vision in earlier chapters, but it is important to reinforce how essential it is that your vision leads the project, not vice versa. Vision is a quality that allows you to set your company and your brand apart from others. Without vision you will have great difficulty putting any distance between you and your competitors – in any marketplace, not only online.

Today your site may be a sales channel; in the future it may be the keystone of your customer relationship. In terms of customer engagement, today your site may be about transactions; in the future it may be about immersion in the brand and about customer retention.

Today you may measure success simply by sales volume; in the future it may be customer retention rate, the lifetime value of a customer, or share of the customer's wallet.

As for business strategy, today you may be building a sales channel; in the future you may be using your web presence to enable the success of other business divisions, or to protect against global competitive threats.

These issues are not academic – even for a small business, it is foolhardy and wasteful to move ahead without first knowing where you are going. It is like ordering a truck-load of bricks and a few bags of cement, and then telling a bricklayer to build you a house that more or less matches the others in your neighbourhood. Until you know what you want to build, why you want to build it, why your customers would want to use it, and what it is going to do for your business, you should not start building your website.

THE REQUIREMENTS OF GOOD WEBSITE DESIGN

Some of the most fundamental errors in website design are unfortunately the most common. Among them are:

- treating the web as a place to stick a brochure, rather than as a phenomenon that should fundamentally shift the way you market your brands and do business
- managing a web project in the same way as any other project, rather than as a specialized customer-interface project
- failing to use professional information architecture (using a website structure that mirrors your organization instead of reflecting the things a visitor wants to do)
- designing pages to look 'cool' rather than to provide an optimal user experience that works in the reality of the user's environment
- writing linear content, or simply copying offline content, rather than writing in a style that has been optimized for online readers and search engines
- structuring your site as if visitors will all arrive on the home page and navigate to deeper pages, instead of designing powerful landing pages for incoming links.

There are a number of requirements for an effective website design. If you do not get the first four right, it doesn't matter how well you do the rest. Your site should be designed so that:

- it is aligned with your vision and business goals
- it is integrated into your marketing and promotion strategy
- it has a clearly defined purpose
- it is customer-centric
- it is intuitive and usable
- it contains deep, rich, relevant content, yours and your visitors', in line with an overall content strategy
- it is architected using information-architecture principles
- it is well presented, with a look and feel that is professional and appropriate
- it is technically sound, and is appropriate for the target user's environment
- it protects the privacy and security of users
- it can be maintained without major rework or resources
- it can be measured and its performance continuously improved
- it is search engine friendly.

These principles apply to the design of any website, no matter what its size. The only difference is scale, and how much time you allocate to ensuring that you adhere to the principles.

TESTING YOUR WEBSITE

I use the term 'customer-centric design' often. How do you go about

> @ It can take you six months to a year to design a website, or it can take you six days. But if anyone tells you it can be d one in six hours, without first asking you about your vision, business objectives, customers, or any of the other considerations mentioned above, they don't know what they are doing.

making sure you have designed your website for the use of the customer, rather than for your own expediency? The most common approaches involve personas and scenarios, and usability testing.

PERSONAS AND SCENARIOS are nothing new to the world of marketing, and they have become a vital component of website design. A persona is a sharply defined fictitious person who is representative of the type of visitor who you expect to come to your site. Scenarios are typical situations or circumstances under which the persona may visit your site. You may work with many different personas, depending on your business and your markets, although it is usual to have no more than three or four. Each persona is built up into as 'real' an individual as possible, with a name, a photo, a family background, and (if appropriate) a job and an income. You describe his or her hobbies, preferences, anxieties, behaviours and abilities. You also define his or her internet technology environment. For each persona, you provide a context, their goals, their pain points and the major questions to which they need answers.

All of these elements can then be taken into consideration when creating the scenarios necessary for conceptualising your site.

Far from being a caricature, each persona must seem as real and as individual as possible. Everyone working on the web project needs to 'get to know' each persona. The personas become the filters through which you talk about focus, design, functionality, conversion funnels and usability. You use them to do virtual walk-throughs of whatever it is that you are developing, to see whether what works for Francois (a 24-year-old mechanic with a passion for computers and mobile phones) will also work for Zelda (the 65-year-old retired teacher with four grandchildren, whose exposure to the internet has been limited to email so far).

The advantage of working with personas is that they provide a human face that forces designers and developers to think through the eyes of someone other than themselves — they essentially provide a consistent challenge to the common problem of self-reference. They help you to empathize with the feelings of your site visitors. Most importantly, they help everyone involved to have a consistent, non-fuzzy framework for evaluating the customer-centricity of every decision, for each major target consumer group.

From the perspective of the marketer, personas also help to define specifically what content and functionality you need on your site, and how you want visitors to access it. By identifying the most compelling needs and problems of your target visitors, you avoid placing too much emphasis in one place while dropping the ball in another. Personas help you to define emerging and definite visitor needs, and the kind of solutions, purchasing decision-making assistance and online experience that you need to provide. They also help you to decide on the information architecture and the conversion funnels that you need in the structure of your site. For example, you may want to provide short cuts for Francois, but longer or more supportive paths for Zelda. Personas also provide a great framework for evaluating the strengths and weaknesses of your competitors' sites.

Finally, your personas help you with emarketing outside of site design. They help you enormously with structuring and designing your digital communications strategy. Whether, and how, you use email marketing, pay-per-click, banner advertisements or social media can be strongly influenced by the customer-centric insights that personas can provide.

The down-side of personas is that their development is not an exact science, and some of your team members may not take them seriously enough to be useful across the board. For web metrics people, personas can be an irritation because there is no way to map hard performance data back to personas, except perhaps in email marketing. But in most cases the benefits vastly outweigh the objections.

USABILITY is a vast field, which could occupy several bookshelves. It is the single most important characteristic of any website, yet it is often dismissed or relegated to afterthought status. Website visitors are not on your side, and they are not forgiving. They are not interested in having to make the effort needed to compensate for the inadequacies you build into their experience. A site that has usability flaws is not a quality site and will always lose its customers if a more usable site comes along. Usability is not about how much irrelevant stuff a user can do on a site; it is about how much relevant stuff a site can do for the user.

> Usability is not about how much irrelevant stuff a user can do on a site; it is about how much relevant stuff a site can do for the user.

Usability is not confined to websites – it applies to the design of everything we interact with in our daily lives. Usability research would have revealed its weaknesses. If you observed how a selection of target users actually used the machine, its deficiencies would have been apparent and ideas for improvement and innovation would have emerged.

Usability is a quality attribute that measures how easy it is to operate a user interface. It is the extent to which a system allows its users to complete their chosen tasks efficiently, effectively and satisfactorily. Usability has six quality components:

 LEARNABILITY: How easy is it to figure out how to use the system and to accomplish whatever goal you are trying to accomplish?

> @ The classic example of usability was the video cassette recorder or VCR. Unless you had a Ph.D., or were under the age of eight, you could never master this device, now gone forever thanks to the personal video recorder (PVR) or TiVo. And why? Because, in the design of the VCR, the simple matter of customer-centric usability was ignored.

- ▨ EFFICIENCY: How much time does it take to accomplish your goal, and how complex or demanding are the processes?
- ▨ EFFECTIVENESS: To what extent are you able to achieve what you set out to do?
- ▨ MEMORABILITY: If you come back tomorrow, or next week, will you have to struggle to figure it out all over again, or is it easy to remember what to do?
- ▨ ERROR MANAGEMENT: How easy is it to make mistakes, and, if you do make mistakes, how easy is it for you to recover from them?
- ▨ SATISFACTION: How satisfying is the experience, to what extent would you be willing to repeat it, and would you want to recommend it to a friend or family member?

The most important of these six quality characteristics is the last one — satisfaction. If you get this feature right, the deficiencies in the earlier attributes are forgiven. Then again, if you get the earlier attributes right, you are likely to get a high score on satisfaction. A satisfying experience is important in a web 2.0 world, where online consumers tell everyone about their experiences, good and bad. Beyond mere satisfaction, you want to make the experience your site provides remarkable — so good that people are compelled to talk about it and advocate it to their networks of contacts.

Among the usability questions you could ask yourself about your site's design are:

- ▨ How easy is the site to use?
- ▨ How easy is it for each persona to find the information they need?
- ▨ How easy is it to buy something?
- ▨ How legible is the text?
- ▨ How easy is it to navigate around the site?
- ▨ How easy is it for a visitor to know where they are, where they have been, or what they should do next?

If you currently have a website, consider doing a formal usability audit, preferably using objective outsiders. The reason for doing this is simply that the people involved in creating the site have an intimate knowledge of how it works, and are therefore not capable of seeing it objectively. If you use an outsider to run an audit through the eyes of each persona, you will be able to identify opportunities for dramatically tuning up the performance of your site.

Some of the things you would look at in a site usability audit are:

- NAVIGATION: Does the site give a clear indication of the current location, and does it provide navigational elements that let visitors go to other contextually logical parts of the site?
- HELP: In those areas where visitors are most likely to be confused or need guidance, is it provided in a readily accessible and intuitive way?
- WORKFLOW: How well does the site support visitors in the completion of their tasks?
- ERROR MANAGEMENT: Does the site make it hard for visitors to make errors, and, if they do occur, are the errors clearly documented, and are easy ways provided to correct them?
- CONSISTENCY: Is your site internally consistent, that is, does it use the same terminology, linking structure, colour coding, navigation framework and icons throughout?
- FUNCTIONALITY: Is the functionality that is needed to accomplish the goals of each persona available, logical, efficient, effective and satisfying to use?
- CONTROL: Will the different personas feel as though they are in control, or will they feel uncomfortable or insecure?
- VISUAL CLARITY: Is the look and feel of the site appealing, uncluttered and scannable, so that the purpose of each page, and its individual visual elements, is immediately obvious?
- LANGUAGE LEVEL: Does the site use a level of language that is appropriate for the different personas who will visit it?

⚄ LANGUAGE STYLE: Does the site use a style of communication that is appropriate for the different personas who will visit it?

Unlike market research, which establishes a sample and tries to project data for the population using various statistical tests of significance, usability testing usually involves running a controlled experiment to see how well visitors can use the site. You are not interested in hard data; you merely need a good indication of where problems might lie. Most website usability testing involves watching a few people trying to do something specific on your site, and observing whether the site actually delivers on its intended purpose.

A usability test involves creating a 'scenario' – a situation that you would expect to encounter among your target visitors. Scenarios serve two purposes: they force designers to focus on the requirements of the site, and they shift the design focus from art or technology to the way activities should be carried out. For example, Zelda has come to your ecommerce site to buy a book as a gift for her gardening-enthusiast neighbour. She has a set budget, but she has no idea which book to buy. How does your site support her decision-making process? Another example: Francois had one bad experience too many at his bank today and has come to your bank's site to explore options for moving his account. How does your site help him to give you his business with confidence?

Another aspect of usability that is fast becoming a legal requirement in many countries is accessibility – ensuring that your site is accessible to people with disabilities. Technology has made it possible for vision-impaired people to read and use websites through assistive devices such as screen-reading web-browsers. To make your site accessible you have to take these requirements into consideration when designing and architecting your site and its content. For example, screen-reading web browsers cannot 'see' images, instead they read the image 'alt tag' to convey the description of the image to the user. Therefore 'alt tags' need to be written for people with sight disabilities rather than simply for

Throughout the process of designing your website, usability should be your constant reference point. You will tend to use formal usability testing as an audit mechanism for your existing website, as a user research tool during the discovery phase of website design (during which you try to find out more about your users and your competitors) and as validation (when you are testing hypotheses, changes or redesigns).

search engines. Another accessibility feature that sites should provide is the possibility to change the font size without the design breaking. It is best to build these considerations into your site design at the outset, rather than having to retro-fit these features into your site at a later stage.

During the test, the person performs the required tasks while observers watch.

There are many test instruments in the usability arsenal. Testers often use paper-based prototypes, which allow you to test before a line of code is written. You can also use pre-test and post-test questionnaires to collect qualitative feedback on the site you are testing. Another popular technique is to ask test subjects to think aloud as they perform their tasks, or to use a piece of equipment that tracks their eye movements while looking at the screen.

These phases are part of the seven steps involved in website design and development.

THE SEVEN-PHASE APPROACH TO WEBSITE DESIGN AND DEVELOPMENT

Every business website or microsite should be designed and developed according to a professional methodology that involves seven phases. Even a small project should pass through these steps — although you may choose not to spend much time on some of

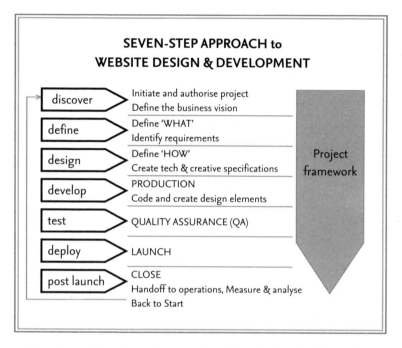

SEVEN-STEP APPROACH to
WEBSITE DESIGN & DEVELOPMENT

discover	Initiate and authorise project Define the business vision
define	Define 'WHAT' Identify requirements
design	Define 'HOW' Create tech & creative specifications
develop	PRODUCTION Code and create design elements
test	QUALITY ASSURANCE (QA)
deploy	LAUNCH
post launch	CLOSE Handoff to operations, Measure & analyse Back to Start

Project framework

the phases, they all require some thought and a few decisions. The seven phases are:

1. DISCOVER: This is the phase at which you initiate and authorize the web project, and define the business vision.

2. DEFINE: You now move to defining what it is that you are going to build, and identifying the requirements of the site.

3. DESIGN: In the design phase you define how the site is going to be built by creating specifications for both the technical and the creative components of the site.

4. DEVELOP: Now you actually go into production, write the code, create the visual and graphic design elements, develop the content and build the website.

5. TEST: In this phase you do your final quality assurance (QA) and testing to ensure that the site works as intended.

6. DEPLOY: In phase 6 you launch your site, that is, you make it available on the web.

7. POST-LAUNCH: Once you have launched your site, you close the project and hand it over to operations and maintenance. You also start to measure and analyse its performance.

@ You will have noted that actual building of the site — writing the code and creating the graphic elements — does not happen until phase 4. It is worth reiterating at this point that you should not rush into building a site until you have clarified what you want to build, why you want to build it and what the site has to do for your business. The planning and thinking phases are crucial.

@ Each of these phases may be complex or straight-forward, depending on the nature and scale of the web project. The bigger and more complex the project, the more formal, documented and signed-off each phase should be.

There is not enough space in this book to cover the details of the process of website design, but here are some of the essentials of each phase.

PHASE 1: DISCOVER

Before you begin, you have to define the purpose and the business case for this marketing investment. All of this should come out of the vision-building and strategy process covered in Chapter 4.

Be specific about who makes up your target audience, what you know (and need to find out) about them and why they will find your site compelling. At this early stage you need to define what kind of user experience you want to provide. Remember that the reason for building your site is to satisfy the needs and solve the problems of the customer.

During this phase, you should define the scope of the project. You should specify not only what the project will cover, but also what it will not cover. You also need to define what the constraints of the project are. Typically these fall into the categories of budget, time, risks and resources.

The documentation you would need to generate in this phase includes a statement of work, a project charter, a scope statement and a project plan.

PHASE 2: DEFINE

Once authorized, the project kicks off and the process of defining what has to be built gets under way. It is critical that the project team defines the business requirements for the site and that a competitive analysis is conducted. The strategy for designing and developing the site is determined. It should answer questions about how much will be outsourced, what technology will be used and how content will be sourced. Any necessary exploratory user research takes place in this phase. The result of this phase is a creative brief and, if appropriate, a prototype model of the solution to be built.

The documentation you will generate in this phase includes a preliminary requirements document, the competitive analysis, the project strategy, any user research reports and the creative brief.

PHASE 3: DESIGN

This step cannot be skipped if you want your site to deliver. The design phase is about creating a great user experience that supports the site's business purpose.

It is during this phase that you define the information architecture (IA) for the site, structure a site map, and decide on the page and process flows. IA defines the organization of your site. At the site level, this is mainly determined by your navigational structure. Navigation should be simple and clear, both in terms of structure and labelling. It goes beyond the buttons, tabs or lists that are on the periphery of the site content, and includes all the internal buttons, clickable images and links that define your contextual cross-linking architecture.

Navigation exists only to help different visitors find their way around in multiple different ways. A site that is hard to navigate will also be difficult to test and maintain, and, in addition to spoiling a visitor's experience, will drop your ranking in search engines.

A site that is hard to navigate will also be difficult to test and maintain, and, in addition to spoiling a visitor's experience, will drop your ranking in search engines.

At page level, IA determines how each page is organized, how the content is broken down into 'chunks' for easy reading, how eye-stopping artefacts such as headings and hyperlinks guide visitors to where they want to be, and how chunks of content connect with each other.

In this phase you create and apply your personas, and define the relevant scenarios for activity on your site. You also create the content strategy for the site, which specifies where the content will come from and how it will be managed. As part of the content strategy, you need to define which templates you will need for the different page types you wish to use.

For each page or page type, you put together what is called a wireframe, a sketch of what information or functional components need to be on the page, and approximately where these elements should be placed in relation to each other. Wireframes are a planning and visualization tool for representing the proposed layout, function, structure, priority of information or content of a web page. A wireframe attempts to separate the look and feel of the site from the way it works and reads, by presenting a stripped-down, simplified version of the page without any design distractions. A wireframe is not a design for the page.

A designer and an information architect will then together turn the wireframes into draft page designs (or comps). If the creative brief calls for animation or video, their storyboards are created in this step.

A key consideration to all of this is your search engine optimization (SEO) strategy, which will play a major role in defining the site map, page flows and content strategy. Finally, you may decide to do some usability research to validate your draft designs and processes, before they incur further production costs.

The documents that you will develop in this phase might include detailed designs for personas, scenarios, the site map, page and process flows, content strategy, wireframes, page comps and storyboards. You would also need to document your SEO strategy and any usability testing that was done. Essential documents at the end of this phase are the final business requirements document, the technical design, the final project management plan and the plan for maintenance handover after completion. Now, and only now, are you ready to start building your website. And as you have designed the site thoughtfully, the development phase is a truly 'production and construction' phase.

> Online, people do not read, they scan. So divide your content into small discrete blocks or chunks, and use headings and hyperlinks to let visitors' eyes know when to stop moving.

PHASE 4: DEVELOP

If you have done a good job in the first three phases, this phase should go smoothly and produce exactly what you expect. The previous phases were largely driven by marketing. In this phase your technical people and your creative artists and writers get down to work. In the development phase, the coding, technical infrastructure, databases and back-end systems are created or integrated.

Your designers produce final artwork and imagery, as well as the look and feel of the site and its component pages. Any graphics production work for animations or video is done, as is photography and photo manipulation and layout work, all within the context of the already defined page comps.

Also in the development phase, your writers produce the text content and enter it into the site. Content must always be written for the web and for your particular audience. Online, people do not read, they scan. The only exception is perhaps in cases where their primary purpose is to read, such as magazine or literary sites. Otherwise, divide your content into small discrete blocks or chunks, and use headings and hyperlinks to let visitors' eyes know when to stop moving. Because the web is an intimate and personal medium, a less formal or colloquial style may be appropriate — but this depends on your business and your target audience. You will have made a decision about this earlier, as part of the content strategy.

As development occurs, each page must be meta-tagged to make the site search-engine friendly and to ensure that, if a page does show up in search results, the listing is compelling and informative.

Finally, in the development phase you put together the plans for testing the site in phase 5.

PHASE 5: TEST

The site you built in phase 4 is a test site. It is not yet live on the web, nor should it be until you have done all the necessary quality assurance tests. In this phase you make sure that things work the way they are supposed to in all the target technology platforms, browsers and bandwidths.

You conduct a site test and a regression test to make sure that you can undo any changes without breaking the system. You do a rigorous test on functionality, making sure that your ecommerce and back-end processes are working perfectly. You also do a performance test and a traffic-volume stress test to make sure the site can handle the hits.

On the user experience side, you test the usability of the site one last time. As a site is tested, it is often necessary to make compromises or deviate from the original plan. While these changes may not have an impact on technical operations, they can have unexpected domino effects on usability.

You also need to test content and design, proofreading every word and examining how the design looks in every likely browser, operating system, version and screen resolution. At each stage you write up the defects, fix them and write up reports.

Finally, you get the sponsors of the project, the website's 'clients', to test the site (this is called User Acceptance Testing) in any way that they choose, and to sign off that the site is acceptable.

Then you go live.

PHASE 6: DEPLOY

In this phase you cut across from your test site to the live site.

To do so, you should have a release plan. A small site may simply be switched over. A large site with complex back-ends may require hours of work before the site is successfully cut over from its test environment to the live production environment. The reason for having a release plan is to make sure that everything that needs to be cut over actually is. This is not as trivial as it may seem, since it may involve changing reference addresses within the site and testing each one as it is changed. Your release plan needs to contain contingencies for situations in which things may go wrong — Mr Murphy has a way of showing up uninvited at the most critical times. If you launch a site and find out that the live site is not working, you should know what your backup plans and procedures are.

Once you have launched the site, you test and fix anything that may have gone wrong. As a marketer, you ensure that the timing is right and that all the necessary communication and press releases go out.

PHASE 7: POST-LAUNCH

Of course the project is not over once you have launched the website. The development team has to do a project review, typically a 360° review, so that any lessons learned are used in future projects. The project must be brought to closure and all documentation should be archived. Any contracts with outsource companies must be terminated.

The developers need to hand over the project to operations and maintenance. There should always be a maintenance plan and service-level agreement to ensure continuity of service, and it may be necessary to train various members of the take-up teams — particularly if your site uses content management systems.

Lastly, you need to ensure that your site metrics and analytics kick in, and that you take all the necessary initial performance measurements to establish a baseline.

Now your only remaining task is to ensure that online consumers know about your site and find it relevant enough to warrant a visit. We'll start to explore how that happens in the following chapter.

Search engine marketing | 8

I f more than half of your website's traffic should be coming to you from search engines, you have to make sure that you are using them to best advantage. Search marketing strategies have five components:

- **NATURAL SEARCH ENGINE OPTIMIZATION (SEO):** this seeks to ensure that your pages will achieve great rankings in the search listings
- **CONTEXTUAL ADVERTISING (PPC OR PAY-PER-CLICK):** to ensure that your pages will appear within the advertising or 'sponsored listings' sections on search results pages
- **PAID INCLUSION:** this makes sure that search engines index your site quickly and often
- **CONVERSION ENHANCEMENT STRATEGIES:** these ensure that more visitors take the actions you want them to take once they arrive at your site
- **WEB ANALYTICS:** to allow you to measure and improve on the results generated from your search marketing campaigns.

This chapter will cover each of these five components. But before this, let's look at why search matters and how search engines work.

HOW SEARCH ENGINES WORK

In 2006, the world generated 161 billion gigabytes of new digital data. This volume is thought to be 3 million times the information in all the books ever written. It is growing at an accelerating pace, more than doubling each year. By 2010, it is forecast to hit 1,000 billion gigabytes (a zettabyte). This is new digital information — in addition to the vast amounts produced in each previous year.

How does anyone ever find anything in amongst all of that? It is not surprising that search engines have become massive businesses, and information architecture is the hot career choice of the decade.

Where your website is concerned, the quaint old notion that 'if I build it, they will come' doesn't cut it any more. Your web pages are snowflakes in a blizzard of data. People need to know that you exist. More importantly, they need to see your web pages as compellingly different, so that they will chose to come to your site rather than to any one of the thousands of others out there.

If you want people to see you as better than their other options, you need to get search engines to see you the same way.

> **If you want your page to get into the top two or three out of thousands for any given keyword, your site has to be one of the very best in its field.**

There are basically two ways in which everything on the web is classified and indexed. The first, and oldest, is by directories. A directory takes the same approach to websites as a librarian takes to books. Each site can only occupy one slot. Directories are run by human beings who take their time to determine where each site belongs.

There is only one directory you need to worry about. It is called DMOZ and you find it at dmoz.org. DMOZ is the foundation of the web, and all the major search engines build off it. You have to submit your site to DMOZ, and then wait, often for many weeks, for someone to get around to looking at it.

If you are not already in DMOZ, it can take Google a very long time to find you. Google is not a directory; it is a search engine, the second way in which information is sorted and identified on the web. While directories are run by people, search engines are automated. Their fieldwork is done by small bits of code called bots or spiders.

This code scurries around the web, following hyperlinks. Every page it encounters is absorbed and taken back home, where it is deposited in a vast database that indexes web pages.

When a spider absorbs a web page, it takes the visible text, the hidden code, the names and addresses of pages and files that the page links to, and the details of pages that link into it from elsewhere. The indexer takes all this information and crunches through it in detail. It then comes up with an understanding of what the page is about.

When someone enters a search query, typically a word or phrase, the search engine retrieves all the pages that relate to the query. It processes them by means of an algorithm that looks at more than 100 different characteristics, and then ranks the pages according to how relevant they are to the query, how good the content is, and how important the page is relative to all the competing pages on the web that are about the same theme. If you want your page to get into the top two or three out of thousands for any given keyword, your site has to be one of the very best in its field.

A keyword is a word or short phrase used to encapsulate the essence of a web page. Search engines use it to classify what a page is about, searchers use it as a search query to find pages that may solve their problems, and marketers use it to trigger advertisements that will lead searchers to their site. Search engines derive the keywords for a page from a number of places, including:

- the content and context of the web page
- the anchor text of inbound links to that page
- the title, description and keyword meta-tags in the code of the page
- the description of the page in web directories
- the tags assigned to the page by social bookmarkers
- the algorithms of the search engines themselves

The algorithms of search engines are complex mathematical and statistical models that weigh and interpret all of the factors associated with a page, in isolation and collectively. Since search engines compete with each other to deliver the best possible search results to their users, their algorithms are black boxes, and are guarded more closely than the recipe for Coca-Cola.

The dominant force in search, at least for now, is Google. Google's share of the search market varies from country to country and from survey to survey. Most reports give Google a US search-queries share of around 64 percent. Yahoo runs a distant and receding second, at around 21 percent. MSN/Live, Microsoft's search engine, is doing quite well at 8 percent. There is not much room left for anyone else, and since MSN abandoned its recent attempt to acquire Yahoo's search business, the future of Google's competitors is rather uncertain.

In the United Kingdom, by contrast, Yahoo has almost disappeared, and Google gets more than 91 percent of search queries! Data for

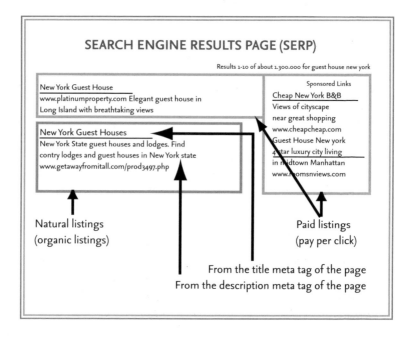

SEARCH ENGINE RESULTS PAGE (SERP)

Results 1-10 of about 1.300.000 for guest house new york

New York Guest House
www.platinumproperty.com Elegant guest house in
Long Island with breathtaking views

New York Guest Houses
New York State guest houses and lodges. Find
contry lodges and guest houses in New York state
www.getawayfromitall.com/prod3497.php

Sponsored Links

Cheap New York B&B
Views of cityscape
near great shopping
www.cheapcheap.com
Guest House New york
4 star luxury city living
in midtown Manhattan
www.roomsnviews.com

Natural listings
(organic listings)

Paid listings
(pay per click)

From the title meta tag of the page
From the description meta tag of the page

other countries, where available, indicates that Google is much stronger outside the United States than it is at home. The sole exception is China, where Baidu gets two thirds of all searches, Google has only 20 percent of the market, and Yahoo! is barely measurable.

Search engine results pages (SERPs) are the point of departure for consumers who have gone to the web looking for an answer to a question, or a solution to a problem. These people are hot prospects, because they have actively expressed a need for a solution that you can provide. There is never a more appropriate or contextually relevant time to get your message in front of their eyes. The SERP is the battleground of permission marketing.

You have two ways to communicate your solution. First, there are the natural results of the SERP, which run down the left-hand side of the page. Secondly, you can use sponsored links (or pay-per-click advertisements), which appear on the right and at the top of the page.

Let's focus on the natural results first. Here are three results that were returned in response to a search for 'mag wheels':

:: Wheelies - Jacob's Mag Wheel Repairs
Wheelies specializes in the refurbishing, repair and sales of 2nd hand mag wheels for panelbeaters, repair shops and individuals.
www.wheelies.com/

:: Groovy Motorsport
ABOUT US | CONTACT US | HOME. Products. home | products | services | profile | contact | enquiries. Copyright © Groovy Motorsport 2007.
www.groovms.co.uk/products.php?step=2&catid=1&cat1=Mag%20W heels/controller?act=MakeModelAct&categmag=26&modelid=12397

:: MagMaster - Wheels Repairs
MagMaster professionally repairs your damaged mag wheels to new condition.
www.magmaster.com/ - 8k - Cached - Similar pages

The top line of the listing is the title. The second line is a snippet of the description. Both are pulled directly from the **title meta-tag** and the **description meta-tag** that appear in the hidden code of each page on your site. You can decide what you want these tags to say, and each important page on your site should have a different title and description. It is a marketing decision, as important as deciding the headline of an advertisement in the *Times*. Do not abdicate this decision to a programmer!

The bottom line of each listing is the URL, or web address, of the page. You have a great deal of influence over this URL. It can be gobbledegook, as in the case of Groovy Motorsport, or it can reinforce the marketing message, as in the case of Wheelies. Gobbledegook URLs typically get produced automatically by databases, but can be designed to be more informative and friendly, if your programmers are willing to make the extra effort. It can be tricky to change this once your site has been built, but if you specify it beforehand it is very do-able.

If you have achieved a top ranking in the natural results, you should not waste the opportunity to attract a click. Every word that appears in the listing of your page is within your control. Do not blow a great opportunity to get a hot prospect to come to your page by displaying something insipid like:

Products
ABOUT | CONTACT | PRODUCTS | SERVICES
http://www.signinn.com/authentication.aspx?turl=mwebpers&psid={
5B30411F-57AD_497B_8776_70C56775BDA}&sn=Global&sa=500
000&surl=http://www.signinnn.com/signin/core_transfer.aspx?loc=ht
tp%3a%2f%2fwww.signinn.com%2fhome%2fhome.aspx&lg=e

The above is not a compelling, well-crafted marketing message.

The reason why it is so vital to get a top ranking for your most important pages, is that two-thirds of searchers never move on to page two. They seldom even scroll down on page one. To make matters worse, since Google introduced its universal search which, instead of simply listing results in text form, now includes space-hungry videos and photos in the listed results, the number of results that can fit on page one has declined.

SERP heat-maps (an eye-tracking image of the screen, which shows as hot-spots the places where a searcher's eyes spend their time) are even more scary — they show that searchers' attention is mostly on the top two or three results. If searchers don't see what they want, instead of going to the next page, they submit a modified search term.

Two-thirds of searchers never move on to page two. They seldom even scroll down on page one.

Good rankings are not optional, they are essential.

The only way to guarantee good rankings would be to know how the algorithms work and to build a site that exploits this knowledge. Since these algorithms are constantly changing as search science evolves, you would never keep up. But there is a whole industry of search-watchers who try to estimate the algorithms based on the impacts on rankings of certain actions. As a result, there are some rules of thumb that make it relatively easy to get good rankings. These guidelines form the basis of search engine optimization.

NATURAL SEARCH ENGINE OPTIMIZATION

In the first place, you cannot get good rankings if search engine spiders do not visit you. So you have to register your site with Google, Yahoo and MSN/Live.

For Google, go to google.com/addurl/. For Yahoo, it is submit.search.yahoo.com/free/request. For any others, just find their 'submit a site' or 'suggest a site' page. Once on these submission pages, simply enter your site's URL, for example, http://www.yoursitename.com. Before you do so, make sure that you have registered with DMOZ.org.

The question is, how worthy is your site? Once the spiders come calling, will they like what they see, or will they prefer the sites of your competitors?

The more customer-centric you are, the better able you are to get good rankings. Your website will be designed to address certain specific needs of your target audience and will use the kind of language and structure to which they will respond most positively.

Google likes usable customer-centric sites — after all, Google's objective is to serve up the sites or pages that are most relevant for each user's query. So if you build a site that is geared towards serving customer needs, then it follows that Google will like you. It is obviously not quite as simple as that — but the very important point is that many 'specialists' spend their time trying to crack the holy grail of Google algorithms when they should be spending that time making sure that their sites are well architected, that they pay attention to the usability and relevance of their sites and to the quality and depth of their content. Customers like this, and because that is what customers are trying to find, Google is doing its best to match their needs. There is no substitute for good site design and well structured content. You may crack the Google code, but no sooner have you done that, and you'll be left behind again by the latest algorithm changes. So your first objective must be the quality of your site. Then you can optimize it and refine and fine-tune it. The long-term success of your ebusiness is about being customer-centric. You cannot build an ebusiness without continually striving to achieve the best possible relationship with your online consumers, and that means constantly looking at your user experience through their eyes.

If you craft your site for your customers, you accomplish two things. You ensure that visitors relate to the content better than they might to your competitors' content. And it helps you to ensure that search engines associate your pages with the kind of keywords that your target customers will most likely be searching with.

But simply using the language of your customers is not enough. To get great rankings, you have to have the best site in its field, across

> @ In seeking to understand your customers, you should also
> seek to understand the kind of terminology they would use
> to characterize their problems or their needs. They are
> looking for a 'sales training course', not a 'persuasive
> communication skills development seminar'. They want to
> get a loan from a 'bank', not a 'financial services provider'.
> They want a 'tummy tuck', not 'abdominoplasty'.

a wide range of dimensions. To achieve this you have to tweak the hidden code, the information architecture and the visible content of your site. The information that follows relates mainly to Google, because it is such a dominant engine, but what goes for Google tends to be true of Yahoo! and MSN Live as well.

Here are 10 steps to search optimising your site. There are many other things you can do to improve your rankings, but these 10 are essential:

1. Do competitive intelligence studies. See who comes up when you search for 'your' keywords and look closely at their sites. Examine their site structure, keyword themes and tags, as well as the depth and quality of their content.

2. Polish up your title, description tags and URLs. They are your neon signs on the SERP. Never leave their wording to programmers. Try to capture the essence of the page and the compelling reason to visit. Resist the urge to put your brand name first in the title or description tag – searchers do not know your brand, or they would have gone right to your site. Lead with the keyword and a solution for the searcher; add your brand later if you have space, or put it in the description tag. You have 45 to 50 characters for the page title. Use them!

There is another tag called the keywords meta-tag, which

appears in the code of each page. Into this tag you can load all the words that are associated with the page, as well as a list of common misspellings, transpositions and foreign equivalents. But don't pin your hopes on the keywords meta-tag, because Google ignores it. Google's view is that if your search engine has a decent algorithm, it doesn't need to be told what a page is about. There was a time, way back in the early days of the web, when the keywords meta-tag was the most important tag. Today it is a has-been. However, it is still used by lesser engines, so make the effort for the important pages on your site. But don't load it with more than a dozen terms, because the seach engines that do look at it do not usually look beyond that.

3. Put alt tags on all important images. Spiders are blind and cannot see what is in a photograph or graphic. Annotate each visual image with an alt tag so that the spiders get a better idea of what is on your page. Do not fall into the trap of 'keyword stuffing', putting as many instances of your keyword on the page as possible, often through using the keyword as an alt tag on every single image, including invisible ones used for creating spacing. This is another early-days technique for making search engines aware of the content theme of a page, but today, far from help your rankings, you will be penalized for it by the better search engines.

4. Put descriptions in all files such as PDFs or .docs. Most spiders cannot read Word documents or Adobe PDF files. But they can read the descriptions of the files that you enter under file properties. Simply right-click on the file name, select properties, and enter a meaningful search-friendly description. Depending on the software application you use, you may be able to enter a title, subject, keywords, and comments.

5. Name all your links with keywords. Google considers the text used in a hyperlink (known as 'anchor text' and typically appearing

in blue and underlined) to be a very important indicator of what the linked-to page is all about. Try to use as your anchor text the keyword associated with the destination page. So instead of using 'For more about our spa facilities **click here**' use 'Read more about our **spa facilities**'.

6. Give text alternatives to all your Javascript, video and Flash content, as you do for photographs. Spiders cannot see what is in Flash content or movie files, which is why so many Flash-based sites get poor search rankings. Spiders simply see a series of big red Xs. Google's spiders are now able to read the text in a Flash, but the jury is still out on whether it does so in a reliable way, and much Flash content is not designed to be too literal anyway. Spiders are also unable to read mouse-over text. So if you have animated menus in Javascript, make sure that spiders have another way of navigating your site. Spiders cannot push buttons either, so any content that can only be accessed with drop-downs or selection boxes, or by pushing buttons, will simply be bypassed.

The best solution is to make sure you have a site map and that spiders can find it (through what is called a robots.txt file). A site map is a standard document, conventionally named sitemap.xml, which lists the unique addresses of all of the pages on your site and, optionally, their relative importance and the frequency with which they change. Spiders always look for a sitemap.xml file when they arrive on your site.

7. Structure your site according to keyword themes. It is better to have a large number of pages than to have all your content crushed into a few pages. Each important page on your site (i.e. every page you want people to find) should have only one keyword theme. The more crowded your page is, the larger the number of different themes it covers, the harder it is for search engines to figure out what the page is about. If they find the information unclear, they will give it poor rankings, because they would rather send their customers (the searchers) to pages that are clearly directly relevant to the search term.

Make sure that you repeat the keyword on the page, but don't overdo this — three or four times is enough, especially if you are also using the keyword in your alt tags. You can use semantic variations, since Google has a great vocabulary and knows how to work with similes.

8. Submit your site to directories and search engines. Allow enough time for them to do their job. Even the most brilliant site will not get top rankings overnight (unless, of course, it goes viral).

9. Build inbound links from quality sites. It is absolutely essential to have links pointing to your site from other sites that deal with similar topics. But they should be quality links from reputable, authoritative, well trafficked sites. If someone called Guido says he can get you 10,000 links overnight for 500 bucks, politely ask him to leave. The use of link farms — that is, banks of phoney sites that are set up to propagate inbound links to your site — is not only pointless, it can get you black-listed by search engines, as happened to BMW, who were kicked off Google for a few bleak days in 2006 for trying to outwit the system.

> **It is absolutely essential to have links pointing to your site from other sites that deal with similar topics.**

You can see who is linking to your site by typing link: followed by your URL in the Google search box. All the links that are returned will be inbound links to your site. You can do the same thing for your competitors' sites too. This gives you a great starting point for deciding which sites you want to link to yours. To identify other sites, search for the keywords that you want to 'own' and see who gets listed.

You need to have a linking strategy that sets about identifying which sites you want to get links from, and how you will go about getting them. If you have a really good site with lots of relevant useful information, or an unusually good user experience, the authors of good sites will naturally want to link to your site, since doing so enhances the user experience for their visitors. If you have a site with nothing to recommend it, don't hold your breath. You can also explore 'link bait' to attract other sites to link to you. Among the things that seem to attract a great deal of attention are communities and forums; movies (pull them in from YouTube so that YouTube pays for the data transmitted and you don't have to pay for it yourself; competitions; online tools; guides and tutorials; reviews; interviews and surveys. Make sure that whatever you do is relevant to the context of your site and delivers real value.

10. Measure, analyse and review. Optimization is not a once-off activity. It is an ongoing process, so you have to put in place the systems to measure how you are doing, and to continuously improve your SEO performance.

SOCIAL SEARCH COMMUNITIES

In addition to Facebook-style networks, there is an emergent type of social search community that will have a massive impact on the future of the web – and on emarketing. They are currently being referred to as social book-marking services or social search services, and include sites such as Digg, del.icio.us, StumbleUpon, Reddit and Furl. There are dozens of such services, some of them receiving tens of millions of unique visitors every month. Social book-marking is, in essence, a way of publicizing your list of favourite sites.

If you find a web page that you think is great, instead of adding it to your favourites list (or bookmarks) in your computer's browser, you add it to your public list on Digg, or whatever social book-marking site you are a member of. When you 'Digg' the page, you have the option of describing what the page is about and scoring how good you think it is. You describe it by attributing keywords or tags to it. Anyone else can use Digg as a search engine. When they search for particular terms or keywords, Digg shows them the relevant tagged pages that have been ranked highest by members.

Why would you use Digg or del.icio.us rather than a powerhouse search engine like Google? Because Google does not understand the context of the web pages it ranks. It is limited to inferring what each page is about, based on the words on the page and the subject themes of other pages that link to that page. If you were reading an article about repairing a broken suspension on a Land Rover while exploring the Zambian bush, you might tag the article with terms such as 'adventure travel', 'tools to take on an off-road trip' or 'Zambian safaris'. Google would attribute none of these to the page. Community-based search adds rich layers of context and examines content across different dimensions. It also adds a qualitative judgement, which Google cannot hope to generate automatically.

> Community-based search adds rich layers of context. It also adds a qualitative judgement, which Google cannot hope to generate automatically.

To compensate, Google's algorithms attach an increasing amount of importance to the tags that social book-marking sites have attached to the pages that they list. Until those algorithms change, which is an ongoing process, it can give your rankings quite a boost if you get your site bookmarked in the more popular social search tools. I will return to this in more detail in the chapter on buzz marketing.

CONTEXTUAL ADVERTISING (PAY-PER-CLICK)

Not every page can get the top ranking in natural search listings. But you can ensure that your page gets seen on the first page of the SERP by making sure that relevant search terms trigger the appearance of an advertisement. Google's contextual advertising programme is called AdWords. AdWords is the service by which advertisers get

Google to place contextually relevant ads, both on SERPS and in the web pages of their network of online publishers; AdSense is the service by which publishers sign up to receive contextually relevant ads from Google AdWords advertisers.

All search engines provide a facility for you to advertise on their SERP using a limited-text advertisement. Most commonly, these advertisements appear when a keyword that you have previously nominated is searched for. You pay the search company only if someone clicks on the advertisement. If several companies want the same keyword to trigger their advertisements, these advertisements appear one below the other.

The ranking of the advertisements is determined by a combination of the maximum you are willing to pay for a click (known as your 'bid') and the quality of your advertisement. Google calculates advertisement quality by looking at how relevant the text of your advertisement is to the keyword, how well the advertisement matches the landing page on which searchers arrive when they click, and the rate at which your advertisement is clicked in comparison to the other advertisements. The exact algorithm is, of course, never made public, and it changes periodically. In early 2007, the amount you bid for a keyword was the most important factor; by 2008, the quality of the advertisement had become most important.

As an advertiser, you do not have to restrict your advertisements to appearing on Google's SERPs. You can elect to have your advertisements appear on the pages of other online publishers. Google has thousands of partners who provide placeholders on their pages for Google advertisers. The Google AdSense system examines the content of those pages, determines what keywords apply, and then posts whatever advertisements are most relevant. If you are advertising a five-star spa and wellness centre, and one of Google's publishing partners is running an article on the top spas of the world, your advertisement may appear alongside the article. Once you leave the SERP, your advertisements no longer have the tight Google restrictions and may contain images or video too. You also are given powerful but easy-to-use tools that let you select specific online publications where you want your advertisement to appear.

The reason why contextual advertising is so appealing and why it attracts a large share of online advertising budgets is that advertisements appear to individual searchers at a time and in a place when they are most receptive to it. On a SERP, they are looking for answers that you can provide; on a publishing-partner page, they are reading an article to which your advertisment is directly relevant. This is about as non-intrusive and contextually relevant as advertising can get, and it provides marketers with an opportunity to speak directly to the current needs and interests of consumers.

Many people will tell you that they never even look at the sponsored links on Google because they know they are advertisements, yet a substantial portion of Google's US$21 billion revenue comes from people who click on those ads. Savvy searchers use them all the time, because they know that they will not find the best site for their needs in a simple Google listing. The sponsored links are advertisements placed by smarter companies who are willing to invest in getting a searcher's immediate attention.

As an advertiser, here is how it works.

- You select which keywords you want to bid on for your particular page
- You craft an advertisement that will be triggered by these keywords
- You decide how much you are willing to pay per click for each keyword
- You decide what your daily budget cap will be (there is no minimum)
- You decide what geographic and time targets you want to apply (for example, only searchers in Central London, or Utah, or Portugal should see my advertisements, only on weekends)

Your advertisements will appear immediately when people within that demographic search using your keywords, and Google provides you with a host of easy-to-use tools to monitor your advertisement's performance and manage your keywords.

Google is, of course, not the only advertising network on the web, but it is the biggest and most user-friendly. There are many others, including Yahoo Search Marketing, Microsoft adCenter, Kanoodle and MIVA Monetization Center. Like many of the smaller advertising networks, MIVA has its own exclusive contracts with select online publishers, mainly in Europe. If you want your advertisement to appear in any of Condé Nast UK's online pages (for example, Vogue, Condé Nast Traveller or GQ), you need to work through MIVA; their system and pricing are not that different from Google's.

> **Think of PPC almost in the same way as direct marketing: if you are getting a 100:1 return, you are not spending enough.**

DEVELOPING A PAY-PER-CLICK CAMPAIGN

As with any traditional advertising campaign, you need to have a media strategy that targets your consumers where they are most likely to be receptive to your message. Sophisticated emarketers do not put all their eggs in the Google pay-per-click basket.

If you want to run a pay-per-click campaign, here are the stages that you need to go through:

STAGE 1: DISCOVER: Collect and analyse all the information that you have about the online communications medium, the target consumer and the past performance of your site. Research your competitors too. Then structure a pilot PPC campaign that will run for two to four weeks. The pilot can be quite extensive and should involve trying many different things so that you can later discard what does not work well.

STAGE 2: EVALUATE: Let your pilot campaign run, and monitor it closely. Examine your keywords, advertisement copy, landing pages and bid strategies and decide which approaches performed best.

STAGE 3: EXPAND: Based on what you learned in the pilot campaign, increase the scope of your advertising for those elements that showed good potential. At the same time abandon the elements that under-performed. You can think of PPC almost in the same way as direct marketing: if you are getting a 100:1 return, you are not spending enough. Keep increasing the budget until your performance targets are achieved.

STAGE 4: ENHANCE: Routinely fine-tune your campaign by tweaking keywords, the copy of your advertisements, the effectiveness of your landing pages and conversion funnels, and your bid strategies. Take advantage of how easy (and instant) it is to A/B test online. A/B testing involves creating two versions of an advertisement, a landing page or some other element, such as a registration form. In pure A/B testing, the two items to be compared are identical except for one specific difference, such as a headline, a call to action, or a colour. You route half of your visitors to each variant and monitor their actions to see if there is a marked difference in performance between the two. If you are really concerned that the difference may be due to chance you can A/A/B test, creating two identical 'control' versions which, if chance is not an issue, should both perform in a similar way.

KEYWORD BIDDING

When you bid on keywords, you need a strategy. An SME may handle keyword bidding manually, but a larger company, such as an ecommerce site with several hundred thousand items in its catalogue, will have to use automated systems. Three out of four searches use keywords of three words or less. But one in four uses longer, more specific search queries. Decide whether you will bid on short, generic keywords, which are often both expensive and non-targeted, but get searched often. Also decide whether you will bid on your own brand names, simply as a defensive strategy. You may also think about bidding on long-tail keywords — those terms that have four, five or more words in them and are available at extremely low prices. They are not used often by searchers, but anyone who does use them has a very clear idea of what they are looking for and is a highly pre-qualified prospect.

MONITORING YOUR CAMPAIGN

In PPC campaigns, continual performance monitoring helps you not to waste money. If only 2 out of 100 people who click on your advertisement end up buying something from you, your 'conversion rate' is 2 percent. If it costs you 40 cents every time your advertisement is clicked, each sale is costing you $20. This is known as your 'cost of conversion'. A conversion is not necessarily a sale, but an act by a visitor that you consider an important step toward making a commitment (such as downloading a spec sheet, signing up for a newsletter, or asking to be contacted by a sales representative). If you know the business purpose of your site, you know what you consider a conversion.

The challenge is to reduce the cost of conversion. There are a number of approaches to try:

- Find cheaper keywords, or lower your bids.
- Word your advertisement more clearly for better qualified clicks; make sure that you are explicit enough to ensure that only those who are seriously interested in your advertisement click on it. You want higher conversion rates, not a large volume of visitors.
- Use landing pages that flow from the keywords used; there should be no disconnection with what the clicker is expecting. Landing pages should address the visitor's problem directly and build momentum towards conversion.
- Tweak the conversion power of your site and use well-crafted conversion funnels that maximize your chances of closing sales.

- Increase the budget for keywords that bring you visitors who convert.
- Abandon keywords that don't bring you visitors who convert.
- Tweak your scheduling to maximize impressions at times that get higher conversion rates.

Search marketing attracts the lion's share of many emarketing budgets, partly because it is so cost-effective and partly because it is so measurable. Because it is a hot issue, many businesses that used to be website designers are now also offering SEO services. For most marketers, the idea of outsourcing search marketing is very appealing, but you do need to be careful of who you deal with. Make sure that you set up a service-level agreement that specifies what the outsourcers will do for your site, initially and ongoing, and how they will report on their performance. Establish that they will handle both SEO and PPC. Check their references and ask to see a sample performance report. Above all, if they promise to submit you to a hundred search engines and get you a thousand inbound links, or guarantee you rankings, head for the door.

Online advertising 9

Despite the reluctance of many advertising agencies to fully embrace the web, it has provided incredibly fertile ground for genuine innovation and creativity. There was the first-ever banner advertisement, way back in 1994, in which AT&T presciently asserted 'Have you ever clicked here? You will!'. There were the wonderful moving parts of the Honda Accord, in the 'cog' ad that virtually invented viral video. Burger King's bizarre but addictive webcam starring a disturbing guy in a chicken suit, who became known as Subservient Chicken. Then there was Dove's brilliant 'Campaign For Real Beauty', showing in time-lapse video the transformation via cosmetics and Photoshop of an ordinary woman into a stereotypical billboard beauty; and its controversial 'Onslaught' and 'Pro Age' sequels.

All these campaigns have leveraged the web's power to stimulate discussion and foster experience-sharing. The campaigns were not messages, but catalysts. While artistic creativity has been an essential ingredient, the real brilliance was in the way the campaigns were conceived to gain permission from consumers to propagate an idea.

The term 'permission marketing' was first coined by marketing guru Seth Godin. The essence of the concept is this: you can market intrusively, by barging into a consumer's space uninvited, or you can market when that consumer gives you permission to do so. The latter will arguably produce better results than the former. As people gain more and more control over when and how they consume media – and the marketing messages they harbour – it becomes easier for them to filter out irrelevant messages and harder for marketers to break through using conventional approaches.

It has always been important for marketing messages to be welcome guests rather than gatecrashers in the consumer's conscience. In conventional media, the timing, context or relevance of a message will nearly always be out of synch with the consumer's current interests. Unless consumers want to notice your advertisement, it is merely static interference. They don't need personal video recorders or TiVo to fast-forward through your advertisement, their brains simply bleep it out. How do you grab people's attention for long enough to make them willing to change their focus of attention and latch onto your intrusive message? Creativity.

Advertisers have come to rely on creativity to seduce consumers away from their preferred focus of attention. All the money, timing, polish, talent and finesse go into crafting a message that is as perfect as possible and so different that it becomes remarkable. When all parts come together, awards are won, champagne is quaffed and consumers talk fondly of the advertisement, though whether they remember the brand behind it is another matter. When things do not gel, which is the case more often than not, the result is simply more of the same invasive, irrelevant noise that has always detracted from the pleasure of watching a movie or reading an article.

Media buyers try to achieve relevance by matching products to media where the target market might be (for example, by advertising cars in ad-breaks during episodes of *Top Gear*, or placing running-shoe advertisements in sports magazines). But this is matching mega-segment advertising to mega-segment media, not connecting solutions to the specific concern of an individual consumer. Each individual consumer, with his or her particular interests, problems or concerns, is presumed to be as receptive and malleable as the next, at least within the target group.

Marketers may never know whether the annoying intrusions of advertising is causing people to move away from traditional media, or whether it is because people prefer to have greater control over their media consumption. But marketers do know that once advertising starts to become intrusive online, people abandon a site rapidly: when advertising began inundating MySpace, the mass migration to Facebook was inevitable.

As marketers move from 'broadcasting at' consumers offline to 'engaging with' consumers online, they move from a reliance on the creative to a reliance on the innovative. Creativity does not become less important online, it raises its game and acquires new dimensions, new opportunities, and new constraints.

It is a common misconception that marketers can simply invoke the web as merely another medium, and that there is nothing inherently new in emarketing. They look at the technology and what it appears to be able to do, and squeeze current thinking into its constraints and capabilities. However, then you have essentially the same marketing mechanism as before, but on digital steroids. There is a belief that you don't have to change your world view or marketing philosophy, since all you are looking for is the ability to reach more people at a lower cost than you could achieve through mainstream media.

> **Think about what you can add to your customer's brand-engagement processes that was previously not possible. This usually requires you to change your world view.**

This is a dangerously limiting, short-sighted view of what emarketing is or can be. Yes, digital steroids could make campaigns more effective, not merely more efficient, but steroids are generally not renowned for making anything smarter. It is this kind of limited thinking that produces that ultimate manifestation of dumbed-down emarketing, the blinking banner. Instead, you should be striving to use the tools to improve the quality of marketing. This does not require anything as mundane as re-thinking your message or positioning; it requires that you think about what you can add to your customer's brand-engagement processes that was previously not possible. And by definition, this usually requires you to change your world view.

A fundamental change has already taken place in the way companies interact with their consumers, and their marketing and communication models have to evolve accordingly or, better, have to regain the initiative. Marketers' willingness to accept the validity of the 'canned message to the masses' model of emarketing should have died with the market for interactive CD-ROMs.

The major branding and loyalty-building advantage that the internet has over any other medium (and it is a huge advantage) is that it fosters peer-to-peer communication on a previously impossible scale. And you don't need to have hi-tech tools to do this; you can use tools that are now part of everyone's daily life – email, chat, social media, threaded discussions and the ever-expanding array of widgetized applications that let people continuously share their every thought and action. Without a desire to use these tools to improve the effectiveness of our marketing processes significantly, without a belief that you need to evolve beyond 20th-century media thinking, emarketing may not become an evolutionary step forward. It may, indeed, be relegated to being the same as television advertising, but with a bigger audience on a smaller screen at a lower cost.

> The major branding and loyalty-building advantage that the internet has over any other medium is that it fosters peer-to-peer communication on a previously impossible scale.

To get true synergies out of the digital potential, marketers will need to think across the dividing lines of online and offline, above-the-line and below-the-line. You need to perceive the media through which you market in the same way as consumers perceive them: not as isolated deliverers of discrete messages, but as complementary places in which to have engaging personal experiences that grow relationships. This 'blended marketing' is a hybrid concept that can de-polarize some of the issues and create a more efficient and effective interface with your target markets. The concept of combining traditional and online marketing processes is not new – just as combining above-the-line and below-the-line marketing is not new. But it is typical for above-the-line traditional marketing to dictate budgets, timing, messaging and creative, leaving online to try to fit all of that into a medium quite unsuited to the offline brief. By endorsing a blended marketing approach you tell people that it's okay to experiment and use the tools and methods that seem sensible, rather than be blinkered by old-media creative processes.

Technology that does not change the way you do things has no value. The raison d'être for technology is performance improvement, and the desire to improve performance in turn drives the development of technology. You cannot separate them. Technology spawns opportunity. Refusing to grasp opportunity because you fear failure is more tragic than failure itself. In emarketing, failure usually results from not rethinking your marketing models.

Technologies such as the telephone and email have had a significant impact on the way people talk, write and communicate. Certain components of those activities may not have changed – you still need to open your mouth and use the 26 letters of the alphabet (except when sending an SMS) – but there have been huge changes in the effectiveness, timeliness, relevance, structure and application of both talking and writing as a result of those technologies, none of which were conceived by their inventors. The same holds true for emarketing.

Today, the world is changing faster than anyone can comprehend. The 'technologies' that people talk about in emarketing are already implemented, usually better, in consumer-centric phenomena such as social networks, blogging, shopping comparison engines, and SMS collaboration services. Massively mainstream digital services like Facebook, Twitter and MXit, dominate popular culture for a short while, then are gone, driven out by competitors who are better able to anticipate and adapt to rapidly changing user needs. The competitive environments in which companies operate are increasingly dynamic and increasingly chaotic. The amount of knowledge generated and shared every day is growing exponentially. For companies to survive, all of their people – not only their marketers – need to learn how to interact with customers in ways that are very different from those that were adequate even five years ago. Senior managers need to be willing to abandon their 20th-century comfort models and live on an edge characterized by dynamism, risk-taking and innovation. They should be steering the boat, or they may drown in its wake.

This is not revolution. It is pragmatism. Use the tools that work, but use them to facilitate speedier, more relevant, less centralized, more customer-centric models, where marketing is driven by shared experience and customers create their own content. It is easy to do, and it works. Most failures in emarketing result from an approach that changes nothing, uses the internet as a cheap broadcast medium for advertising content, and puts even more distance between customers and marketers.

In the minds of many advertising executives, emarketing is taking on a life of its own – as if it exists outside their control. Every survey over the past five years has had corporations calling for ever greater percentages of marketing to be done online. So is the traditional agency an endangered species?

Optimistic advertising agencies say that the web will make their lives easier or richer. Pessimists see themselves losing their livelihoods. Pragmatists scramble to enrol in courses that promise to teach them web authoring skills. But what if you don't want to become a Dreamweaver expert or a Flash guru? What if you see marketing as much too important to be left to the coding geeks?

A computer equipped with Microsoft Word will not make an untalented person into a world-class writer, nor will a blogger account. But a good writer might exploit such tools where appropriate and relevant. If blogging had been around when James Joyce wanted to write, he would have been drawn to it as a form of unfettered self-expression, requiring neither editor nor publisher.

(Imagine reading Ulysses in blog-sized chunks, with every day's episode coming to your RSS reader from Joyce sitting hunched over his mobile phone in the corner of a pub.)

Good marketers, like good writers, will exploit new technologies only in so far as they help to fulfil their vision. The tool may influence that vision, but it should never be allowed to corrupt or dominate it. The ability to understand customer needs, analyse the marketing environment, interpret the objectives and constraints of the customers, conceive a marketing process that will be effective and manage its creation and deployment is not yet available at the click of a mouse.

The skilled, committed, 'old-school' professional will remain integral to marketing no matter how cool the digital evolution becomes. Marketing is a process. No matter how exotic the enabling technology, you need to remember that at the beginning and end of every business process is a human being. Every process is conceived and architected by people to achieve goals that are decided on by people. In a decade or so, machines and software may start to evolve themselves. But in the meantime the electronic systems that we have are products of – and servants to – real human beings.

Naturally, human beings change, sometimes rather rapidly. Marketers should be in tune with the evolving needs of their consumers. If, on average, a group of consumers is indicating that they form loyalties or make purchasing decisions better with processes or experiences that are wildly different from those the marketer has grown comfortable with, the marketer must adapt. This is not easy to do. Even if individual marketers see the benefit of a fundamental shift in approach, their colleagues or managers may be sceptical — even outright hostile — to a move away from established 'best' practices.

> You now see advertisers doing things that would have been heresy a decade ago. Brands are being unshackled and consumers are being invited to publicly help them evolve.

One of the paradoxes of emarketing is that you need an open mind to see and embrace the potential of the web, yet many emarketing practitioners are incapable of seeing beyond their new-found techno-centric comfort zone. There is a bigger context out there, an ever-changing marketing landscape. It is one you cannot see clearly while you remain buried in your chosen technology du jour. True marketing professionals are able to keep their heads and exercize all their options when all those around them are clutching at macromediocrity.

The technologies available today are simply tools. The marketer is the craftsman. He or she is an indispensable conceiver, creator and driver of the marketing process, whether those processes are online, offline, interactive, immersive, emailed, search-based, socially networked, YouTubed, SMS-based, rich-media or drawn with a stick in the sand.

THE STATE OF ONLINE ADVERTISING

What exactly is the state of online advertising? By early 2009, worldwide online advertising expenditure amounted to about 10 percent of all advertising. In the United Kingdom, online advertising had passed television ad spend by 2008, was 6 times the size of radio advertising, and had attracted as much revenue as all outdoor and magazine advertising combined. In the United States, total online advertising spend in 2008 was about US$24 billion, a figure that is forecast to rise to US$29 billion in 2010. In the developed nations, for the past few years, online advertising expenditure has been growing at rates that vary between 25 percent and 50 percent a year.

ONLINE BRANDING

Marketers are rapidly finding that online environments can be very good for developing brands. After all, great branding and web commerce have a lot in common. All great brands start with a compelling vision based on profound customer insight. They have a deep understanding of the cultural context, values, needs and aspirations of their customers. They seek to empathize and engage with their customers in scenarios in which they can add most value.

The converse is true of branding that is not great, the second-tier variety whose existence is entirely dependent on repeated assertions of its importance, but who patently has no interest in empathising with consumers on any real level. Brands do not usually start out being uninterested, they become the victims of bureaucracy or of lazy or expedient marketers, even in huge corporations.

There has recently been a growing sense of disquiet among many marketers, prompted largely by the growing transparency that the web imposes on markets and marketing. The internet is a vast focus group. If you take the trouble to listen, you hear things that can be quite disturbing.

You now see advertisers doing things that would have been heresy a decade ago. Brands are being unshackled and consumers are being invited to publicly help them evolve. Companies are backing off from their more aggressive modes of marketing and starting to engage more in a participative mode of exploration. Brands are still claiming to care about consumers, only this time they appear to mean it.

In February 2004, Jim Stengel, global marketing officer of Procter & Gamble stood up at a conference and asserted, 'We're applying antiquated thinking and work systems to a new world of possibilities … The traditional marketing model is obsolete.' That upset a few people, but they got over it.

Then in March 2007, Stengel stood up at another conference and said, 'Building relationships through our brands is the future of marketing. It's not about new media models or new tools. It's about engaging with people in a two-way relationship. It's about seeking to understand the other person rather than trying to control their actions. That's why we're changing. That's why we're committed to building brands that stand for something meaningful to consumers rather than just telling and selling.'

Unilever has followed the same lead. Its recent campaigns have turned conventional marketing inside out. Dove's 'Campaign For Real Beauty' is aimed at girls between 8 and 12 and their parents. It targets girls before they reach the age at which peer pressure, magazines, television and celebrity cults (and advertising) make them dissatisfied with the way they look, giving them a distorted idea of what real beauty is. Dove provides online discussion forums where girls can talk freely about how they feel about their appearance. It provides free self-esteem workshops right across the country, which do a tremendous amount of good. And at the same time, Dove locks in brand loyalty among parents. The Dove campaigns have leveraged the web to achieve massive word-of-mouth marketing and viralized campaign videos. The company used the web to create a sensitivity to a problem, to communicate its solution, and to deliver much of that solution.

Dove is a great example of what brands have to become in a web-connected world where jaded online consumers are untrusting of marketers, prefer to connect with peers and want to be able to have their say. Brands have had to become more authentic, more generous and more engaging if they wanted to engender any credibility, trust or affection. This is not easy to pull off. Beauty products lend themselves to this approach, but what about insurance or fast-food franchises? Given the right brief, customer insights and freedom to innovate, marketers will continue to produce remarkable online branding experiences.

The immediate challenge for advertising agencies is waning credibility with their own clients. In recent American surveys, most marketers (both client-side marketers and advertising agencies) said they would not recommend their agencies to a colleague. In another study, only 10 percent of the chief marketing officers in the United Kingdom and the United States said they seek to partner with large advertising agencies for online marketing. More than half of them believe that traditional, large advertising agencies are ill-suited to meet online marketing needs. To senior marketers in these countries, the most important factors in choosing an agency today, in order of importance, are:

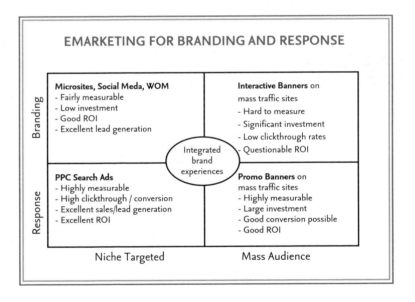

- quality of creative
- innovation and strategic value
- cost
- sophistication of analytics
- proficiency in emerging, interactive or digital media
- traditional print, offline and media buying services

Marketers are anxious to work with agencies who can help them not only define a digital strategy, but make it happen in practice.

EMARKETING FOR BRANDING AND RESPONSE

Branding

Microsites, Social Meda, WOM
- Fairly measurable
- Low investment
- Good ROI
- Excellent lead generation

Interactive Banners on mass traffic sites
- Hard to measure
- Significant investment
- Low clickthrough rates
- Questionable ROI

Integrated brand experiences

Response

PPC Search Ads
- Highly measurable
- High clickthrough / conversion
- Excellent sales/lead generation
- Excellent ROI

Promo Banners on mass traffic sites
- Highly measurable
- Large investment
- Good conversion possible
- Good ROI

Niche Targeted   Mass Audience

As online marketing establishes itself as not only a mainstream medium but, in some places, as one of the largest media, traditional ad agencies have to work really hard to develop their perceived expertise to meet the demands of their clients. They need to become more flexible, manage web projects and work across media. They need to be more willing and able to measure the performance of their initiatives. They also need to develop good models for building synergy among advertising and PR online, and offline. It is time to stop thinking about 'online' as a single medium and start thinking about it as multiple channels, each capable of delivering a different marketing advantage, each capable of having an amplified impact if innovatively integrated with the others. The diagram on the previous page illustrates how diverse the online marketing communications tools are, and how targeted they can be.

If the two primary goals of marketing are branding and response, and you look at both mass and niche markets, you can draw up a grid with four quadrants. You can then ask yourself, 'What online approaches are best suited to each quadrant?'

If you want to achieve branding goals in a mass audience, banner advertisements placed on mass-traffic sites are the most effective approach. This is the closest analogy to print, TV, or outdoor advertising, and one with which traditional marketers are most comfortable. The notions of reach and frequency seem to apply, and many online media are willing to pay agencies for placements. The purpose of banners is to raise awareness, so the fact that they typically have low click-through and conversion rates is irrelevant. After more than a decade of experience with banner ads, most marketers agree that they provide a poor return on investment, since costs per impression are high and overall effectiveness is low.

But recent research by Specific Media shows that while the direct connection between banner advertisements and purchases is low, there can be a significant indirect connection: brands that use banner ads are searched for in Google and other search engines much more frequently than brands that do not run banner ads. In travel and tourism, banner ads lift search by a massive 260 percent. A similar impact is felt in the financial services sector.

Unfortunately, in the consumer goods sector, where brands are probably a lot more familiar, banner ads appear to have little impact on search volumes.

The more interactive the banners are, the better the ROI. Rich media banners can be particularly effective, because they immerse the consumer in the brand for an extended time without taking him or her away from the original page. Rich-media banners can roll out over the page, are bandwidth-friendly, and can contain video, animation, games and navigation. Activity within the banner is totally measurable, telling you where the mouse was pointed, how long the viewer spent in which sections, and which items within the banner were clicked. You can think of rich-media banners as nanosites.

If you want to achieve response in a mass audience, promotional banners on mass-traffic sites are the best approach to take. These banners require a large investment, but can provide a good ROI. Click-through rates are relatively good and the performance of such banners is highly measurable.

When rich-media banners are used for promotion, they can achieve great results. For example, Hollywood has used rich-media banners to promote upcoming movies. On a website whose context is movies, you might see a banner ad about an upcoming feature film. Roll your mouse over the banner and it expands across a portion of the page to reveal a small website. On that site you can click links to run trailers, download images, see actor profiles or reviews, and even buy tickets through an imbedded ecommerce facility. All of this activity happens without you having to leave the original page on which you first saw the banner. The company placing the banner can get full metrics, including what items were clicked and how long each visitor spent on each section, allowing the performance of the banner to be tweaked and improved.

If you are looking for response from a niche audience, the best approach would be search-based pay-per-click advertisements. They provide excellent ROI, are highly measurable and can be tweaked and fine-tuned in real time. If designed well, PPC campaigns can produce excellent click-through and conversion rates and are very good for generating sales or sales leads.

If you have branding goals in a niche audience, many of the web 2.0 social network tools are invaluable. Branded microsites, targeted social media, word of mouth (WOM), viral video and competitions can all be leveraged to build rapid awareness and interest in a brand. These options produce a good ROI, are fairly measurable (though in some cases measurement can be difficult) and typically require a low initial investment. Unlike other branding activities, many campaigns in this area produce some excellent lead generation as a by-product.

> **If you are looking for response from a niche audience, the best approach would be search-based pay-per-click advertisements.**

For any significant marketing campaign, you would not focus only on one of these quadrants, but would structure an approach that integrates them all – and in addition integrates your online and offline marketing too.

Just as with website design and search engine marketing, the specific mix of advertising tactics you select will be determined by your business objectives, your strategy, your insights into online consumers, and the character and values of your brand. Yet no matter how focused you get, advertising will never be an intimate or personal communications vehicle. For that, email marketing has no equal.

Email marketing 10

The first email message was sent 40 years ago. Since then, email has consistently been the biggest application on the internet. There are nearly 2 billion email addresses in the world. 72 billion email messages are sent every day. More than 9 out of 10 of them are spam.

Anyone who tells you that email marketing is easy, is fooling themselves. But if you pay attention to the details, email marketing can be an incredibly cost-effective way to achieve your marketing goals. On average, for websites that are experiencing good growth in their visitor numbers, 1 in 5 visitors arrives as a result of clicking a link in an email message.

Like PR, email is currently undergoing a renaissance. Ten years ago, email marketing was driven by copywriters and graphic designers. Companies would create a broadcast message, put together their databases and blast out an undifferentiated email to their list. Then spam came along, and consumer sensitivities became a lot more acute.

At about the same time, web analytics started becoming easier to manage. It was possible to get a clearer idea of the impact of email campaigns. Best of all, it became easier to evaluate the connection between creative decisions and market reactions.

Today, things have changed dramatically. The creative process for email campaigns is different from other broadcast media, because marketers have learned to target and segment their messaging. Marketers now seek to engage in an ongoing relationship with their customers, and email is a vital agent in that process.

Spam has made everyone wary. Companies are much more cautious in how they use their lists and are a lot more respectful of customer wishes.

When website visitors sign up to receive email information from a site, it is good practice to work with a double opt-in process – in fact, in the US this is a legal requirement. What is double opt-in? When a visitor provides his or her email address (the first opt-in point), the site sends an email, asking the person to click a link in the email to confirm that he or she really wants to sign up. Once that has happened (the second opt-in point), the site sends another email, welcoming the registrant and reconfirming what was agreed. It is a quick and simple automated process that serves three purposes: First, it ensures that the registration was legitimate. Secondly, it provides an opportunity to manage expectations, and to upsell. And thirdly, it provides an audit trail of evidence so that if, at any point in the future, the recipient reports the site as a spammer it is easy to defuse the situation.

Your website may not be the only place from which you are getting people to sign up, so it is important to stay permission-consistent across all address sources. For instance, people may be signing up in-store, from your brochures, or in a phone conversation with your call centre. You have to avoid inconsistencies between the online and offline opt-ins by making sure that the process followed and the permissions granted are identical. Consistency does not apply only to the permission you are getting, but also to the customer information you are asking for. It does not help you to collect first and last names on the site, but not on the paper-based sign-up form.

Even companies who have a perfectly clean opt-in list tell me that they are nervous about email marketing because they might be thought of as spammers. In this regard, you need to have two concerns: your customers' attitude to you, and the law.

Customer attitude management entails that you ensure that you send them what they are expecting to receive, at a frequency they

@ Spam is generally considered to be any unsolicited commercial communications, typically mass-market, originally using email, and now using any electronic medium. The name is derived from the Monty Python sketch in which a restaurant customer is unable to order anything that does not contain copious quantities of Spam, while a chorus of Vikings at another table sings the virtues of 'Spam, wonderful Spam.' (You will find it on YouTube's Monty Python video channel).

anticipate, and that you send them something that it is always relevant and useful. You provide easy (ideally one-click) opt-out capabilities in each email, so that if you are annoying them, they can get off your list without a problem.

At first most countries' laws had no teeth where spam was concerned, but this situation is changing quickly. European and American legislators have come down hard on spammers, invoking harsh penalties for anyone who transgresses the law. The toughest legislation is in the US, where the latest updates to the Controlling the Assault of Non-Solicited Pornography and Marketing (CAN-SPAM) Act have made it harder than ever to get away with sending unsolicited email.

The main provisions of CAN-SPAM are:

- You may not use false or misleading header information ('From,' 'To,' and routing information)
- You may not use deceptive subject lines
- You must provide a one-click opt-out method, and you must honour opt-out requests within 10 business days of receiving them
- You must identify commercial email as an advertisement and include the sender's valid physical postal address

Any business in the US that wants to do email marketing of any kind must digest the latest version of CAN-SPAM and be sure to adhere to its requirements, in detail. The law is very clear, but it has many complex details that you must simply become familiar with.

For example, people opting in to a list from your website cannot be required to provide information other than their email address and their opt-out preferences. When they want to opt-out, you cannot require them to do anything more than send a reply email or visit a single 'unsubscribe me' web page. If people click to an opt-out page, you cannot take them first to a page on which you make an offer to try to retain them; nor can you require that they enter a password to ensure that the person making the opt-out request is in fact the original subscriber.

In Europe, while EU legislation provides guidance, it is left to each individual nation to pass its own laws. The EU's directive on privacy and electronic communications is a lot gentler on marketers than CAN-SPAM, allowing a number of exceptions to the opt-in requirement. For example, where natural persons (consumers) are concerned, email marketing messages can only be sent to those who have opted-in. But you have the right to send emails to already existing customers, marketing products similar to those around which a buyer-seller relationship was established, where those customers have not opted out of receiving such messages. You do, of course, have to offer an easy opt-out mechanism in those emails. What about non-natural (legal) persons? You are entitled to send commercial emails to business owners and employees without their prior consent, but, again, must provide an opt-out mechanism. The Federation of European Direct Marketing maintains regular updates on (and interpretations of) EU data protection initiatives, and for anyone wanting to do extensive email marketing in Europe this is a good place to start.

Clearly, you have to turn to the law of your nation or state for guidance, but you can also look at established best practice among ethical mass mailers. Commonly accepted best practices of ethical mass mailers include:

- provide truthful message headers, subjects and content
- provide an obvious, simple unsubscribe process (one click is ideal)
- always actually de-list those who wish to unsubscribe
- provide the physical address of the sending company
- provide an accessible, transparent privacy policy
- use opt-in addresses only, ideally double opt-in, and never use opt-out addresses
- never use third-party lists unless you know they are opt-in
- if your list is not opt-in, state clearly that the content of your message is an advertisement, solicitation or commercial message
- don't harvest or scrape addresses from the web
- don't provide addresses to third parties without express permission.

If you stick to these guidelines you will probably be within the law anywhere in the world, and you are likely to keep your customers happy at the same time. Irrespective of what is required by the letter of the law, no legitimate business should want to do anything that might endanger a customer relationship.

CREATING AN EMAIL CAMPAIGN

In putting together a successful email campaign, you obviously have to adhere to the strategic guidelines covered earlier in this book (see Chapters 4 and 5), particularly making sure that you have a clear vision and well-defined business objective and that you stay customer-centric.

Creatively speaking, the single most important thing you need to keep at the top of your mind when creating an email is what you want people to do with it, that is, your 'call to action' (CTA). You work so hard and jump through so many hoops to get the attention of the recipient. When you finally have their attention you need to be very clear about what your message is, and what you want them to do. The answer to this question hinges on your objectives. If you don't know where you are going, you'll burn precious opportunities. Not setting objectives is almost inexcusable, because it is so elementary.

When you start down the road to designing your email campaign, make sure that you and everyone on your team knows what your objective is, why customers should care and how you are going to capture their attention. You can test your email easily – even by simply asking some colleagues, friends or family to look at the email and tell you what they see first and what they think the email is about. Because the call to action is so important, make sure that you reinforce it by providing multiple ways of carrying out the desired actions. By the same token, don't clutter your email with distractions — avoid letting the customer slip away from you through lack of focus.

Then you need to create minimum performance specifications for your email. Typically, they would be:

- tested for multiple email clients and versions
- of an appropriate width (about 650 pixels)
- bandwidth-conscious
- tested for effectiveness in preview windows
- tested for effectiveness with image-blocking
- spam filter tested.

Some of the terms above may need a little explanation.

An email client is the software that you use for sending and receiving emails. On your PC or Mac this may be Outlook, Eudora or Opera. On the web it may be Hotmail, Gmail, Yahoo! Mail or one of many others. One thing is certain, your target market will not all be using the same email client as you. Why does this matter? Email clients are not as predictable as web browsers. They all render HTML code differently, and different generations of the same email client work quite differently too. This means that if you send out an email that is coded to look great in only one email client, using colours and fonts and images in a carefully crafted layout, the addressee may well receive something that looks like a badly designed work in progress.

You have to design an email that will work in all the most common email clients, and test it to be sure that what the customer receives is exactly what you sent. Or take the strategic decision, based on testing, that you don't care.

A further complication is that the vast majority of people preview their emails without opening them, using a preview window in their email client. Three quarters of the time these windows are horizontal. You have to design your email so that the most important call to action is visible, no matter what. This means putting it in the top left-hand corner, the 'sweet-spot' where most designers want to put your logo. If you must put your logo at the head of your email, put it on the right and use the space on the left to display your most compelling stimulus to open the email.

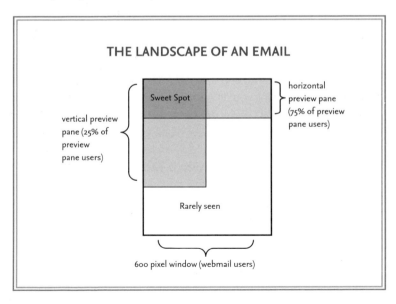

THE LANDSCAPE OF AN EMAIL

Sweet Spot

horizontal preview pane (75% of preview pane users)

vertical preview pane (25% of preview pane users)

Rarely seen

600 pixel window (webmail users)

There is another complication: most email clients by default block images from downloading. If you have designed your email to be dependent on photography, or if you have put all your text into a picture as an image, your email recipient will have no idea what the email is about. So you have to ensure that your design uses HTML text in the top left-hand corner of the email, and that the text is a strong call to action.

Many major email marketers have simply given up trying to get it right, and place a clickable link at the top of their email stating, 'if you can't see the images click here for a web version'. At least the web version will be viewed in a browser, and browsers render code a lot more predictably than email clients. This may be a cop-out, but it's a pragmatic tactic in an increasingly chaotic technical environment. Sadly, even this is not a perfect solution, since it relies on only the subject line and the sender's name to provide the stimulus to go to the web version.

The width of your mailer has to be around 650 pixels, since this is the default width of the most popular web-based email clients (though, of course, there is no industry standard). If your design is wider than this, the recipient will have to scroll horizontally to see the message. Horizontal scrolling is simply not acceptable.

Bandwidth consciousness should be part of your design philosophy in anything you do online, particularly if you have a large proportion of users accessing the internet at dial-up speeds, or who are conscious of the cost of every kilobit of data they download. Keep the size of your email low, ideally under 100KB. Don't saturate it with large high-resolution photographs. Recipients may resent that, and, in most instances, will not stick around long enough to see the images anyway.

Image blocking is often the default setting in email clients these days, and a lot of users never change their defaults. Because so many viruses, worms, and other malicious software programmes travel embedded in images, it is considered sensible to download only images that come from a known reputable source. In older versions of email clients it was possible to click a button to enable images in a particular email; today it is frequently quite difficult to work out how to enable images. If you embed the images in the email, instead of following industry norms and linking to images hosted remotely, you risk triggering spam filters, or, worse, causing paranoid recipients to block all future mailings from you. None of this is good news for graphic designers, who have to learn to be a lot more creative with text and colour, and to let go of the notion that a picture is worth a thousand words.

> **The two most important indicators to an email recipient of whether or not to open it are the 'From' and 'Subject' sections.**

Finally, spam is a problem in that your email message has to fight its way through dozens of spam filters at every step along its route. It is possible for a perfectly innocent email to get blocked before it gets to its intended recipient. So before sending your email, you have to run it through a spam checker such as SpamAssassin to see if it has any problems. This check is free, takes only a second, and most bulk email services will do it for you.

Because of people's growing suspicion of spam, much of the creative effort in designing an email must go into getting people to open the message when it arrives. The two most important indicators to an email recipient of whether or not to open it are the 'From' and 'Subject' sections.

Focus your creative effort on the subject line. You only have 50 characters, so make the most of them. If your recipient target group are mobile phone or BlackBerry users, you only get 15 characters for the subject. This is a challenge, but it imposes good discipline. Subject lines that fit into the 50-character limit get much greater opening rates than longer subject lines. To save subject-line space, place your company or brand name in the 'From' section.

Here are some guidelines for creating successful subject lines:

- synergize with what you put in the 'From' section
- front-load your subject line, with compelling words at the beginning
- do not be clever with words; stay clear and direct
- set a deadline ('only four days left')
- don't inadvertently trigger spam filters with all capitals or repeated exclamation marks
- don't over-promise
- review historical subject-line performance
- be honest and truthful
- test alternative subjects on a small sample of your list

Most web designers like to use cascading style sheets (CSSs) to code web pages. CSS is a kind of shorthand, in which you label the formatting of different sorts of content (e.g. headings, indents, captions, links) only once, then use those labels throughout the code rather than repeating the formatting. CSS provides a logical and efficient approach to coding a website, and it is generally considered a best practice. However, you should never use it for emails. Many email clients do not render style sheets correctly, and some of the popular ones strip out CSS completely, leaving you with a really messed-up email. To format your email code, you have to use in-line styles, where every item is individually marked with the code that specifies how it should be displayed.

Here are some other best practices for email marketing:

- ideally, you should code emails by hand since HTML design tools can add code that causes chaos. Microsoft Word is one of the worst offenders. Otherwise, use good tools such as Dreamweaver, and then manually remove any unnecessary code.
- always validate your code (use the free tool at validator.w3.org/)

- test your email in as many email client environments as possible (use tools such as Lyris EmailAdvisor at lyris.com/products/emailadvisor/).
- always send a text version along with your HTML version (known as MIME encoding), as many email users have clients set to 'plain text only'. If HTML comes in as plain text it is displayed as gobbledegook.
- provide many links within your email, since click-throughs increase with the number of links.
- include a link to a forward-to-a friend form on your website.
- include a subscriber-management section after the footer. This should contain fields such as contact, change my email address, update my profile and unsubscribe).
- finally, always design a landing page that synchronizes with your email piece. It will provide a seamless integration with the clicked-from message and will smooth the path to conversion. The landing page should focus on the goal of the campaign, channel the context of the click and contain no extraneous clutter (not even your usual site navigation). The next steps should be obvious and intuitive to the customer who lands on this page.

As with any aspect of emarketing, before launching into creating an email piece that is beautifully designed and illustrated, take the time to be clear on your strategy. Consider whether a simple text message might not achieve more for you. Text is personal – it is how your friends and colleagues communicate with you. Polished HTML is perceived as commercial, and therefore as impersonal.

In the US, email marketing provides a return on investment in excess of 50:1.

If you are a known brand with a customer base that relishes receiving your messages, you can afford to go the all-photo route, with a link to a web version for those with images suppressed. If you are a personal services business, try testing a personal text message against a more elaborately designed commercial message, and measure which is more effective for your objectives.

With all the complexities that haunt email, why would you want to use it for marketing? Because overcoming the problems is simply a matter of technical or creative detail. The strengths of email as a strategic marketing medium are hard to deny.

Email lets you personalize messages and offer relevant content, directly to the mailbox of the recipient, without them having to go to the web first. It has viral marketing capabilities, since it is easy to pass on. Emails allow you to test variations quickly and inexpensively, and they are easy to track and evaluate.

Email is one of the fastest ways of both generating and following up on leads. It incurs no printing, paper or postage costs. In the US, email marketing provides a return on investment in excess of 50:1. It gives customers an opportunity to stay engaged with the brand, even if they do not want to go to the web, so email is a great complement to your marketing mix. Carefully used, it can become integral to developing and maintaining personal relationships with customers.

Buzz marketing 11

The dream of emarketing in a web 2.0 world is that customers who already know and love you will enthusiastically advocate you to other members of their social networks. Those other members will be sufficiently stimulated by the endorsement that they will visit your site or try your product, and in turn they will recommend you to the members of their networks. With only three or four layers of endorsement (known as degrees of separation), you can theoretically reach millions of customers in no time at all, without having to pay the media bill for traditional marketing.

Generating and sustaining this snowballing effect on the web is known as buzz marketing, viral marketing or social media marketing. It dangles in front of marketers the prospect of high-impact marketing at a very low cost. But, with rare exceptions, it does not work out that way.

With traditional advertising, there is a relatively low up-front production cost, and the bulk of the budget is consumed by what you pay to the media for placement. As a marketer, you are heavily involved at the beginning of the process where conceiving and producing the advertising takes place, then once your media schedule is set you effectively sit back and wait, or at least play a much more passive role in the campaign. With buzz marketing, your active involvement grows with the success of the campaign, because it is all about engaging with the market and forming relationships at a human, conversational level. It requires a real ongoing time commitment from someone who understands your products and brands, empathizes with the target market, and can spontaneously carry on a brand conversation without needing constant supervision or editorial clearances.

In other words, buzz marketing requires a continuously engaged professional communicator (or team of communicators); so it is not a cheap low-level tactic. It also requires policies that allow less restrictive controls over what a company may say about its brands, and how it may be said. Like politicians, most brands are socially dysfunctional – they retreat from holding spontaneous conversations with their customers in a public forum out of fear that they might say the wrong thing, be asked an embarrassing question, or otherwise feel exposed. Like politicians, they are more comfortable on the podium where they are in control and can endlessly regurgitate their talking points.

> **Buzz marketing requires a continuously engaged professional communicator; so it is not a cheap low-level tactic.**

For social media marketing to work, brands (and the people who control them) need to learn not only how to hold a conversation, but how to be the sought-after conversationalist in the room. Without those social skills, brands, like banner ads, will be disregarded wallflowers quietly hanging around at the fringes of the party, or worse still, resented intruders.

SOCIAL MEDIA

Using social media for marketing is still a nascent science. As with all things new, the concept is subject to gross oversimplification, scepticism and hype. The believers say that social media marketing will fundamentally change the dynamics of brand communication forever; the nay-sayers claim that it will never work, because people in a social mindset block out commercial messaging. But each is talking about a different aspect of this big multi-faceted concept called buzz marketing.

Let's look at the sceptics first. Big companies have been experimenting with marketing via social networks for some time, and have generally experienced disappointing results. Procter and Gamble, for example, have created branded product pages on Facebook for everything from laundry detergent to teeth-whitening strips, and have run banner ads targeted at members of Facebook who meet the appropriate criteria. Though they do not publish the results, informally P&G employees acknowledge that, with some exceptions, the experiment has failed. A banner ad in a social network is as welcome as an insurance salesman at a neighbourhood barbecue. People on Facebook are there to engage with their friends, not to interact with brands, so banner ads are less relevant and more intrusive than they would be alongside a contextually relevant article in a news or magazine site.

That web users have flocked to join and actively use social networks is hardly surprising, given that the single most useful thing the internet does is facilitate human connections. By early 2009, Facebook had more than 220 million active members. (Despite its high profile in the news media, though, Facebook received only 20 percent of the visitors to US social network sites, with MySpace attaining 68 percent of visitors). LinkedIn, a network for business professionals, had 30 million members, with more than a million more joining every month.

@ To an old-school media buyer, online social networks are an obvious place to advertise, since that is where the audiences are. But, unlike Google searchers who are on a quest for a solution, or TV watchers who are passively resigned to interruptive advertising, social network users are actively pursuing personal interactions around themes that defy prediction.

Just because someone has the words 'football' and 'travel' in his member profile does not mean that this is all he talks about online, or that your banner advertising trips to sporting events will even be noticed. Nor does the fact that someone does not list 'health' and 'beauty' in her profile mean that she is not a good target for your organic skincare ads. In fact, at the time of writing, Facebook does not even allow you to target the intersection of two elements like 'health' and 'beauty'.

Click-through rates on banner ads are low on social networks, but this does not mean there is no branding impact. Sometimes, when your analytics tell you that you failed, you need to look again to be sure you are measuring the right metric against the right goals.

> **The herd mentality is a powerful ally if you are adept at steering it. But once a stampede toward your competitor begins, there is no stopping it.**

Besides, and this is an important point, banner advertising and branded pages are but small components of what can be done in social media environments and a nominal failure here cannot be used to decry the effectiveness of social media marketing as a whole. As I have said elsewhere, it is a mistake to take offline marketing concepts and try to shoe-horn them into online environments. Rather, you should look at the environment through your target customer's eyes, understand the processes that the customer seeks to go through, and try to work out how you can add value in a way that also contributes to your marketing goals. Design a marketing intervention that goes with the flow, or supports the user's experience, rather than one which cuts across it. Seeking innovative ways to relate to networked customers will be far more effective than being creative within traditional approaches.

What about the believers? Conceptually, there is no reason why social network marketing cannot represent an irreversible shift in the way companies communicate their brand messages. Buzz marketing is an evolution of PR, whose primary purpose is to get the media to talk to their audiences about your products. Journalists have found their importance as a conduit for product reviews being undermined by networked consumers, just as their role in researching and reporting news has been challenged by bloggers.

But experienced marketers know that PR alone is rarely enough to build a brand, increase sales, or sustain loyalty. If you are dependent solely on social media, you will struggle to survive. Appealing as they are for short-term tactical profile building, social networks are at the mercy of the attitudes and opinions of individuals, who can be frighteningly fickle. The herd mentality is a powerful ally if you are adept at steering it. But as Rupert Murdoch discovered soon after buying MySpace, once a stampede toward your competitor begins, there is no stopping it. If your brand is not bolstered by the other strategic approaches to marketing, it can be gone in the blink of an eye.

In Chapter 9 I talked about the need for an integrated strategy, in which each approach should be used to achieve the end to which it is best suited, and in which all your marketing approaches should collectively build solid sustainable momentum for your brands.

For example, when VIBE Media wanted to increase the number of visitors to its urban music and culture website, they ran an online competition for rap musicians. To enter, participants created videos and uploaded them for the VIBE community to vote on. Each entrant was given a widget for MySpace that shared their videos with friends (and friends of friends), and directed them to the website. Once on the site, these visitors engaged with other entries and participated in community discussions. The campaign massively increased the number of videos viewed on the site, and delivered 60,000 new registered members.

Buzz marketing covers a much broader field than merely advertising on social networks. There is an ever-growing array of opportunities to have customers talk about brands online, and innovative marketers are already benefiting from them. The emerging social media landscape requires marketers to be willing to learn about and experiment with different ways of exploiting contextual and behavioural targeting, mobile marketing, games and virtual worlds, user generated content (UGC), viral marketing, and, of course, social networks. You need to become familiar with Twitter, Facebook, YouTube, Whrrl and Digg, as well as their competitors, and you need to stay on top of their evolution into mainstream media.

We will look at how you might use some of these services later in the chapter, but first I'd like to elaborate on the role of the professional social marketing communicator mentioned earlier. If markets are now conversations, companies that take marketing seriously must have the resources to plan, attract, guide and monitor ongoing brand conversations. The conversations are a means to building and sustaining relationships, because ultimately a relationship is what brand loyalty is all about.

Sceptics will tell you that nobody wants a relationship with Coca Cola, American Express, BMW or Chanel No. 5. Consumers may not think of their involvement with a brand in this way, but brand loyalty has all of the characteristics of a relationship: you prefer to be with your brand rather than any other; it makes you feel comfortable and reinforces your concept of who you are; the brand understands your needs and responds to them; you feel reluctant to switch to something new and even feel guilty about considering such a move; you want your friends to know about your feelings and to approve of your choices; and you will come to the defence of your brand whenever it is criticized.

A social marketing communicator has to facilitate these relationships, not casually or reactively, but in a planned strategic way, without being rigid or dogmatic.

A communicator must plan to engage with a mix of different media and forums, including social networks, user generated content, and word-of-mouth. A social network is any community where people can establish relationships with other people. Obvious digital examples are MySpace and Facebook, but wikis like Wikipedia, product-review sites like TripAdvisor, ecommerce sites like

Amazon.com, auction sites like eBay, and virtual worlds like Second Life are all social networks. You have no way of knowing how reliable or credible the people you encounter online are, so the really successful social networks use reputation systems to help identify useful contacts. Amazon.com, for example, allows people to rate the usefulness of individual book reviewers, so you don't waste your time reading reviews that nobody thought worthwhile; eBay has a system where buyers can rate sellers and vice versa, to help newcomers feel more comfortable about who they transact with.

User generated content (UGC) is now an expected feature on most websites. People like to feel that they influence their world and that the influences they have are persistent. Everyone has a natural desire to feel important or to differentiate themselves, and they happily do this on the web by expressing opinions, publishing ideas and sharing creative output. So encouraging web users to discuss your brands in a public forum is an important part of engaging with them. In considering what purchases to make, consumers are now more knowledge hungry than ever before. They want as much objective data as they can get, particularly comparative data, but they also attach great value to the subjective views and actual experiences of other consumers. UGC immediately humanizes products in a way that no spec sheets or marketing spin can ever do. What a marketer has to say about a product is interesting; what technical details reveal is useful; what actual users have to say is golden.

That is why every month more than 25 million people consult the reviews of real travellers on TripAdvisor.

A recent campaign by Victoria's Secret, the lingerie retailer, is a good example of an innovative approach to generating awareness. Victoria's Secret, whose marketing has often been light-hearted, put up a microsite called Pink Panty Poker. On the site you could play strip poker with supermodels. You were placed in a room with five models (male and female) and dealt a hand of cards. A simplified poker engine allowed you to play out the hand. The loser of each hand then removed an item of clothing, using a slide-show approach rather than video. The site had no overt marketing support, but it went viral, attracting half a million unique visitors per day. Each visitor spent on average eight minutes on the site, immersed in a Victoria's Secret branded environment.

The internet has fundamentally changed word-of-mouth marketing, allowing product advocacy to spread further and faster than ever before. A recent study by Yahoo! found that product advocates have a 2:1 conversion impact across categories. This means that people who endorse a brand online produce on average two additional customers. In addition to simply talking to friends and colleagues, they spread their views in a host of digital ways, on social networks, by instant messaging, in chat rooms, by Twitter, via SMS, on their blogs, on review sites, or by placing comments on other people's blogs, product websites or online articles.

> **People who endorse a brand online produce on average two additional customers.**

If you see a great movie, read an inspiring book, stay in a fantastic hotel or discover a wonderful restaurant, you are likely to go out of your way to share that experience with as many people as will listen to you. You do so partly out of a desire for others to benefit, partly out of the ego satisfaction that comes from being the first to discover something, and partly out of a need to bond using your positive experience as a pretext. If your experience has not been good, you are less likely to make an effort to communicate it.

Sixty percent of people who advocate products online simply believe that good brands are worth talking about. They spend more time promoting a brand than they will being critical of it, and nearly 90 percent will write something positive about a purchase they made or an experience they had. Sadly, just as having a great website is not enough to get you traffic, having a great brand experience is not enough to get you widespread recommendations. You have to seed and nurture the advocacy process.

The tools you have available to do this are those that attract or facilitate most social interaction, both via traditional computers and mobile devices, including YouTube, Facebook, Twitter, MySpace, Whrrl, Loopt, MXit, Flickr, and dedicated branded microsites. There are, of course hundreds more, and many new ones emerge every day. These are merely tools; what you do with them will depend on your market, your strategy and objectives, and your ability to innovate.

As a social marketer, one of your challenges is to stay on top of developments to be sure you do not miss an opportunity to engage your market. Because their specific capabilities are changing every day, this book is not the place to talk about the tactics to use with any of these buzz marketing tools. But let us explore some of the strategic approaches you might take to using just a couple of them.

> Having a great brand experience is not enough to get you widespread recommendations. You have to seed and nurture the advocacy process.

VIDEO

Online video has proven to be one of the biggest phenomena of the internet. By 2009 there were 600 million people around the world who watched video online regularly. There are 3 popular ways in which online video can be used by marketers:

- The first is to emulate TV and advertise within the video, either by attaching 15 or 30 seconds of pre-roll that plays before the video begins, by placing an ad in a footer beneath the video, or even by overlaying a text ad on top of the video. The Google AdWords service, for example, allows you to run text ads beneath other people's contextually selected videos on YouTube, on a pay-per-click basis. The so-called 'in-stream' video advertising approaches are a very powerful way to get attention, and have significantly greater awareness impact than putting video ads in banners. Like most intrusive advertising however, it can backfire and has a limited impact on how favourably people perceive the brand advertised.

🔲 The second way video is used is to provide content on websites. Useful video can add tremendously to lead generation, sales, repeat visits, referrals to friends and customer relationships. Whether it is a resort hotel, a piece of software, a business service or a fashion item, video demonstrates the appeal, utility or context of a product in a way that is hard to achieve with any other medium. The production quality of video plays a significant role in people's willingness to watch it. If you are putting your own video content on your site, it is probably best to stream it as Flash video from a professional video server, rather than hosting it on a free service like YouTube. This way you have total control over how the end product will look. That said, YouTube-hosted videos have proven very successful in many marketing applications, particularly where the content involves interviews, people talking about an issue, how-to demonstrations, or documentary-style footage. YouTube and its competitors are getting better at providing quality video – it can now handle High Definition and widescreen content – so it may rapidly become an appropriate server for professional video.

🔲 The third way video is used is as a catalyst for viral message distribution. Videos that have the right appeal can go viral very fast, but creating or selecting such content is not an exact science. The web is littered with failed attempts to 'go viral'. Half-hearted efforts to push product with video designed to make people want to share it with their friends seem to lack the authenticity required to make the social headlines. Remember, people forward content as a pretext for bonding so if your video does not provide a valid pretext for your target market, it will not do much for you. It is a mistake to view viral video as something easy and inexpensive to produce. If you do not have access to extraordinarily intuitive talent, producing video that should go viral requires clear insights into the target market, a carefully conceived strategy, a tight creative brief, a lot of innovation, and the time to do good testing. These things rarely happen, and most viral campaigns are given as much budget as a run of flyers to be slipped under windscreen wipers at the local mall.

Content aside, if you want your video to have the best chance of going viral, keep it short (ideally less than 30 seconds) and avoid making it an overt advertisement, unless the advertisement has a real 'wow' factor, as do those for Sony Bravia, Dove Real Beauty, or the classic Honda Accord 'cog' advertisement.

A good example of how video can be used to virally generate awareness is Blendtec's 'Will It Blend?' series, which demonstrates the power of their blender as it takes on the task of pulverising items such as golf balls, a video camera, and even an iPhone (watched 6 million times on YouTube alone). In a similar whacky vein, Cadbury's 'In The Air Tonight' drumming gorilla video achieved the kind of impact that makes viral video worthwhile, getting more than 3 million views and producing tremendous secondary buzz among bloggers and the traditional media. Levi Strauss ran a video that was viewed nearly 5 million times, showing guys doing elaborate back-flips to get into their jeans.

While YouTube is extremely popular as a way to watch small video clips (it has half of the market), it is not the only way that people watch video. In second place is Yahoo! Video, though its traffic is less than an eighth of YouTube's. Video watching on MySpace is almost as big as on Yahoo!, and because it benefits from the snowball effect of social networks, can be a great place to seed any video that you want to go viral. Other video sites include Metacafe, Revver, and DailyMotion which is effectively the YouTube of Europe. Blip.tv is a publisher-friendly free video distribution site that is used by independent programme producers to air their content, as well as by marketers to serve videos to their websites.

Finally, there are the sites run by content producers in the movie and television arena. These media companies have been forced to provide their own shows online, simply because so much of their programming was being pirated anyway. Hulu, a joint venture between television networks News Corp and NBC Universal, has come from nowhere to tremendous popularity, because it allows you to watch last night's shows for free in your browser. Hulu streams many shows to the web simultaneously with broadcasting to TV audiences, and, in some cases, makes them available on the web a week before the TV broadcast. The BBC is also providing current programme content online, as are countless other TV broadcasters around the globe.

YouTube has attained its success in part because it has been generous. Anyone can run a YouTube-hosted video on their own website or blog for free, without even having to pay for the bandwidth. To plug a video into your page, all you have to do is copy the video's unique YouTube share code and paste it into the code of your page. As a marketer, YouTube offers you the ability to upload your videos into your own branded folder, where they can be watched by YouTube visitors. Those visitors can post comments and share the video on their own sites (you can easily block this, but why would you?). YouTube is America's second most used search engine, and it is not that difficult to help searchers find your video if you give thought to the tags or keywords that you associate with it.

Being found is one thing; being clicked on is another. Be sure to provide a compelling name for your video and give it an informative description. Every video has a thumbnail image, but if you do not provide one the system uses a frame from somewhere in the middle of your footage. So be sure that you provide a recognizable and intriguing thumbnail when you upload your clip.

If you do a lot of video work, a free service named TubeMogul can save you hours. You upload your video to TubeMogul, then it disseminates it for you to the major video sharing sites. It automatically converts your video to each site's required format, and it provides detailed metrics on viewership, monitors comments, and emails you reports. It also allows you to schedule deployment, so you can go live at the right time for your campaign. The service will submit your videos to all of the major social bookmarking sites as well, making it a powerful tool for anyone trying to get the most out of video marketing with limited resources.

MOBILE

Even the most basic mobile is capable of receiving short message service (SMS) messages, the stripped-down but always-available equivalent of email. Many people's concept of mobile marketing is limited to SMS spam, but it can and should be a lot more sophisticated than that.

Axe deodorant (sold as Lynx in Australia, New Zealand, Ireland and the United Kingdom) recently provided a novel approach to integrating mobile audiences into a viral campaign. The target market for Axe is teenage boys (or men with a teenage sense of humour), and the unspoken promise of the brand is that its user will become irresistibly attractive to beautiful women. The marketing goal was to provide an experience amusing enough to the target group that they would want to

Many people's concept of mobile marketing is limited to SMS spam, but it can and should be a lot more sophisticated than that.

spend time immersed in it and recommend it to their friends. But there was also a need to extend the brand experience beyond the website and inject it into the life and conversations of the visitor. The mobile phone was an obvious choice. Axe created a microsite called Booty Tones, structured around the theme of a little black book which listed various types of women and their associated ring-tones. 'The Head-case' for example had the Twilight Zone theme tune; the ring-tone for 'The Tease' was the theme from Mission Impossible. You could download the ring-tones and apply them to girls in your phone contacts list. If you were with your friends and your phone rang with an unusual tone, the conversation might turn to Axe and the Booty Tones site.

The fact that Axe is owned by the same company that owns Dove was not lost on the cynics, but nobody could accuse either brand of not being authentic, engaging and generous to its specific constituency.

In early 2009, there were 3.5 billion mobile phones in use around the world. Eight out of ten people on the planet live in range of a mobile network, and even in the poorest countries, 80 percent of urban populations have access to a mobile phone. As more and more phones become web enabled and capable of sophisticated multimedia and interactivity, they bring the dream of true anytime, anywhere marketing within reach.

A phone that connects to the internet is most commonly referred to as a 3G phone (for third generation), though 3G is really just the entry level. Technologies such as HSDPA (high speed data packet access) now give phones much faster web access. Irrespective of the technology, a mobile phone in data mode is accessing the web, and is capable of doing pretty much what a web-connected computer can do. Today's mobile phone is simply the next evolution of the laptop. The phone has become another device through which to interact with email, social networks, websites, search engines, microsites, UGC content, web widgets, and streaming video. So anything in your emarketing strategy that was intended for those using a computer could be accessed by those using a 3G phone.

There are free online tools (such as http://ready.mobi) that will show you what your site looks like in a host of popular phones.

To provide the best possible user experience to people browsing your website from a mobile phone, you need to have a '.mobi' website designed for mobile browsers. Your main website, whether it is a .com or .co.uk or .de site, should recognize when a visitor is using a mobile browser and automatically transfer them to the .mobi site. This site is inherently simpler than a fully-fledged website. It typically uses drill-down architecture, and uses the phone's numeric keys as short-cut options for links.

A well-managed mobile site prioritizes links by popularity, so users do not have to scroll far to get to where they most often want to go. The site will usually have many lightweight pages, with minimal use of graphics and images, and will be structured to fit a small screen of about 200 by 250 pixels, in portrait format. Mobile sites are most usable if they have a single column of content, with navigation buttons across the top and bottom of the page. The iPhone and its imitators are changing this rather rapidly, and as wide-screen phones become more popular they present fresh challenges to mobile site designers.

Every brand and model of phone has a different screen or uses a different browser. Mobile browsers are quite forgiving if your site is designed for them, and are rather good at reformatting your .mobi site to fit most models of phone. As you would for websites built for computer screens, always test your site rigorously. There are free online tools (such as http://ready.mobi) that will show you what your site looks like in a host of popular phones. Phone browsers are not forgiving, however, of normal sites that have been designed for desktops or laptops. These sites are typically badly scrambled to the point of being unusable when viewed on a mobile.

Today it is essential for every website to have a mobile equivalent, and for that mobile equivalent to be thoroughly tested in multiple phone browsers and operating systems. This is true not only for websites, but also for landing pages linked to from mobile devices. For example, if your email marketing message is opened in a mobile, and the call to action is clicked, you should identify the browser type being used and serve up a landing page that will work well in it – irrespective of whether the recipient has a small-screen Nokia running Symbian as its operating system and Opera Mobile as its web browser, an iPhone running iPhone OS and Safari, a G1 running Android and Chrome, a Blackberry running RIM OS and Firefox, or any of dozens of other possible combinations. You will find that a .mobi site can be made to look good on most phones, but will often look worse than your main non-mobile website on a large-screen smart phone.

For an example of mobile website simplicity at work, BestBuy.mobi is hard to beat. BestBuy retails thousands of consumer electronics items, but their mobile presence is process-centric, not product-centric. The opening screen has no images or graphics and loads instantly. The only things on the page are a product search box, and a store locator dropdown. The footer, persistent on each page, contains a clickable telephone number to order by phone and a link to a privacy policy.

If you search for 'iPod shuffle' you get a list of products and prices, prioritized by popularity. Click on one of them, and you are taken to a page with a small product photo, a customer rating score (with a link to customer reviews), and a brief description of the product. You are also given a clickable link that lets you phone to order, along with the SKU and model number, eliminating the possibility of confusion and shortening the time it takes to place the order.

Whether you are planning a shopping trip, or doing a price comparison in a competing chain, you can immediately find the information you need without being interrupted by promotional distractions or cross-selling pitches. The site adds real value to the customer's shopping process, and in turn adds a service dimension to the BestBuy brand that helps to make the relationship stronger. If you are good at standing out from your competitors on the desk-bound internet, how much more influential could you be if you could use the web to communicate with potential customers wherever they happen to be, especially in-store at the point of making a purchasing decision?

This complexity is as real for advertisers as it is for website owners. Before you commit a large budget to mobile advertising, be sure that your ads will work properly on the host site for all types of phones. With worldwide mobile advertising spending expected to top $15 billion by 2012, you do not want to pay out for impressions that couldn't impress.

Mobile devices have the capacity for applications that other media cannot provide. It is important for marketers to innovate, and to go beyond merely replicating for the phone user their conventional online marketing approaches. Ideally, marketers find a way to integrate all of their marketing activity, and mobile phones may provide the catalyst.

A company called i-lincc lets marketers tag their advertising in offline and online media with a short branded alphanumeric code, such as 'BMW320' or 'HILTON'. When you see an i-lincc code on billboard, TV or print ads, or on product packaging, you can send it by SMS message to the i-lincc number (+833 1000, a local call anywhere in the world). You immediately receive rich information about the product, along with links to landing pages, websites, or click-to-buy phone numbers. The i-lincc system recognizes the location of the phone making the enquiry, and can send local markets tailored messaging in the right language. I-linccs may rapidly become mobile resource locators, combining the uniqueness of bar codes with the spontaneous usability of SMS, and will find applications way beyond conventional product marketing. They are used, for example, in books to provide information about authors or references, on hazardous product shipments to provide safety data, and on consumer electronic items to provide a short-cut to instruction manuals. The essence of the i-lincc is that it assists people in satisfying their impulsive desire for more information at the time and place where that impulse is stimulated, adding value to their knowledge-gathering process. (My personal i-lincc is

GODFREY.PARKIN and if you SMS it to +833 1000 you will receive more information about me and get a clickable list of information resources that go along with this book).

SOCIAL NETWORKS

Much of this book deals with social networks, so there is little more to be said. The possibility of connecting with your customer base in those places where they gather together has obvious appeal to online marketers. But often these networks are viewed as simply another medium, rather like a niche magazine or a local radio station programme, where a qualified target group can be addressed en masse. There has been much disappointment with the results that marketers get from, for example, running banner ads in social networks. But why do people gather in these networks in the first place? They do it to exchange information and experiences, and to bond, with other people who share their interests. Even the most passive members participate, by consuming the conversations, insights and advice of others. People do not spend time in social networks to consume advertising. Their minds are active, and their attention is more focused here than in any other web environment on interacting with user generated content. Banner advertising is simply ignored; intrusive advertising is resented.

To have a presence in a social network is inexpensive and simple. But it is not enough. Whether you have a branded page in Facebook or a fully-customized environment in MySpace, unless you make the effort to engage in a useful and personal way with your target market, your efforts may be wasted. The best way to benefit from the social network frame of mind is to add value, by providing tools, applications, functionality, insights or environments that support whatever activity your target market is engaged with.

One of the more obvious approaches is to provide applications or 'apps' that interface with the network's database to allow the user to do what the network itself does not. Most social network apps are amateurishly conceived and badly programmed, but this does not get in the way of people wanting to use them. Many of the more popular apps deal with sending virtual gifts, and their relevance to branding is not immediately obvious. Other apps allow you to add dimensions to your personal profile. For example, TripAdvisor provides an app which lets you identify on a world map all of the cities that you have visited. This map becomes part of your member profile. You can, at the click of a button, see the maps of people in your list of friends, and scan them to see what cities they have visited. This is interesting, but not useful. How much more valuable would it be if you could click on a city and be shown friends (or others) who have been there recently? Doing this without taking you away from the social network page, through a rich-media microsite, would make the app both useful and non-disruptive.

The best way to benefit from the social network frame of mind is to add value, by providing tools, applications or environments that support whatever activity your target market is engaged with.

The future of social network marketing will probably lie in a combination of sophisticated app design, intelligent database mining, and personal conversational communication.

If there were any doubts about the collective power of social media in a web 2.0 age, they were dispelled in 2008 when a new Johnson & Johnson advertisement for Motrin was withdrawn within 48 hours. The advertisement appeared to suggest that mothers who wore their babies in a sling were making a fashion statement. The objections started with a few outraged comments from mothers on Twitter, then grew rapidly into a storm of blog postings, articles hyped by Digg, discussions on social networks like CafeMom, and even protest videos uploaded to YouTube. Johnson & Johnson stopped running the ad and their VP of Marketing posted a fervent apology on the Motrin website.

There are a few lessons in this. First, it does not take many networked individuals to make a great deal of noise and to convey the impression that they represent the entire market. Second, engaging rapidly with customer buzz makes for powerful PR, so you need to be constantly monitoring what is being said online about your brands. Third, whether it is positive or negative, buzz can go viral frighteningly fast.

Imagine being able to harness the passion that a few Motrin moms felt, in favour of your brand rather than in contempt of it. Using your insights into your market to seed and nurture the conversations that will build durable profitable relationships between your brands and their users is what buzz marketing is all about.

The future of marketing 12

Should humanity survive the next few hundred years, people will probably look back at the early decades of the 21st century and think of that time as the marketing revolution, much as people today think of the last decades of the 18th century as the industrial revolution. The sacred cows of marketing dogma will be put out to pasture, and the previously ingrained best practices of advertising will sneak out of town under cover of darkness. And while advertising agencies will probably be there forever, marketing departments may be decimated and their inhabitants diasporized into all the far-flung operational units of their organizations.

Like most significant revolutions, it will take time, and those who are most affected by it are unaware of the significance of what is happening. The harnessing of fire, the invention of the wheel, the concept of zero, all had an irreversible impact on the nature and pace of change in the societies that reluctantly embraced them.

The evolution of marketing has been stunted for many decades, simply because, until recently, the volume of knowledge did not grow significantly, the pace of change was pedestrian, and the nature of change was linear and predictable. A conventional approach to marketing was adequate for those circumstances. Not any more.

A 'renaissance man' of the 1600s may have been more comfortable with languages and the classical arts than the average university graduate today, but he had far less knowledge. Even 60 years ago it was possible to put all of the significant knowledge in all fields of endeavour into a few bookshelves. In 1943 the chairman of IBM estimated the total world demand for computers at five. Today the world generates more new data in a day than our grandparents were exposed to in a lifetime. You can no longer cram everything there is to know about a particular subject, let alone all the knowledge of the world, into a single head. And if you could, you would never be able to find what you needed in time to be effective.

Small wonder that Google is the darling of the stock market, while industrial-age giants such as Ford and General Motors have been downgraded to junk-bond status. Society now places far more value on those who can find information instantly than on those who merely manufacture 'stuff'.

POWER SHIFT

Marketing, as we have known it, provides fuzzy benefits, and has a return on investment that nobody expects to measure accurately. But that can change. Traditional advertising focuses on telling people intrusively about a product at every possible opportunity, and on trying to stimulate a purchase; Google focuses on helping people find a solution to a problem when they need it most.

Corporate marketing has to follow the Google 'search-and-connect' model instead of the General Motors 'produce-and-sell' model. Even today, marketing purists often sneer at social networks and consumer-generated content, insisting that brand messaging should be defined and conveyed only by marketers. They undervalue collaborative marketing networks, regarding them as potentially dangerous or subversive. They fervently believe that consumers must be led, child-like, through pre-determined communication paths mapped out and controlled by a central authority. They overestimate the power of their influence in a world suddenly flooded with alternate sources of information and the tools, such as Google and social search networks, for filtering the useful and credible from the noise and spin.

However, marketers no longer need to see themselves as guardians of sacred brand dogma, and have to stop seeing consumers as naïve and malleable. Marketing is a framework for understanding and relating to consumers. As consumers change — and they are doing so dramatically — there is no excuse for perpetuating marketing processes that are no longer relevant or appropriate.

Twenty-five years ago the internet triggered a big bang in knowledge and personal communication. Many ebusinesses made rapid progress in exploiting the opportunities as they emerged, building real-time ecommerce systems, personalized services and ubiquitous access to information. By contrast, most marketers are still building basic websites. They need to start thinking about new ways to foster relationships that accommodate the real needs of customers and leverage all the data, systems, economies and connectivity that online consumers now take for granted.

> **Emarketers need to see the end product of their endeavours to be not polished websites or award-winning banners, but delighted consumers, increased brand performance and achievement of business objectives.**

Instead of focusing only on marketing content, brand objectives and the outdated and inadequate concepts of advertising, marketers should craft their marketing processes to match the processes by which their customers want to engage with them. If you build websites, your web designers need to adopt some marketing thinking, so they have a better chance of being able to understand customers according to the criteria that those customers consider important.

Emarketers need to see the end product of their endeavours to be not polished websites or award-winning banners, but delighted consumers, increased brand performance and achievement of business objectives. Maybe then marketers will have a better chance of surviving, or even guiding, the online revolution.

More and more people who only last year were 'marketing professionals' are now describing themselves as 'digital strategy practitioners'. Strategy purists become very prickly when a marketer presumes to take on this kind of title, because strategy is considered special. It has its own language and rituals and codes of conduct. It seeks to transform organizations, hopefully for the better. To the hard-boiled no-nonsense business person, digital strategy is prone to hype – more alchemy than action. But to digital strategy insiders, it's a tough, disciplined and highly specialized field that seeks to improve the way organizations work.

Marketing focuses on improving the performance of brands and product categories; digital strategy focuses on a bigger picture, improving the performance of support systems, structures and processes, as well as branding. The 'as well as' is where the conflicts between digital strategy and marketing arise, and where the synergies are to be found.

As more marketers discover the implications of having an online customer base, they seek to engage with their markets on the web. But one of the most significant changes that the web has wrought is that marketing is no longer a one-way street. Marketers can no longer get away with 'talking at' their customers as an anonymous group. You have to engage with your customers as individuals, in a two-way conversation, and this means you need to get the facilities and resources in place to nurture relationships and hold those conversations. Typically this means changing corporate infrastructure, policies and processes far beyond the traditional remit of the marketing department.

There are few situations in which traditional marketing alone will produce the desired business result, where systemic changes would not be beneficial. Indeed, marketing is sometimes a complete waste of time and money if the environment, structures, systems or processes do not change to support and reinforce the marketing investment. You can get a hamster to run faster in its wheel, but unless you remove the wheel, your hamster won't win you any races.

CENTRALIZATION VS DEMOCRATIZATION

There is growing acknowledgement that the best place to leverage local marketing is deep in the flow of customer experience, not from a remote central bureaucracy. Yet, while everyone else is adopting more web-centric thinking, which is all about decentralized, spontaneous, loosely networked activity, many marketing departments are looking for more control, not less. Corporate marketers are beginning to use technology as a pretext to force a re-centralization of marketing via corporate content management systems or by copying central marketing processes and plugging them into decentralized locations.

As hardened silos of command and control give way to ephemeral spheres of influence, organizational entities that have always relied on centralized authority need to rethink the way in which they stay in control. Digital strategists are accustomed to hopping across silos and forging odd trans-hierarchy alliances. Marketers need to be doing the same.

> **Organizational entities that have always relied on centralized authority need to rethink the way in which they stay in control.**

Why are so many marketers reinventing themselves as digital strategists? It may be because marketers don't get taken seriously enough by management. The 'marketer' label is a handicap that ring-fences their perceived effectiveness areas and deprives them of the ability to voice the need for changes credibly beyond the four Ps of the company's brands. And it places a barrier in the way of their influencing or driving those changes.

Digital strategy professionals are often horrified when marketers attempt to go beyond their brief. Granted, strategists are highly trained in what they do, and a bumbling amateur may do more harm than good. But experienced marketers often have much deeper hands-on insight into competitive or consumer relationship issues than anyone gives them credit for. In pursuing digital strategy initiatives, it is a good idea to tap into the expertise and creativity of marketers and salespeople, because they are the nervous system of that part of the organization that comes into contact with the consumer. They see, hear and feel more than many central managers do, at a level that is raw and unfiltered; and they are exposed to the systemic problems and opportunities through the eyes of their customers.

Perhaps marketers are in a good position to interpret for their brands how best to engage with the increasingly digitally savvy population of online consumers.

THE 'TECH' GENERATION

Generation Y, generation neXt, generation Y2K, generation E, newmils, echoes – those born between 1981 and 2001 have many labels. Whatever you call them, those who have come into the world since the launch of the Apple III personal computer are more different from their previous generation than any group of people in history. As these people enter the marketplace, they present a significant challenge to marketers. Or perhaps marketers present a challenge to them.

The term 'tech generation' is being used more and more frequently in business to describe those late generation Xs and early generation Ys, who are now in their early to mid-20s and a prime target population for many marketers. They have been immersed in digital technology their entire lives. Computers and networks are not daunting to them – they may have had a PC at home the day they opened their eyes. They are as comfortable with the shifting ambiguities of relational data, organic networks and distributed applications as their predecessors were with hierarchical structures, delegated administrative work and central control. They can type an SMS message with their thumbs on a phone keypad as fast as a 1980s touch-typist keyed in text on an IBM Selectric. They don't use the same vocabulary, of course, and they leave out most vowels and pay no attention to grammar, but they communicate very fast and very effectively. But to those who are not attuned to the nuances of tech gen digital shorthand, their communications are as baffling as birdsong.

These born-digital 'natives' are often at odds with the way things are done by traditional 20th-century businesses, and strategic management has much to learn from them about thriving in markets soon to be dominated by digitally savvy consumers and competitors.

> @ The implications for marketers are significant: if knowledge flows, and the processes that leverage them, are evolving in real-time despite your best efforts to corral them; and if your product communication channels have become irreparably corrupted; and if peer-to-peer communication, distributed expertise and experience sharing are the de-facto norm among your target consumers, what purpose does old-school brand-centric marketing management serve? All it does is get in the way of progress, preserve dysfunctional power structures, and slow down your own evolution.

Even in cultures as committed to central control as Microsoft and the US military, 'digital natives' have put sufficient pressure on those in command to stimulate significant shifts in strategy. This happens not by using conventional channels, but by ignoring them completely and behaving in a way that is perfectly natural to someone who 'gets' the web. Disruptive technologies have bred a disruptive generation. The approach of these new consumers to making sense of the chaos in the world is so undeniably sensible, so effective, and so compelling that older generations have been inspired to follow suit.

New-consumer behaviour is not limited to the younger generation. In the United Kingdom and Japan, people over the age of 65, popularly labelled 'silver surfers', have become the demographic group who spend most time and money online, and are actively engaged in social networking. Someone in the market for a digital camera or a natural eczema cure turns to fellow consumers on the web for product reviews and advice, rather than make do with the limited data and subjective spin provided by marketers or retail salespeople.

Digital consumers make fast decisions, sort through complex information and dexterously juggle knowledge resources. Those whose sole contact with the internet is email, find such people chaotic and believe they have the attention span of a gnat; in reality, they are merely parallel processing. Their lifetime of digital experiences dictates their approach to information seeking and decision-making.

New consumers are not the same kind of people marketers were studying and marketing to 10 years ago. Do you continue to treat them the same, subject them to the same communication processes, force them into the same models and behaviour norms? Do you try to suppress and channel their inherent vitality and flexibility, or do you exploit and encourage it for the good of your brands? To do so you probably have to slaughter many of the sacred cows of the marketing profession and seek out new models, not only for emarketing, but for marketing itself.

One thing is certain: every year will bring more and more digitally converted consumers into your markets. Like the nomads who gradually infiltrated and overwhelmed the culture of the citizens in Kafka's story 'An Old Manuscript', they will appear and begin to dominate culture and change norms. Will you be left marginalized in your own campaigns, unable to join their conversations or to influence your direction, or will you seize the opportunity to find and nurture new, more effective ways to communicate, to build customer relationships and to grow your brands?

THE VALUE OF INFORMAL MARKETING

The impact of innovation varies in inverse proportion to its cost of proliferation. So why is it that so many marketing professionals conspicuously ignore the potential for brand performance improvement offered by informal marketing? Now that the internet facilitates the kinds of human interactions that make informal marketing so effective, the relevance and impact of formal marketing may diminish even further. Do you as a marketing professional stand by and watch your empires being sidelined by MySpace, widgets and Twitter, or do you try to take a leading role in defining and refining emerging-marketing paradigms?

There will probably always be a need for formal marketing and diligent brand management. But customers are no longer the uninformed, compliant people they used to be. Consumers are learning, and marketing people need to get their heads around what that means. According to studies by the organizational learning consultancy firm Capital Works and others, corporate employees learn three times

> **You need to have a mentality that sees failure as a stepping stone for moving forward rather than as proof of the need to turn back.**

more from informal experiences than they do in formal training courses. Those informal learning experiences include interacting with co-workers, modelling peer behaviour, trial and error, social support structures, networking, ad-hoc mentoring and so on. The implication for marketers is obvious: if people learn so little from structured communication, perhaps marketers are putting too much effort (and way too much budget) into traditional media messaging, and not nearly enough into fostering informal brand conversations. Or perhaps consumers will simply get by without marketers.

Anthropologists and particle physicists agree that there are things in this world that cannot be observed without changing them in the process. Can marketing professionals, whose frame of reference is formality, understand how informal marketing takes place in their own consumer bases, and engage that process without breaking it? Can marketing departments, with all their post-industrial-revolution baggage, rise to the challenge and achieve the kind of post-knowledge-revolution changes that are both necessary and inevitable? The challenge is to facilitate, not dictate, and to nurture and focus those aspects of an informal marketing environment that can leverage what people do naturally. You need to create a marketing culture that encourages grass-roots innovation, experimentation, socializing and networking. You need to make time for talking and for listening. You need to have a mentality that sees failure as a stepping stone for moving forward rather than as proof of the need to turn back. And you need to start a movement, top-down, to dissolve organizational silos and the tunnel vision they produce, and to provide the facilities that make it easier for customers to engage with each other in the context of your brands.

What is more, as an essential component of your corporate nervous system, you need to foster a renaissance in performance measurement and marketing analytics. As the web barrelled its way into corporate life in the early 1990s, many people hoped that it would have a liberating effect on how people go about their work of brand performance improvement. For the most part, it has not.

Instead of cultivating and liberating brand experiences, companies build websites that reinforce their ivory towers; instead of opening people's eyes, marketers put them to sleep; instead of personalising experiential marketing, they deliver mass-market packaged advertisements. Instead of encouraging people to explore and innovate, they force-feed them on spam, hoping that their expectation of anything better will eventually fade away.

It may be that in the business world, projects that stray too far from conventional thinking will not be funded. Exploration and experimentation are frowned upon in corporate marketing, because it is not only financially risky, it threatens to rock the boat if it were to be successful. Change is so ubiquitous it has become a cliché. Yet many corporate marketers don't want to go there. To us, 'innovation' is about boldly trying to run a self-funding SMS competition, or converting our clickable links into animated 3D icons.

The recording industry discovered the power of informal networked collaboration when music consumers started doing things in a radically new and – to them – eminently sensible and efficient way, using peer-to-peer file sharing. But not only music files were shared; long before Facebook came along, the web facilitated a boom in knowledge sharing, with discussion forums, gossip boards, fan blogs, newsgroups and specialized communities of interest that did more to promote musicians than the marketing budgets of the record companies could ever have accomplished.

Music recording companies were left looking silly and marginalized, and had to resort to petty legal actions against their consumer base to maintain a failed business model. Let's not allow the recording industry to be a model of what is to become of marketing generally or advertising in particular. Marketers need to maintain some influence over the evolution of marketing, because what crystallizes from the informal consumer-led bottom-up flux, while it may be 'right' for the personal objectives of individual customers, may not be 'right' for the business objectives of a corporation.

THE PROGRESS BOOM

Perhaps you remember the arcade game 'Space Invaders'? The more attackers you shot down, the more they spawned and mutated, and the faster they moved until, inevitably, you could not keep up – game over. Welcome to 21st-century marketing.

Change management used to mean dealing with single adjustments in an organization. Now change is altogether different. It's pervasive, relentless, unpredictable, non-linear and frighteningly fast. This has implications for the concept of marketing and for the nature of the marketing role.

Progress is like a sonic boom; you only know it is coming once it has already hurtled past you. Today, people become aware of opportunities and threats only when they are choking in their dust. By the time marketers have created a marketing strategy or simply an advertising piece to address an issue, the issue is no longer relevant or its context has altered. By the time you have configured your resources to exploit an opportunity, it is gone.

Marketers used to be able to take weeks to develop 30 seconds of advertising, knowing that it would be relevant and effective for long enough to generate a healthy return on investment. This is no longer true. In those areas where a company's differential advantage is generated and sustained – inside its nervous system – the inherent smartness of the business and the speed and effectiveness with which communication takes place are the keys to competitive success.

@   Individual marketers and entire companies need to be able to better anticipate, generate or react to change. This means that marketers (and the processes and external agencies that support them) have to become smarter, faster, more far-sighted, more flexible, more collaborative and more synergistic. It is becoming more vital than ever to identify and build the analytical thinking, communication and decision-making skills of individuals at all levels, as well as in teams and business units.

It is not enough to re-cast marketing as 'relationship-building', important as that shift may be. To stay relevant and effective, marketing has to be performance-driven and pro-active, which means being a formative part of company thinking and of company workflows, rather than an after-the-fact service to the business.

Marketing professionals have to be willing to change their perceptions of what they do and of what 'good practice' is, and they need to challenge the perceptions of others in management. The polished high-production-value 30-second movie may no longer be relevant. Marketing departments as central conceivers, administrators and disseminators of branding dogma may no longer be relevant.

Business needs to lose the notion of marketing as a series of campaigns and instead see it as an integrated collection of perpetually evolving customer engagement processes. With performance improvement as a goal, appropriate technologies should be used to collapse advertising development lead-time — or to eliminate traditional advertising completely. Marketers should create dynamic customer engagement processes that directly leverage the connections and experiences of their customers. And they should integrate brand owners, marketing managers and business partners directly into the actual relationship-building process.

> **Rapid adaptation requires an ability to understand, anticipate and embrace change, and the only way to do that is to build an organization of people who are continuously curious.**

The accelerating pace of change in business means that all consumers have to absorb more data, more frequently, in less available time. Consumers need to fit media into their lives, rather than fit their lives around chunks of media consumption. Marketers have similar constraints in their job: you have to develop and update more messaging more often, taking less time to do it. If marketing is to survive as a relevant function in business, marketers have to mutate, spawn new ideas and move ever faster. Your best salvation may lie in collaborative teamwork with your customers.

At today's accelerating pace of change, organizations which are most willing and able to adapt rapidly will outperform the rest. In fact, they will be able to create the changes that keep their competitors reeling. Rapid adaptation requires an ability to understand, anticipate and embrace change, and the only way to do that is to build an organization of people who are continuously curious. This allows for micro-refinements and mini-innovations throughout an organization, and collectively facilitates bigger changes in organizational direction or nature. The notion of 'the learning organization' does not quite cover this concept, nor does the doctrine of continuous improvement. The focus of these terms is on process, not on the human beings who define and drive those processes.

Advocates of the traditional approach to marketing find the very notion of disruptive change abhorrent. The larger the organization, the more protective it tends to be of its brands. Their brands have been conceived and nurtured with immense attention to detail. Once a brand has matured, it gets locked into place by rulebooks and style guides and brand bibles, and any attempt to challenge or change any aspect of it is typically met with very uncreative bureaucratic obfuscation. However, if modern brands are to be dynamic and adaptive, business needs to rethink the nature of brand management.

Curiosity is what makes people learn from early childhood – a fascination with everything new, and with its potential impact on us, makes us who we are. Children ask questions, experiment, push their boundaries, and operate in 'what-if' and 'yes, and' mode. Children are constantly trying to look over the horizon. But as people grow up, the more organigram-defined and cube-farm-constrained they become, and the more creatively complacent they get. People's major focus is on following the routines that keep them employed. You are taught, or conditioned, not to question the status quo or to step beyond the bounds of your defined job. In any field of business today, that complacency is dangerous; in the field of marketing it can be fatal.

The attitude to emarketing that is still often voiced by experienced creative businesspeople is sometimes outright negative. It is not unusual to hear statements such as, 'it will never replace classic marketing', 'creativity can't find full expression' and 'it's only good for certain kinds of product'. People are ready to pass summary judgment on 'emarketing', a broad label that covers a huge range of activities, processes, technologies, applications, content and quality. How can you pass judgment on emarketing as if it is already formed, when all you can see right now are the tentative beginnings of a whole new approach to communication? How can you let your view of the entire industry be driven by your most recent experience of it? Perceptions of what emarketing is vary enormously, in both its intellectual definitions and its practical manifestations.

Marketing professionals should embrace change and experimentation, rather than resist it. Yet many don't. Emarketing, as it is typically practiced today, often leaves a lot to be desired. There are three main reasons: first, marketers want emarketing to cut their budgets and make their lives easier, and they accept – and expect – that communication quality must suffer as a result. Secondly, marketers are currently obsessed with tools and technology instead of with applications and customers. Finally, marketers have difficulty seeing the internet as an incredibly powerful communications medium, not merely as a very poor broadcast medium.

Properly used, the web can make marketing an organic, experience-sharing journey that gives consumers far more ongoing one-on-one contact with brands and fellow consumers than could ever be achieved via television or print. It would be delightful if more marketing designers would get their heads around the concept of allowing networked consumers more influence.

Ten years ago, email was considered to be for geeks only, and would never replace 'real' communication, with paper and signatures and all the important intangible values that tangibles allegedly provide. Today, anyone without an email address is thought of as quaint.

A VISION FOR THE FUTURE

The web became almost ubiquitous worldwide, in only a little over 5,000 days. If you do not embrace it, you will be left behind. It is not owned or managed by anyone, and it grows like a virus because its users invent and share applications for it.

Marketing should be the same – liberated, viral, empowering and compelling. Emarketing will mutate so rapidly that marketers won't be able to define it. But it will work, and it will always be an evolutionary leap ahead of what people thought of as marketing in the previous year. Marketers need to drop all of their prejudices and focus on 'what must be' instead of on 'what was'. With vision, you can steer marketing to be fabulously richer and more essential than it has ever been. Let's drop the 'e' and focus on marketing. The 'e' is already so ever-present that it is beginning to look and sound pretentious, irrelevant and more than a little silly. Stop talking about banner marketing, or search marketing or social network marketing and focus on describing a marketing experience in terms of its consumer relationship outcomes, not its technology or media components.

The drive to implement large-scale enterprise emarketing 'solutions' typically leaves marketers, and their agencies, with a sense of being left behind, rather like running for a train that is pulling out of a station. Senior management, already comfortably aboard, yell at you to run faster and to mind the gap, but this does little to diminish the panic of your impending loss of control.

Marketing is going through some fundamental conceptual and operational shifts. New ways are emerging daily to satisfy marketing objectives, and marketers and their agencies are having to learn new skills and take on new responsibilities. The way companies perceive brand development, and the path to it, is in flux. Marketers need to be able to exercise some influence over the systemic changes in their organizations, and they need to be equipped to guide their brands through the transitions.

Courses in web development will not help you prepare for the future. A technical skills-set is less relevant in a marketing career than your ability to analyse and understand markets and to devise processes and models that can make customer engagement happen better, faster and in a more relevant manner. In the blink of an eye you will be outsourcing most of your technical development anyway, so don't think that those skills will make you indispensable. It is more important to have conceptual skills, project management skills and the skills of an agent of change.

Change facilitation, or 'change agentry', as it is popularly termed in the United States, requires few skills that a competent marketer does not already have. It mainly requires a different attitude to your role and an ability to step back and see the bigger picture. It also requires a willingness to keep on learning — and unlearning — perpetually. Here are some things you can do to improve the way you facilitate change:

- Try to become comfortable with letting go of established ways of doing things. You cannot see necessary innovations and exploit the opportunities they provide without acknowledging that some current practices are possibly outmoded.
- Never become so arrogant about your knowledge or competence that you refuse to have an open mind. A passion for learning often requires a certain disdain for what you already know.
- View change in marketing as cross-functional. Think and communicate in ways that emphasise the big picture, business objectives and bottom lines. Try to stop yourself, your colleagues and management from obsessing about a few details at the expense of a balanced perspective.
- View your role in terms of the corporate vision. It is easy to be distracted by bright, shiny objects if you do not have a strong commitment to a clearly shared vision.
- Focus on the outcome of the change rather than the change itself. This should be self-explanatory for marketing people (it is not the campaign but its impact on market performance that matters), but far too often businesses get sidetracked by managing and selling features rather than benefits.
- Do not impose change where you can generate a desire for it — develop processes that inspire your agencies, your colleagues and your managers to initiate and create the changes. People will readily buy into change once they have clarified in their own minds what changes are needed and the benefits of making them. (Anyone in marketing who does not have skills in basic consultative selling should sign up for a course.)
- Resist the me-too mentality that pushes you into change simply because everyone else seems to be doing it. Be aware of the disastrous consequences that this kind of approach has sometimes had in emarketing and learn from past mistakes.

Challenge conventional wisdom, especially if you don't understand it and it seems like the emperor's new clothes!

◪ Learn to understand the dynamics of change. The more familiar you are with how change happens, the less formidable it becomes. A good way to do this is to expose yourself to innovation almost out of habit, preferably by reading outside of your normal field and engaging in discussions with marketing professionals outside your organization. Join an online discussion forum or social network, get an RSS reader and subscribe to some innovation-focused content.

Ed McCracken, founding chief executive officer of Silicon Graphics was fond of saying that in order to survive change you have to be the one creating the chaos. Silicon Graphics computers were objects of lust for every graphic artist, animator and games developer on the planet throughout the 1980s and 1990s, and the company was celebrated for its continual innovation. Soon after the turn of the century, they quietly shut down. The pace of change in the marketplace had been too much even for them.

The evolution from traditional marketing to web-enhanced marketing is not a one-off event. It is only the beginning of a perpetual evolution process that will accelerate over time, becoming more and more chaotic and complex as it does. Those who will thrive as marketing professionals in this environment are characterized by their ability to see beyond the immediately obvious, their willingness to embrace disruptiveness and generate innovation, and their capacity to leverage the power of informal networks. They use deep insight into their consumers as a starting point for everything they do, they are committed to defining clearly-focused sharable visions, and they never start any project without stating its commercial objectives. They are strategists who look for ways to make things happen, who continuously hone their skills as a change agent. If this describes you, you are well on your way to becoming a true 21st-century marketer.

Building an effective
online business

The following section provides you with a practical methodology for creating and implementing an ebusiness strategy and its associated emarketing strategy. It is structured as a series of questions and exercises designed to get you thinking about your business, its vision, its capabilities and its customers. Answering these questions in sequence is not necessarily easy, and may require quite a bit of thought and discussion.

Try not to do this all in your head – actually committing your thoughts to writing is a vital part of committing yourself to action. Get yourself a dedicated spiral-bound notebook and make it the journal in which you record your ideas and responses. You will find that in many cases your answers in one section cause you to rethink earlier answers in another section. This iteration is a necessary part of polishing your strategic thinking, and an essential process for developing viable operational plans.

You will find that the insight and effort required for answering the questions or following the exercises gets more complex – and more specific – later in the process, as you move from the more abstract conceptual thinking to the real planning commitments. A large organization following this methodology may take weeks of discussion and internal consultation before every stakeholder is happy with the project. A small to medium enterprise might initially go through the methodology in only a day or two.

Thinking through each of the following aspects helps you to develop a comprehensive picture of your marketing landscape, and to build a robust approach to succeeding in it. It is important that you consider every one of the aspects covered, even if, after consideration, you decide that it is not currently relevant to your particular situation. As with most 'best practices' you do not have to do absolutely everything immediately – depending on your time and resources and the scope of your project you might go for the 20 percent of the work that delivers 80 percent of the result. Or you might decide to roadmap a more ambitious roll-out over 18 months or 3 years. But at least, when you decide to not do something, you know why you are not doing it and have made a conscious assessment of the likely consequences.

As has been stressed throughout the book, ebusiness is not a minor add-on to your existing enterprise. It represents a fundamental change in approach and philosophy. Answering the questions posed here with honesty and inspiration will help you to kick-start that revolution in thinking, and move you rapidly into successfully marketing your business online.

The approach is broken down into sections as follows:

A: Strategy and planning

B: Customers

C: Your Website

D: Search engine marketing

E: Online advertising

F: Email marketing

G: PR

H: Metrics

I: Revise your strategy

A: STRATEGY AND PLANNING

A1 – MISSION

Describe the mission of the project, initiative, business or department for which you are building an effective online business.

Your mission statement should briefly but clearly define the core purpose of your organization – its raison d'être beyond the obvious notions of 'grow profits' or 'gain market share'. In a few sentences it should reflect the motivations and aspirations of employees and customers for working with you. Effective mission statements are inspiring and easy to communicate. Typically, a mission statement outlines what the organization is now. It focuses on today, identifies your customers, your critical processes and your level of performance.

A2 – VISION

Describe the vision of the project, initiative, business or department for which you are building an effective online business.

Your vision statement should briefly but clearly define your broad aspirational image of the future that your organization is aiming to achieve. It is a description of the organization size, structure, role, relationships, reputation, achievements and sphere of influence. Your vision statement describes in a couple of sentences a picture of your desired future, as if you were there right now (written in active present tense). It is often helpful for your vision statement to state what you are not doing too.

A3 – ENVIRONMENT SCAN

What are the relevant characteristics of your current and immediate-future operating environment? Briefly categorize all the important factors as strengths, weaknesses, opportunities or threats (SWOT).

There are layers of detail in this exercise that can make it unwieldy. Try to focus on those factors that affect the project, initiative, business or department for which you are building an effective online business. Be aware, though, that online businesses seldom exist in isolation, and that whatever you, your customers or your competitors are doing offline can be very relevant to your online situation.

STRENGTHS   **WEAKNESSES**

OPPORTUNITIES   **THREATS**

A4 – PRIORITIES
From the above SWOT analysis, what are your strategic priorities?
- What are the most attractive (viable) opportunities to pursue?
- What strengths should you leverage most?
- What threats do you HAVE to deal with?
- What weaknesses must you sort out, or plan to live with?
- What is the burning light you will follow?

A5 – OBJECTIVES
Reframe your priorities as a set of strategic objectives.
Objectives are outcomes, and they are the result of your activities. They are closely linked to your vision, but expressed in concrete, measurable terms. So think medium to long term (two to five years).
- What are your strategic business objectives?
- What customer problems or desires will your online initiative address?
- What are the dimensions and time frames by which you will measure success?

A6 – OBSTACLES
What are the things that will make achieving your objectives difficult?
There are always issues that will get in your way. If you anticipate them, you stand a good chance of overcoming them or finding a way around them. Typically, obstacles will fall into categories such as functional (marketing, production, admin), processes, competitive, technological or financial. What are your issues? Which of these can you defeat? Which ones do you need to circumvent?

A7 – STRATEGIES
[You will revisit this step once you have completed all the exercises in this workbook.]
Describe, without too many specifics, the general approach you will take to get from where you are now to your objectives, and how you will be handling any obstacles in the process.
You can usually take a number of alternative approaches. What are the

alternative broad-brush approaches to getting to your objectives? Which is/are most viable? What will be your chosen path?

A8 – OPERATIONAL PLANS
[You will revisit this step once you have completed all the exercises in this workbook.]
Look at your strategy and ask yourself what actions you need to take to put flesh on its bones and make it specific, step-by-step and actionable.
Who will do what? When do the major steps need to be taken and in what sequence? How much will all of this cost? What resources do you need? How will you obtain them? How will you start? How will you stay on track? It may help you to use headings such as budget, website development, customer service, search-engine optimization, linking strategy, pay-per-click, advertising, e-mail marketing, offline marketing, public relations, internal systems and processes, metrics and reviews.

A9 – PROJECT MANAGEMENT
[You will revisit this step once you have completed all the exercises in this workbook.]
Whether you are doing everything yourself, managing staff or using outside contractors, you need to refine your operational plans further into projects. Which projects can you identify in your operational plans? Then break each one down into granular detail.
Each project should have clear tasks, roles, dependencies, timelines and budgets. Manage the project plans ruthlessly, but creatively, using project management disciplines and tools. You will find Microsoft Project is a very useful tool to help you structure and manage projects. Ideally, let a trained professional project manager take responsibility for bringing each project in according to specifications, on time and within the budget.

B: CUSTOMERS

B1 – YOUR TARGET CUSTOMERS
Define who your target customers are.
Remember that an online presence gives you an opportunity to expand your customer base geographically and address completely different customer segments from those you have had in the past.

B2 – CORE COMPETENCIES
What are your core competencies?
Think not only in terms of the 'things you do well' but also in terms of what value you can add to your customers' processes.

B3 – PERSONAS
Describe the various personas into which your customers may fall. A persona is a characterization of a typical customer type that helps you to

look at your solution through the eyes of different customers.
Give each persona a name, personality and attitudes, background and behaviour patterns. For example, the busy business executive, the young single adventure traveller, the tech-savvy online shopper, the risk-averse investor.

B4 – PROBLEM SCENARIOS/TASKS
Describe the problem scenario(s) that each of your personas would have.
How would these problems make them look to your ebusiness to help them solve it. What tasks would the personas perform?

B5 – COMPETITIVE ADVANTAGES
Why would each persona come to you for a solution to their problems, rather than to one of your competitors?
For each competitor, state the relative advantages that you intend to build into your ebusiness. Who are your competitors? Enter the most important keywords that characterize your ebusiness into a search engine and follow the links to discover who your major online competitors may be.

C: YOUR WEBSITE

C1 – PURPOSE
Define the purpose of your website.
◆ What are the key business objectives your site will achieve?

C2 – SCOPE
Define the scope of your website.
How far do you want to go? Will an online brochure satisfy your stated purpose, or do you need to provide full ecommerce functionality, or total ebusiness integration? What is the geographic scope of your site? Also define what your site will not do, at least for now.

USABILITY (CUSTOMER-CENTRIC DESIGN)
INFORMATION ARCHITECTURE:

C3 – SITE MAP
Sketch out your site structure (site map). Map out how the different topics on your site will link to or flow from each other, and the navigation paths that visitors will take (information flows).

C4 – INFORMATION FLOWS
For each page type on your site, map out how the relevant chunks of information will be represented, and how the visitor's eye will navigate the page contents.

C5 – PERSONA NAVIGATION
For each of your major personas and their problem scenarios/tasks, trace the navigation process they will have to follow in order to find solutions to those

problems. Rework your information flows within your site map and within each page to minimize time and confusion.

C6 – COMPETITOR ANALYSIS

Look at competing sites online and follow those same problem solving paths for each persona. Identify where you have an advantage, and where you can learn from your competitor's approach.

CREATIVE BRIEF

CONTENT

C7 – DESCRIPTION

Describe the content you will be using on your site.

C8 – LANGUAGE

Define the language style and tone you will use for writing your content. For larger sites with many contributors, create a style guide for writers. If your site information will be translated, you would include translation guidelines.

C9 – LAYOUT

Define how you will lay out your text and what text treatments you will use to make the content of each page easy to scan for visitors, for example, through headings or sub-titles.

C10 – THEMES

Ideally, each page should have a content theme and should focus on only one issue. Revisit your site map and page structures and label them with their respective themes. Be ready to break dense pages into several shorter pages if necessary. For each page theme, find a keyword that relates to the theme.

DESIGN

Design determines the look and feel of your site. It should conform to your overall usability requirements and should support rather than detract from your business objectives.

C11 – MOOD BOARDS

Find (online or offline) any content, imagery, colour schemes, text treatments or layouts that you feel would work well with the kind of tone and style that you want your site to convey. Pull all these examples together into 'mood boards' that help you define the direction for your site's design. If you are working with an agency, they will do this for you, or you can make this part of your briefing to them.

C12 – BRANDING CONSISTENCY

Look at your offline branding, if any, to ensure that there is consistency across media.

C13 – IMAGERY

Define the imagery that you will use on your site, both quantitatively and qualitatively. Ideally, create a style guide that becomes your design bible. The style guide will include text and image guides.

◆ **Text:** Define the fonts, sizes, colours, spacing, justifications and weights. If you have HTML skills, define much of this in a CSS (cascading style sheet).

◆ **Images:** Decide on the colour palette, photographic style, file size and type specifications, actual pixel dimensions to be used and where jpegs, gifs and Flash are to be used.

C14 – CONSTRUCTION

Define how your site will be built: from a template or from scratch. If you are using a template, outline the functionality and scope of the template you need, using your earlier site maps and usability exercises (see C3 to C6) as a guide.

C15 – MAINTENANCE

Define how your site will be maintained.

◆ Specify the frequency of updates.

◆ Specify the process (including quality assurance and publishing schedule).

D: SEARCH ENGINE MARKETING

NATURAL SEARCH ENGINE OPTIMIZATION

D1 – KEYWORDS

◆ List all the **keywords** and phrases by which you believe each of your personas may search to find you.

◆ Look at the **keyword theme** for each page and allocate your chosen keywords accordingly.

◆ Rewrite the **content** for each page to maximize the density of keywords, without your text losing its flow, naturalness or feel. (Remember that search engines penalize you for keyword stuffing).

◆ Craft a keyword-rich **title tag** for each page.

◆ Craft a keyword-rich **description tag** for each page. Remember to place the major theme keyword(s) at the beginning of the description and to enter it in the description tag of each page.

◆ Collect all the relevant keywords and phrases for each page and enter them into the **keywords meta-tag** for each page.

◆ Then, and only then, go to DMOZ.org and register your site. Then, and only then, register your site on Google, Yahoo and other search engines.

D2 – LINK POPULARITY

◆ Do a baseline audit of who is currently linking to your site, and to the sites of your major competitors (simply enter link: and the site URL in a Google search, and the resulting SERP is a ranked list of inbound links to the site).

- ◆ Search for and list those sites from which you would benefit having **inbound** links to your site.
- ◆ Define a linking strategy, and approach those sites with which you are willing to have **reciprocal** links.
- ◆ Identify **blogs** and **discussion forums** that are relevant to your site, and decide on a strategy for posting your site address within their content.
- ◆ Examine the **cross-links** within your own site and make sure that they are adequate in number and that they use the keyword theme of the destination page as the <u>link text</u> (that is, contextual links), not merely '<u>more</u>' or '<u>click here</u>', for example, instead of 'find our privacy policy <u>here</u>', use 'find our <u>privacy policy</u> here'.

PAY-PER-CLICK

D3 – FIND KEYWORDS
Use Google's keyword tools to identify related or alternative keywords to those you have already identified.

D4 – RESEARCH AVAILABILITY AND COST
Go to Google AdWords and research your major keywords to see how many competitors are using them and how much they cost.

D5 – SEEK OPPORTUNITIES
Identify some keyword opportunities that your competitors are ignoring, and look for longer phrases or long-tail terms.

D6 – ADWORDS STRATEGY
Draw up a budget and a strategy for an AdWords trial campaign.

D7 – ADWORDS ADVERTISEMENT
Craft your AdWords advertisement, making sure that you conform to Google guidelines and that your advertisement uses the keywords that would have caused it to pop onto the SERP.

D8 – ADWORDS METRICS
Become familiar with Google's AdWords metrics and track the progress of your trial campaign. Use the lessons you learn to help you structure a pay-per-click strategy for more significant follow-on campaigns.

E: ONLINE ADVERTISING

E1 – MEDIA
Identify the sites to which your target customers may be drawn and on which you can advertise. To find more sites, search using your major keywords.

E2 – RATES AND REACH
Identify each site's advertising rates and conditions, and any visitor demographics that it can provide.

E₃ – SHORTLIST
Short-list the sites on which you will be able to advertise.

E₄ – DRAFT ADVERTISEMENT DESIGN
Sketch out the banner advertisement that you will use on each site and determine which placement(s) you will use.

E₅ – LANDING PAGES
Determine on which target page a visitor will land when he or she clicks your advertisement. Avoid wasting a sales opportunity by directing people to your home page if you are able to craft a message-specific landing page instead.

E6 – FINAL ADVERTISEMENT DESIGN
Create, test where possible and submit the advertisement(s).

E₇ – MONITOR
Use your site metrics to monitor the success of your advertisement(s).

E8 – TEST AND ADJUST
Tweak your campaigns. Test different banners and different landing pages, increase the frequency of impressions on sites that deliver well.

F: EMAIL MARKETING

F₁ – COMMUNICATION STRATEGY
What is your email communication strategy?
Decide what you will communicate to whom and how often, as well as how you will measure results. Also decide what the look, feel and tone of your communications will be.

F₂ – DATABASE
Will you handle the database aspects of building and maintaining your lists yourself, or will you outsource this?
If so, to whom will you outsource? Go to MailChimp's and to Constant Contact's sites (and anyone else's site that interests you) to compare their abilities with your own. Then make a decision.

F₃ – INCENTIVES
What specific incentive(s) will you offer visitors to motivate them to give you permission to email them?
Decide how you will build a house list and ensure that the necessary functionality is in place on your website to capture visitors' contact details and permission.

G: PR

G1 – PRESS-RELEASE STRATEGY

What is your press-release strategy? Under what circumstances will you issue a release, and to whom? How will you distribute your releases?

Go to the sites of various online press-release agencies (MyPressportal, PRwire, PR Leap, PRFree) and compare the services they provide, particularly their abilities to search-optimize your release. Select at least one for domestic releases and one for global releases.

G2 – LEVERAGE COMMUNITIES

Brainstorm some ideas of how you could build and use 2.0 communities to generate inbound links and business referrals.

If you decide to pursue any ideas, treat this as a serious marketing communications project, not as a frivolous exercise.

G3 – GENERATE BUZZ

Brainstorm some ideas to generate buzz around your ebusiness or your site.

Define a buzz strategy, making sure that whatever you are doing conforms to your overall business objectives and is in keeping with your brand building goals.

H: METRICS

H1 – GET SET UP TO MEASURE

Sign up either for a commercial metrics service or for one of the free services such as Google Metrics. Get familiar with the tools and functionality.

H2 – VALIDATE DESIGNS

Confirm your design assumptions by looking at what visitors actually do on your site, and modify link labels and navigation terms to increase usability.

H3 – ANALYSE TRAFFIC

Analyse traffic patterns moving to your site and through your site, especially its conversion funnels. Identify where you are losing traffic and plan to make incremental changes to rectify this.

H4 – ANALYSE PERFORMANCE

Define the Key Performance Indicators (KPIs) for each of your emarketing objectives and for overall site performance. Structure a report that you can study on a regular basis to track how well you are doing.

I: REVISE YOUR STRATEGY

Go back to the strategy exercises A7, A8 and A9 and revise your answers in the light of what you have subsequently learned.

3-D VIRTUAL WORLDS: A computer-based simulated environment. Users inhabit the environment and interact via avatars. The environment is usually a two- or three-dimensional graphical representation of the environment. Some examples of such worlds are Active Worlds, Second Life, Club Penguin, Ultima and World of Warcraft.

3G: The third generation of mobile phone standards and technology that enable network operators to offer users a wider range of more advanced services. Services include wide-area wireless voice telephony and broadband wireless data, all in a mobile environment. 3G networks are wide-area cellular telephone networks that have evolved to incorporate high-speed internet access and video telephony.

A/B SPLIT: Refers to a test situation in which two randomized groups of users are sent different content to test the performance of specific campaign elements. The A/B split method can only be used to test one variable at a time.

ABANDONMENT: When a visitor leaves a page or shopping cart. The abandonment rate is the number of users who abandon divided by the total number of unique visitors for a given period.

ABOVE THE FOLD: The part of an email message or web page that is visible without scrolling. Material in this area is considered most valuable because the reader sees it first.

ACQUISITION COST: In email marketing, this is the cost to generate one lead, newsletter subscriber or customer in an individual email campaign; typically, it is the total campaign expense divided by the number of leads, subscribers or customers it produced.

ACQUISITION LIST: A rented list of prospects to which email can be sent. Prospects on a legitimate acquisition list are supposed to have opted in to the list and possess a certain set of characteristics, for example, dog owners who shop online.

ACROBAT: A program from Adobe Systems that captures a richly formatted document and allows people to view it in its original appearance, either as a shared file or on the web. Acrobat files use portable document format (PDF) with the file extension .pdf. To view an Acrobat document you need the freely downloadable Acrobat reader, which can be used as a standalone reader or as a browser plug-in (*also see* **plug-in**).

ACTIVE SERVER PAGE: *see* ASP

ADDRESS BOOK WHITELISTING: When a consumer adds a company's email address or domain name to his or her email address book. This prevents inadvertent 'false positive' filtering out of content that the consurmer wants to receive.

ADDRESS VERIFICATION SERVICE: A retailer resource that provides affirmation that a given billing address agrees with the address kept on file by the credit card companies.

ADDRESSABLE CALLS: A description of phone inquiries that can result in an action or sale; addressable calls are a key metric in pay-per-call search.

AFFILIATE: A marketing partner who promotes your products or services under a payment-on-results agreement; the affiliate relationship may range from simply carrying a button on a web page to entire email campaigns.

AFFILIATE MARKETING: The selling on one website of products provided by other websites. Amazon.com, for example, has thousands of affiliates — sites that capture business for Amazon in return for a percentage of the sale.

AJAX (ASYNCHRONOUS JAVASCRIPT AND XML): A web development technique for creating interactive web applications. It is the most common technique used in web 2.0 sites. Its intent is to make web pages feel more responsive by exchanging small amounts of data with the server behind the scenes, so that the entire web page does not have to be reloaded each time the user requests a change. This is meant to increase the web page's interactivity, speed and usability. Ajax is not a technology in itself, but a term that refers to the use of a group of technologies.

ALERT: An email message that notifies subscribers of an event or special price.

ANALOG (OR ANALOGUE): Analogue signals are typically represented as sine-wave audio signals and imply a continuously changing process measured in amplitudes and frequencies, while digital signals imply a process that is on or off, measured in ones and zeros (*see also* **digital).**

ANDROID: An operating system (and software platform) for mobile devices developed by Google.

ANONYMIZER: A service that acts as an intermediary between a computer user and the sites visited, enabling the user to surf the web relatively anonymously. This service prevents a website from identifying a computer's IP address and blocks cookies. It does not obscure users' activities from their Internet Service Providers (ISP), as the anonymizer service falls between the ISP and the websites visited.

AOL (AMERICA ONLINE): One of the largest online service providers in the United States. It pioneered internet access for the home user in the United States, providing easy-to-use interfaces and email, as well as a huge palette of proprietary online content. It also pioneered online chat for the non-technical user (*see also* **chat, ISP).**

APP: Abbreviation of Application.

APPLET: A small program written in Java and embedded in an HTML page, which is able to connect over the internet only to the computer from which it originated. (*see also* **HTML, Java**)

APPLICATION: A use of a particular technology or software. Online learning is an internet application — the internet applied to education. An application can also be a computer program. Microsoft Word is a word-processing application, a piece of software that is applied in word processing (*see also* **killer application**)

APPLICATION SERVICE PROVIDER: *see* **ASP**

ARPANET (ADVANCED RESEARCH PROJECTS AGENCY NETWORK): The United States Department of Defense network, which has been designed to survive a nuclear attack. This packet-switched, fault-tolerant network was the forerunner of the internet (*see also* **internet, packet switching**)

ASCII (AMERICAN STANDARD CODE FOR INFORMATION INTERCHANGE): A protocol that assigns a seven-digit binary number (a string of seven 0s or 1s) to every letter, number and character on a keyboard to allow transmission of basic text. For example, the letter 'm' is represented as 109 in ASCII. ASCII is commonly referred to as 'plain text' and is the most common format for text files in computers and on the internet. ASCII is used to code text in all UNIX and DOS operating systems, except Windows NT, which uses a more recent code called Unicode (*see also* **DOS, protocol, UNIX, Windows NT**)

ASP (APPLICATION SERVICE PROVIDER OR ACTIVE SERVER PAGE): An application service provider is a company that provides access to applications and services over the internet, relieving its customers of the burden of carrying the infrastructure or expertise required to keep those applications or services in-house. Active server pages are web pages whose content is called from a database, making the pages dynamically configurable to the needs or interests of individual users. (*see also* **application**)

ASYNCHRONOUS: Literally, asynchronous means 'not at the same time', and it usually applies to communication among people on the internet. Email is asynchronous, chat is synchronous. (*see also* **synchronous, chat**)

ATTACHMENT: A text, video, graphic, PDF or sound file that accompanies an email message but is not included in the message itself. Attachments are not a good way to send email newsletters because many ISPs, email clients and individual email recipients do not allow attachments since hackers use them to deliver viruses and other malicious code.

AUTHENTICATION: An automated process that verifies an email sender's identity.

AUTORESPONDER: Automated email message-sending capability, such as a welcome message sent to all new subscribers the moment they join a list. These messages can be triggered by users joining or unsubscribing, or by email arriving at a particular mailbox.

B2B (BUSINESS-TO-BUSINESS): Usually used to describe the nature of a company's business model or transactions, as distinct, for example, from business-to-consumer (b2c). Example: A company that sells data storage space to other companies is b2b; a website designed for individuals to purchase toys is b2c. (*see also* **b2c**)

B2C (BUSINESS-TO-CONSUMER): Usually used to describe the nature of a company's business model or transactions, as distinct, for example, from business-to-business (b2b). Example: A company that sells data-storage space to other companies is b2b; a website designed for individuals to purchase toys is b2c. (*See also* **b2b**)

BACKBONE: A line or series of pathways that forms the major high-speed route through a network. In the context of the internet, it refers to one of several major data arteries on the commercial or scientific networks around the globe. Each of the major telephone companies has a backbone, as do different government agencies. (*see also* **NETWORK, NETWORK ACCESS POINT**)

BACKUP: Backup describes copies of files or databases that are made as a precaution against the loss of the originals in the event of mechanical failure, corruption, accident, theft or other disaster. To back up files is the process of making backups.

BAIDU: The dominant search engine in China.

BANDWIDTH: Bandwidth describes the transmission capacity of a connection and refers to the rate at which you can move data through it. Low bandwidth means a slow connection. Bandwidth can be compared to a pipe — a pipe with a large diameter can pump through a great deal of data, a pipe with a small diameter will let only a trickle through. Bandwidth is usually measured in bits per second (bps). A modem may transmit 56,000 bits per second, or about 3.5 pages of text.

BANNER: Banners are advertising images that appear on websites. Originally static billboards, banners now come in a range of standard shapes and sizes and are frequently animated. Typically, a banner is also a link — if you click on the banner, you are taken to the page it is promoting. (*see also* **linking**)

BATCH TIME: In the days of mainframe computing, most of the work of commercial computers was done in batch processing, usually once a month. All transactions were stored up until the scheduled time to process them, and then the batch of transactions was run. In many businesses today, processes still run in batch time (at defined intervals and in chunks) rather than in real time (as they take place). (*see also* **real time**)

BAYESIAN FILTER: An anti-spam program that evaluates header and content of incoming email messages to determine the probability that it is spam. Bayesian filters assign point values to items that appear frequently in spam, such as the words 'money-back guarantee' or 'free'. A message that accumulates too many points is either rejected as probable spam or delivered to a junk-mail folder.

BIT (BINARY DIGIT): A bit is the smallest unit of computing data, that is, either a one or a zero. There are eight bits in a byte. Bandwidth is usually measured in bits per second (bps) or kilobits per second (Kbps), although many people mistakenly believe it is measured in bytes per second (Bps). (*see also* **bandwidth, bps, byte, kilobit, kilobyte**)

BLACKLIST: A list developed by anyone receiving email — processing email on its way to the recipient or interested third parties — that includes domains or IP addresses of any emailers suspected of sending spam. Many companies use blacklists to filter inbound email, either at server level or before it reaches the recipient's inbox.

BLOCK: A refusal by an ISP or mail server to forward your email message to the recipient. Many ISPs block email from IP addresses or domains that have been reported to send spam or viruses or have content that violates email policy or spam filters.

BLOG (WEB LOG): A blog is a journal, usually written by an individual, published on the web. A blog typically includes thoughts, opinions and commentary on a particular topic, often with a collection of links to related items on the web. Blogs are usually written in diary style, with dated entries. They are increasingly used by journalists and business professionals as a way to publish their thoughts directly, without the intervention of an editor.

BOT (ROBOT): A bot is an automated program that explores the internet to gather information. If you want to find out the price of a particular digital camera, instead of visiting a hundred shopping sites yourself, a shopping bot can do it for you and let you know where to find the best deal.

BOUNCE: A message that is not delivered promptly is said to have bounced. Emails can bounce for many reasons: the email address is incorrect or has been closed; the recipient's mailbox is full, the mail server is down, or the system detects spam or offensive content. (*see also* **hard bounce** and **soft bounce**)

BOUNCE RATE (ALSO RETURN RATE): The number of hard or soft bounces divided by the number of emails sent. This is an inexact number because some systems do not report bounces back to the sender clearly or accurately.

BPS (BITS PER SECOND): The speed at which data moves, also known as bandwidth, is measured in bps. A 28.8 Kbps modem transmits data at the rate of 28 800 bits per second. (*see also* **bandwidth, bit, Kbps**)

BRICK-AND-MORTAR: A term coined by the media to describe companies that exist and do business in some physical form, be it in offices, warehouses, retail stores, campuses or from other premises. (*see also* **clicks-and-bricks, click-and-mortar**)

BRIDGE: A bridge links different local area networks to each other. Bridges keep LAN traffic inside the LAN and redirect data headed to other interconnected LANs. A bridge decides whether a message from you is going to someone else within your LAN, or to a computer on a neighbouring LAN. In bridging networks, computer or hub identities are not locatable addresses. A bridge will broadcast each message to every identity on the network, and only the intended destination computer will accept it. Bridges learn which addresses are on which LAN and so become more efficient at directing messages. Broadcasting every message to all possible destinations would overload a large network such as the internet completely, which is why router-based networks (such as the internet) use addresses rather than identities. In a router network a message can be forwarded only in one general direction rather than in all directions. (*see also* **LAN, hub, router, gateway**)

BROADCAST: The process of sending the same email message to multiple recipients.

BROADBAND: In common usage, this term has come to mean internet access connections faster than 1 Mbps (typically 40 Mbps in the United States and Asia), such as cable modems, ADSL, T1 or T3 lines. Technically, broadband describes a data transmission that entails a medium such as a cable that carries several channels at once, as it does for cable television. (*see also* **cable modem, DSL, T1** and **T3**)

BROWSER: A client software program that accesses and displays resources on the internet, particularly web pages. (*see also* **client, web page, Internet Explorer, Netscape, Mosaic, Firefox, Safari**)

BUZZ: Catch-all term for talk or excitement about a given issue. In the online marketing world, buzz has become a common term in word-of-mouth marketing.

BYTE: A byte is a number of bits that together represent a single character. Usually there are eight bits in a byte. (*See also* **bit**)

CABLE MODEM: A cable modem allows a home computer to connect to the internet using television cables, at speeds nearly 30 times faster than analogue modems. Modern cables have a bandwidth of typically up to 85 Mbps. (*see also* **analogue, modem, T1, bandwidth**)

CACHE: A cache (pronounced cash) is a temporary storage area. Web browsers automatically cache the contents of web pages on your hard drive, so that if you return to the page there is no download time — and you do not have to use your bandwidth unnecessarily. The browser simply checks to see if the page has changed since the last visit and downloads only the changed components. (*see also* **bandwidth**)

CALL TO ACTION: The link or body copy in an email message, web advertisement, etc. that tells the recipient what action to take.

CASE NUMBER: In customer service, the attribution of a specific code or number to a customer request.

CELL: A segment of your list that receives different treatment specifically to see how it responds in comparison to the control (normal treatment).

CGI (COMMON GATEWAY INTERFACE): CGI is a standard way for you to interact with an application through a web server. The server receives your request and passes it to the application, then gets the response from the application and passes it to you, all using a common gateway interface. When, for example, you register on a website by filling in a form, the form has to be processed by an application on the server, probably a database application. The web server passes the information in your form to the database and sends you the response using CGI. (*see also* **application, web server**)

CHANNEL CONFLICT: Channel conflict arises when a company adds online business transactions capability and in effect starts to compete with its other sales channels, such as its own sales force or distribution partners.

CHAT: Chat refers to text-based discussion among two or more people who are on the internet at the same time. It is synchronous and involves users reading and reacting to each other's comments. Chat usually takes place in a chat room, a virtual space manifested as a window on each user's screen.

CHROME: Google's web browser. (*see also* **browser, Chrome, Firefox, Netscape, Safari**)

CHURN: The number of subscribers who leave a mailing list (or the number of email addresses that go bad) over a certain length of time, usually expressed as a percentage of the whole list.

CLICK: In web advertising, a click is an instance at which a visitor clicks on an advertisement and is taken to the target web page. The proportion of clicks to impressions measures how successful the advertisement has been at stimulating interest in those who see it. (*see also* **impressions**)

CLICK-AND-MORTAR: A term coined by the media to describe a company that does business in a physical location such as a retail store (mortar) as well as online (click). (*see also* **clicks-and-bricks, brick-and-mortar**)

CLICKS-AND-BRICKS: A term coined by the media to describe a company that does business in a physical location such as a retail store (bricks), as well as online (clicks). (*see also* **click-and-mortar, brick-and-mortar**)

CLICKFRAUD (OR CLICK FRAUD): In search marketing, any incident of human or automated fraud related to erroneous clicks on paid search advertisements.

CLICKTHROUGH: When a link is included in an email, search advertisement or online advertisement, a clickthrough occurs when a recipient clicks on the link. (*see also* **link**)

CLICKTHROUGH TRACKING: Refers to the data collected about each clickthrough link, such as how many people clicked on it or how many clicks resulted in desired actions such as sales, forwards or subscriptions.

CLICKTHROUGH RATE: Total number of clicks on email link(s), search advertisements or other elements divided by the number of emails sent, page views, and so on. The clickthrough rate is the percentage of advertisement views that resulted in clickthroughs — that is, how many of those who saw an advertisement actually clicked on it. It is an indication of the effectiveness of an advertisement. In general, click rates for banners that are repeated regularly vary from 0.15% to 1%. Some advertisements can produce click rates of 8% or more, but this rate is rare and is usually not sustainable.

CLIENT: In client-server computing a client is a software program on one computer that is used to contact and obtain data from the server software program on another computer, usually over a network. A client is designed to work with one or more types of server. A web browser such as Netscape or Internet Explorer is a type of client designed to access web servers. (*see also* **browser, server**)

CMS (CONTENT MANAGEMENT SYSTEM): A system running behind a website that allows someone to change or update content (e.g. prices, descriptions, images) without needing to know how to write code.

COMPARISON SHOPPING SITES: Similar to search engines, comparison shopping sites or engines allow users to compare products from a variety of sources (websites). Merchants feed product data to the comparison sites and pay for leads or sales generated.

COMPRESSED FILE: A compressed file is one that has been reduced in size by one of many compression programs using a proprietary algorithm. A compressed file must be decompressed by the same program that compressed it before it can be read. Some popular compression programs are WinZip, Stuffit and Unixcompress. (*see also* **WinZip, zipped files**)

CONFIRMED OPT-IN: Inexact term that may refer to double-opt-in subscription processes or may refer to email addresses that do not hard-bounce back a welcome message.

CONSUMER-GENERATED MEDIA (CGM): Any of the many kinds of online content that are generated at user level. Personal web pages such as those found on MySpace are rudimentary examples; blogs and podcasts are more evolved ones. (*see also* **user-generated content**)

CONTENT: All the material in an email message except for the codes showing the delivery route and return-path information. Content includes all words, images and links.

CONTENT-BASED FILTERS: A type of filtration that sorts messages based on strings or keywords that are located within the message. Filtering can take place based on a score that is assigned to some words or phrases, or on binary if/then statements, for example, block if 'free' appears in the subject field.

CONTENT STRATEGY: A content strategy includes the creation, capture, delivery, customization and management of content across an organization so that it delivers a consistent message about that company and is useful to the customer .

CO-REGISTRATION: Arrangement in which companies that collect registration information from users (email sign-up forms, shopping checkout process, and so on) include a separate box for users to check if they would also like to be added to a specific third-party list. Publishers purchase these names outright, or trade in-kind names.

CONVERSION: In internet marketing, a conversion is a click that becomes a purchase. If someone clicks on a banner advertisement, is taken to the target page and actually purchases something, this is called a conversion. The conversion rate (number of conversions as a proportion of clicks) is a measure of the success of the advertising tactic used. (*see also* **click**, **banner**)

COOKIE: A cookie is a small, non-executable data file that a web server saves on your hard drive to 'remind' it about your identity, preferences or behaviour on your future visits to the site. You can view the cookies that websites have placed on your hard disk: Netscape accumulates all the cookies in one file called cookies.txt; Internet Explorer keeps each cookie in a Windows subdirectory called cookies. You can delete cookies, although this may cause things that happened automatically in the past (your password was remembered for you, your site settings were customized, your purchaser data was automatically entered, and so on) not to happen any more. You can also set your browser to intercept cookies. The way in which some websites use and share cookie data has been the subject of controversy and privacy concerns. (*see also* **browser**, **Netscape**, **Firefox**, **Internet Explorer**)

COOKIE CRUSHER: Any software that helps a computer user to block or delete cookies.

COPYRIGHT: Copyright describes the legal right of an owner of intellectual property (such as a document, image or software program) to be protected from abuse of this intellectual property, within the limits of relevant national or international law. In most countries, copyright law gives the owner of a property the exclusive right to print, distribute and copy the work, and denies anyone else the right to do so without express permission of the owner. Copyright applies to the expression of an idea, whether published or not, and once an original work is created and fixed, copyright exists automatically.

COPYRIGHT INFRINGEMENT: Copyright infringement is the unauthorized copying of copyrighted intellectual property.

CPA (COST PER ACTION OR COST PER ACQUISITION): A method of paying for advertising in which payment is based on the number of times users complete a given action, such as purchasing a product or signing up for a newsletter.

CPC (COST PER CLICK): Different from CPA in that all you pay for is the click, regardless of what that click does when it gets to your site or landing page.

CPM: CPM or cost per thousand ad impressions is an industry standard measure for selling advertisements on websites. (The M comes from 'mil' which means one thousand, or from the Roman numeral for thousand.)

CRACKER: A hacker with criminal intent. (*see also* **hacker**)

CREATIVE: An email message's copy and any graphics.

CROSS-CAMPAIGN PROFILING: A method used to understand how email respondents behave over multiple campaigns.

CUSTOMER LIFETIME VALUE: A measure of the total amount a customer will spend with a merchant during the entire time that they are a customer. This value is usually calculated by taking a customer's spending per year and multiplying it by the average number of years they are likely to be a customer. The concept can be expanded to include an estimate of the value of business that a customer brings to a business through referrals.

DE-DUPLICATION (ALSO DE-DUPING OR MERGE/PURGE): The process of removing identical entries from two or more data sets such as mailing lists.

DEFERRED CONVERSIONS OR LATENT CONVERSIONS: Sales that take place following a website session that may result from the session, but where the conversion takes place at a later time or even in a place other than the website. With many online marketing tactics, it is not always possible to discern whether a sale took place as the result of some past interaction.

DENIAL OF SERVICE (DOS): A denial-of-service attack is an event during which a targeted computer or network is bombarded so intensely with traffic that it simply overloads and shuts down. The motivation behind a DoS attack can be political, military or commercial.

DEPLOY: The act of sending an email campaign after testing it.

DHTML: The technology on which 'floating' online advertisements are built. DHTML can be made to sit on top of a page and incorporate movement and sound. DHTML is not typically blocked by pop-up/pop-under blocking software.

DIGEST: A shortened version of an email newsletter, which replaces full-length articles with clickable links to the full article on a website, often with a brief summary of the contents.

DIGITAL: Digital refers to any technology that uses data that is either 'on' or 'off,' represented by ones and zeroes respectively. One and zero are each a binary digit, also called a bit. (*see also* **analogue**, **bit**)

DIGITAL CERTIFICATE: A digital certificate is an electronic 'identity document' that confirms your identity when transacting on the internet. Digital certificates are issued by a certification authority (CA) such as VeriSign or Thawte. The certificate contains your name, a serial number, expiration dates, a copy of your public key (to let others send you encrypted messages) and your digital signature, as well as the digital signature of the CA so that a recipient's browser can verify the validity of your certificate. (*see also* **public-key cryptography**, **digital signature**, **encryption**)

DIGITAL SIGNATURE: A form of encryption that authenticates sender and message using public-key cryptography. A digital signature consists of data appended to a digital message. Your digital signature changes with every message you send. A one-way 'hash function' generates a code from your message, which is then encrypted with your private key to become the digital signature for that message. The receiver recomputes two versions of the code, from the message and from your signature, with the help of your public key. If the codes are the same, the receiver knows that the message has not been tampered with and has indeed come from you.

DIRECTORY: On the internet, a directory is a structured, index-like, hierarchical subject guide that uses hypertext to provide rich layers of subtopics. Directories help users find relevant web pages on the internet. The biggest internet directory is Yahoo! (*see also* **hypertext, search engine**)

DOS (DISK OPERATING SYSTEM): DOS was the most widely used operating system in personal computers until the advent of Windows.

DOMAIN NAME: A domain name is the unique name that identifies an internet site. The internet is divided into different 'domains', which describe the type of site or its geographic location. The letters at the end of an internet address are the domain of that address. These letters tell you what the sites in that domain do (in most cases, .com is a commercial company; .edu is an educational institution; .gov is a government site; .org is a not-for-profit site) or where they are (.ca is a Canadian site; .uk is a site in the United Kingdom; .za is in South Africa). A domain name consists of a name followed by a domain. Each name is unique within its domain. Newer domains, such as .travel and .name are released because the number of sensible names still available is limited. (*see also* **IP number**)

DOMAIN NAME SYSTEM: This is the system according to which computer networks locate internet domain names and translate them into IP addresses. The domain name is the actual name for an IP address or range of IP addresses, for example, britefire.com, Britefire.co.za.

DOUBLE OPT-IN (OR VERIFIED OPT-IN): A process that requires new list joiners to execute an action (such as clicking on an emailed link to a personal confirmation page) to confirm that they do wish to be on the list.

DOWNTIME: Downtime refers to the amount of time that a system is non-operational. If you shut a website down for maintenance, you are incurring downtime. (*see also* **uptime**)

DSL (DIGITAL SUBSCRIBER LINE): DSL is a technology that uses standard telephone lines for high-bandwidth data transmission. Unlike regular dial-up modems, which send data wherever the telephone system wants them to go, a DSL circuit is set up like a dedicated line to connect two fixed locations, usually a home and the nearest central office of the telephone company. DSL allows for bandwidth far greater than conventional modems. It is usually configured for downloads from server to client at speeds of at least 1.544 megabits per second, and uploads in the other direction at 128 kilobits per second. This configuration is called an asymmetric digital subscriber line (ADSL). While ADSL may be advertised as providing 4 Mbps or higher, actual data transfer speeds are usually considerably lower, and drop off the further the user is from the nearest central telephone office. A symmetrical DSL (SDSL) line allows for equal data speeds in either direction. (*see also* **bandwidth, modem, bit, bps**)

DUMPSTER DIVING: This is the act of looking for value in someone else's garbage. In the contexts of computer security and personal privacy, dumpster diving is any technique that is used to retrieve discarded information that could be helpful in getting into a personal computer or network, or which could be used to steal an identity.

DYNAMIC CONTENT: Email-newsletter content that changes from one recipient to the next according to a set of predetermined rules or variables, usually according to the preferences the user set when opting in to messages from a sender. Dynamic content can reflect past purchases, current interests or the place where a recipient lives.

DYNAMIC IP ADDRESS: (*see* **IP address**)

EMAIL: Electronic mail messages sent from one person to another through a network.

Email is the single biggest user of bandwidth on the internet. Email may be in the form of only a text message, though it is common to send files (such as images, spreadsheets or documents) as attachments to messages. Email can often be configured to be plain or formatted text (HTML). (*see also* **HTML**)

EMAIL APPENDING: Service that matches email addresses to a database of personal names and postal addresses. Appending may require an 'OK to add my name' reply from the subscriber before you can add the name to the list.

EMAIL CLIENT: The software that recipients use to read email, such as Outlook Express or Lotus Notes.

EMAIL-FRIENDLY NAME (ALSO DISPLAY NAME, FROM NAME): The portion of the email address that is displayed in most, though not all, email readers in the place of, or in addition to, the email address.

EMAIL NEWSLETTER: Content of some inherent value distributed to subscribers by email on a regular schedule.

EMAIL PREFIX: The portion of the email address to the left of the @ sign.

EMAIL VENDOR (EMAIL SERVICE PROVIDER OR ESP): Another name for an email broadcast service provider; a company that sends bulk (volume) email on behalf of its clients.

ENCRYPTION: The conversion of data into a scrambled format that cannot be read by people who do not have the necessary decryption key to unscramble the data. Simple digital encryption is done by applying a mathematical algorithm to the digital message to be kept secret. (*see also* **public-key cryptography**, **digital certificate**, **digital signature**)

EVENT-TRIGGERED EMAIL: Pre-programmed messages sent automatically based on an event such as a date or anniversary.

EZINE (OR E-ZINE): Another name for an email newsletter, adapted from electronic 'zine or electronic magazine.

EXTRANET: A secured private-content internet made up of parts of the intranets of two or more enterprises. An extranet is usually built to facilitate communication and collaboration among suppliers, customers or partners. It usually uses internet infrastructures rather than private lines, as well as TCP/IP and other internet protocols. Because of this, an extranet usually requires the use of security systems such as firewalls, encryption and digital signatures. (*see also* **intranet**, **internet**)

FALSE POSITIVE: A legitimate message that is mistakenly rejected or filtered as spam, either by an ISP or a recipient's anti-spam program. The more stringent the anti-spam program, the higher the false-positive rate.

FAQ (FREQUENTLY ASKED QUESTIONS): A list of answers to common questions, provided on a website as a way of providing help to visitors.

FILE EXTENSION: The identifier that comes after the dot in a file name, for example .exe, .vbs, .doc or .jpg.

FILE SHARING: The practice of giving a file to another person, or allowing that person to copy it from your computer.

FILTERING: The real-time analysis of a user web page request to determine which advertisement or advertisements to return in the requested page. The web browser of a visitor to a web page sends a request to the server to receive the contents of the page. This request can tell a website or its advertising server whether it fits a certain characteristic, such as the browser type being used or the geographic location of the visitor, or, if the visitor's computer has a relevant cookie, what the visitor's past activity on the site has been. The advertising server can then place an appropriate advertisement.

FIREFOX: A web browser developed by Mozilla as part of an open-source initiative. Firefox is Internet Explorer's greatest competitor and is growing in popularity among web-savvy users as Internet Explorer moves further away from web standards. Firefox currently has around 15 percent of the global browser market.

FIREWALL: A specially configured computer that contains a set of security programs, usually at a gateway server, that allows company employees to access the internet but keeps unauthorized people out of the corporate intranet. (*see also* **gateway, server, intranet, network, LAN**)

FLAMING: The activity of publicly reprimanding or remonstrating with someone online where other parties to the online discussion can witness the 'dressing down'. Flaming is considered to be poor online etiquette (or netiquette) and is a breach of the unwritten laws of online behaviour.

FOLD: 'Above the fold', a term that originated in print media, refers to an advertisement that is viewable as soon as a web page is displayed, without the user having to scroll to see it.

FOOTER: An area at the end of an email message or newsletter that contains information that doesn't change from one edition to the next, such as contact information, the company's postal address or the email address the recipient used to subscribe to mailings. Some software programs can be set up to place this information automatically.

FORWARD (ALSO FORWARD TO A FRIEND): The process by which email recipients send your message to people they know, either because they think their friends will be interested in your message or because you offer incentives to forward messages. Recipients can forward the message through their own email client or by giving the recipient a link to click, which brings up a registration page at your site, in which you ask the person forwarding the message to provide his/her name and email address, the name/email address of the person they want to send the message to and (optionally) a brief email message explaining the reason for the forward. You can supply the wording or allow the person forwarding to write his or her own message.

FRAME: In website design terms, a frame is analogous to a window. A screen can be divided into different sections (frames), each providing different information. The contents of each frame are different HTML files, pulled into the master frame. The use of frames, once common, is rare today. (*see also* **HTML**)

FTP (FILE TRANSFER PROTOCOL): FTP is the most common protocol used for transferring files on the internet. The FTP protocol allows your computer to talk to another computer to download or upload files directly. (*see also* **protocol**)

GATEWAY: A gateway is where one network meets another, or a point in one network that serves as an entrance to another network. It is like a bridge, except that where a bridge simply passes data, a gateway will translate data if it is moving to a different kind of network. The computer that controls traffic at an ISP is a gateway. In a corporate LAN, a gateway is frequently also a proxy server and a firewall. A gateway is usually linked to a router, which redirects the messages that arrive at the gateway. (*see also* **bridge, ISP, LAN, firewall, proxy server**)

GBPS (GIGABITS PER SECOND): A gigabit is equal to one US billion bits per second, that is, one thousand million.

GIF (GRAPHIC INTERCHANGE FORMAT): This image file format is common on the internet. It is especially suitable for images containing large areas of the same colour such as logos, icons or diagrams. The GIF format makes image files smaller than they would be in other image formats such as JPEG. GIF files are not suitable for complex images such as photographs (*see also* **JPEG**)

GB (GIGABIT): One thousand million bits, making it one-eighth the size of a gigabyte (GB), which is one billion bytes. There are eight bits in a byte.

GOODBYE MESSAGE: An email message that is sent automatically to a list member who unsubscribes, acknowledging the request. You should always include an option to re-subscribe in case the unsubscribe was requested accidentally.

GOPHER: Before graphically rich browsers came along, Gopher was the first widely used client-server program for finding and accessing text-based menus of files available on the internet. It is still used today. To use it, you must have the Gopher client software installed on your computer, and you have to access Gopher servers. The client software is freely available. (*See also* **browser**, **client**, **server**)

GUI (GRAPHICAL USER INTERFACE): A GUI (pronounced gooey) is a means to interact with a computer system, which uses images, icons and graphics instead of purely text and code. Originally all interfaces were text and you needed to know commands and syntax to achieve anything (does anyone remember DOS?). On the internet, Gopher changed this, although it was still text based through a point-and-click menu-based interface. Today, all end-user computing uses GUIs, and the design, imagery and navigation systems of the particular program define what is called the 'look and feel' of the program. (*see also* **DOS**, **Gopher**)

HACKER: Any unauthorized person who tries to use a computer system or program by penetrating its security system. Once a term of praise for a programming expert, it has now acquired the same negative meaning as 'cracker' — a criminal hacker. (*see also* **cracker**)

HARD BOUNCE: Message sent to an invalid, closed or non-existent email account.

HEADER: Routing and program data at the start of an email message, including the sender's name and email address, originating email server IP address, recipient IP address and any transfers in the process.

HEAT MAP: An image that shows, for a given web page, where users' eyes go and how long they stay there.

HEURISTIC FILTERS: Filters that attempt to identify unsolicited commercial email (UCE or spam) using reiterative guesswork and past experience, to establish filtering rules. The longer a heuristic filter system is in place and its experience grows, the more accurate it becomes.

HITS: The number of hits or contacts with a site used to be the most common website equivalent of magazine circulation figures. It was once a fundamental determinant of advertising rates. However, as a measure of the volume of visitors to a site, the number of hits is frequently misleading. Hits are counted by a statistical package on a site's server, and the way that program is set up can cause dramatic variations in the results. If a visitor's browser requests a page that has multiple graphics, each graphic may register as a hit if it comes from a separate server. If a visitor returns to the page, it can register as a new hit. If your site has 100 pages and one visitor goes to each of them, this may be registered as 100 hits. If each page has 10 images, that could be 1,000 hits — from only one visitor! If an ISP caches web pages for its subscribers, the first subscriber to your page is a hit, but subsequent subscribers may not get counted because they are instead hitting the ISP's cached pages. A hit is also a term for a match in a search, as in 'that search resulted in 11 hits'. (*see also* **browser, ISP, AOL, cache**)

HOMEPAGE: A homepage is the first page on a website. If a site is a collection of pages like a book, the homepage is the cover of the book. It is usually the page that appears when you enter the site address. A homepage is also the default page to which your browser goes when you start it up. (*see also* **browser**)

HOST: A host is any computer on a network that contains resources that are available to other computers on the network. (*see also* **network**)

HOTSPOT (OR WI-FI HOTSPOT): An access point or area for connecting to the internet (*see also* **Wi-Fi**)

HTML (HYPERTEXT MARKUP LANGUAGE): The programming language used to create and format hypertext documents for use on the world wide web. In HTML you can specify that a block of text, or an image, should be linked to another address on the internet. HTML files must be viewed using a web client such as Firefox or Internet Explorer. (*see also* **client, world wide web**)

HTML SNIFFER: Technology embedded in email software that determines if users' email clients can receive HTML content.

HTTP (HYPERTEXT TRANSFER PROTOCOL): HTTP is the protocol for moving hypertext files from one computer to another over the internet. It requires a HTTP client program on one end, and an HTTP server program on the other end. It is the single most important protocol used on the world wide web.

HOUSE LIST: The list of email addresses an organization develops on its own, that is, your own list that you develop as a marketer.

HSDPA (HIGH-SPEED DOWNLINK PACKET ACCESS): HSDPA is a 3G mobile telephony communications protocol in the high-speed packet access (HSPA) family, which allows networks to have higher data transfer speeds and capacity.

HSUPA (HIGH-SPEED UPLINK PACKET ACCESS): HSUPA is a 3G mobile telephony protocol in the high-speed packet access (HSPA) family with up-link speeds of up to 5.76 Mbps. The technical purpose of the enhanced uplink feature is to improve the performance of uplink-dedicated transport channels, that is, to increase capacity and throughput and reduce delay.

HUB: A hub is like a central switchboard on a local area network (LAN). It simply links computers to each other so that they can communicate. The term can describe a configuration of several devices, which receives data from different directions and forwards it in one or more other directions. You can think of a hub as the centre of a wagon wheel. The computers in a LAN sit at the end of each spoke and communicate with each other through the hub. To communicate with computers on another LAN, say another wheel on the axle, the hub directs their messages through the axle (a bridge) to the other wheel's hub.

HYBRID MALWARE: Any software that combines the characteristics of several types of malicious code, such as viruses and worms.

HYPERTEXT: Any text that contains links to other text, other images or other documents. Hypertext links are addresses that are embedded in that text or images that, when you click on them, will lead to another document (or document section) being retrieved and displayed. (*see also* **HTTP**)

IDENTITY THEFT: A crime in which someone impersonates someone else, using the personal information of the victim as credentials. In 'true-name' identity theft, the criminal opens new accounts (such as credit card or telephone accounts) using the assumed identity, or uses it as a criminal alias. In 'account takeover' identity theft, the criminal gains access to the victim's existing accounts, usually changing the mailing address so that it takes some time for the victim to notice the fraud.

I-LINCC: A unique, often branded, alphanumeric code which, when sent by SMS to the global i-lincc number, returns an email containing relevant information to the sender.

IM (INSTANT MESSAGING): The ability to see easily whether a chosen individual is online and, if they are, to exchange messages with him or her. Unlike email, instant messaging is immediate and facilitates real-time written dialog. Most IM is text-only, although some services allow attachments such as images or even video.

IMPRESSIONS: The most frequently used measure of the potential value of a web page to advertisers. Impressions is a measure of traffic to a page, which is also known as 'eyeballs' or 'opportunities to see'. The number of impressions that a particular web page offers advertisers describes the number of visitors that might see their banner or link. It does not take into account unique visitors, so one visitor hitting the page a hundred times is counted as 100 impressions. (*see also* **hits**)

INACTIVITY: When a list member or registered user has been inactive for some time. There are no industry standards, as inactivity depends on the nature of the relationship and the frequency of communication. For example, a list member who is emailed quarterly wouldn't be considered inactive as soon as one who is mailed weekly.

INFORMATION ARCHITECTURE: Information architecture (IA) is defined as the art and science of organising and classifying information to help people meet their information needs based on principles of design and architecture. As information proliferates exponentially, usability and interaction design are becoming the critical success factors for website and application design. Good IA lays the necessary groundwork for an information system that makes sense to and is usable by users. IA involves the combination of organization and labelling of information, navigation schemes and retrieval mechanisms within an information space.

INTELLECTUAL PROPERTY: Any property that is the product of creativity or invention (such as a document, an image, a song or a computer program) and that does not exist in a tangible form. The ideas and the expression of those ideas that a book contains are intellectual property, but not the book itself. A compact disk is not intellectual property, but the songs it contains are.

INTERNET: An internet consists of any two or more networks connected together. The internet is a loose collection of interconnected networks that all use the TCP/IP protocol. The internet evolved from the ARPANET. (*see also* **ARPANET, TCP/IP**)

INTERNET2: A very high-speed backbone that moves data at 2.4 gigabits per second. (*see also* **backbone**)

INTERNET EXPLORER (IE): Microsoft Corporation's web browser. (*see also* **browser, Chrome, Firefox, Netscape, Safari**)

INTERNET FRAUD: Any fraud that is committed using the internet. This includes identity theft, email scams, online auction frauds or the fraudulent sale or purchase of merchandise or services over the web.

INTERNET PROTOCOL NUMBER: *see* **IP number**

INTERNET RELAY CHAT (IRC): The system for real-time text conversations that was first available on the internet before the graphical web came along. IRC is still in use today.

INTERNET SERVICE PROVIDER (ISP): An organization that provides access to the internet. Most computers are not connected directly to the internet – they connect to an ISP, which is connected directly. Individuals may access their ISP (for example, MSN, Yahoo!, Verizon) by dial-up modem, DSL, or 3G wireless, and companies may have dedicated lines linking their computers directly to their ISP (for example, UUNet).

INTERNET TIME: Internet time essentially means 'very quickly'. The expression implies that a business or technology that is involved with the internet moves and evolves much faster than any that is not involved with the internet.

INTERSTITIAL: *see* **splash page**

INTRANET: A private network contained within an organization such as a company or a university to allow communication and sharing of resources within a defined community of users. An intranet usually consists of interconnected local area networks (LANs) or wide area networks (WANs), which are LANs that are connected over distances requiring dedicated lines. An intranet is usually connected to the internet (or other proprietary network) through a gateway and is protected from unauthorized use by one or more firewalls.

INVASION OF PRIVACY: Any act that intrudes on the individual's right to privacy, which is essentially the right to be left alone by other people. This includes intrusion of personal space, public disclosure of private information, publicity that unjustly defames a person and the theft or abuse of a person's identity. Just as an individual's legal right to privacy varies from country to country and state to state, so do legal definitions of invasion of privacy.

IP NUMBER, IP ADDRESS (DYNAMIC OR STATIC): An internet protocol number, or IP number, is a unique numerical address given to each computer on the internet. (Most computers also have one or more domain names, which are easier to remember.) Anyone who dials your telephone number will always get through to your telephone because it is static or unchanging. Like a phone number, a static IP number is a fixed address on the internet – it belongs to a specific computer. Most internet servers and commercial websites have static IP numbers. If the address of a computer hosting a website changed every time it disconnected from the network, nobody would ever be able to find the site. But many computers connecting to the internet do not have their own unchanging IP number. To save costs, many companies acquire a pool or block of IP numbers that are shared as needed. As each user connects to the internet, a system dynamically allocates an IP number from the pool to the individual's computer. As that user disconnects, that IP number goes back into the pool, becoming available to the next user. This is the basis on which most Internet Service Providers (ISPs) work, too. Every time you connect to Yahoo!, for example, the Yahoo! server allocates your computer an available IP number for that online session. Your IP number will probably be different every time you connect. You are using a dynamic IP number.

IPHONE OS: The operating system of the iPhone and iPod touch developed by Apple Inc.

ISDN (INTEGRATED SERVICES DIGITAL NETWORK): A set of standards for transmitting digital data over ordinary telephone lines. It was the original 'high-speed' commercial connection system. ISDN lines, which have a transmission rate of only 128 Kbps (twice the speed of a 56 K modem) are still widely used by small businesses, although they are slow and expensive compared with T1 and DSL lines. But like all internet-age technologies, ISDN is evolving rapidly. A broadband version called BISDN will soon be available, which will allow transmission rates of 2 Mbps and higher. (*see also* **Kbps**, **DSL**)

ISP: *see* internet service provider

JAVA: Developed by Sun Microsystems, Java is a relatively simple object-oriented programming language designed for the internet. It can be used to build sophisticated applications that run as a distributed process on several computers, but typically it is used to build applets (very small programs) that download safely from web pages and allow users to interact with them. (*see also* **applets**)

JAVASCRIPT: A programming language used in web pages to make them more interactive. JavaScript (from Netscape) and Java (from Sun) are two different programming languages.

JPEG, JPG (JOINT PHOTOGRAPHIC EXPERTS GROUP): A format for image files that are used on web pages, this format is better suited for photographic images than the GIF format. (*see also* **GIF**)

KBPS (KILOBITS PER SECOND): The standard way in which the transmitting speed, or bandwidth, of a modem is described. A 56 Kbps modem transmits data at 56,000 bits (not bytes) per second. This means that a file of 56 kilobytes will take 8 seconds to download. (*see also* **bit, byte**)

KEYWORD: Words that represent or categorize the content of a particular web page. When you search for a web page through a search engine or directory, the words you ask the engine to search for are keywords. Many web pages embed keywords invisibly in the headers of their pages to help search engines categorize them. (*see also* **search engine, directory**)

KILLER APPLICATION: A killer application or 'killer app' is an application for a technology that becomes wildly popular and makes that technology ubiquitous. Email was the 'killer app' for the internet.

KILOBIT: 1,000 bits.

KILOBYTE: Usually thought of as 1,000 bytes, a kilobyte is technically 1,024 bytes.

LANDING PAGE: A web page viewed after clicking on a link within an email; may also be called a microsite, splash page, bounce page or click page.

LAN (LOCAL AREA NETWORK): A computer network in a limited geographical area such as an office, building or campus. (*see also* **WAN**)

LINKING: The process of connecting one section of a document to another using hypertext. A link is a selectable connection that jumps you to a new destination if you click it. The link may be an icon, a banner, or a word or phrase. Typically a link is a word that is identifiable as a link because it is underlined. Linking also refers to connecting one hardware device to another to form a network.

LINKROT: Term describing the process of links going bad over time, either because a website has shut down or a site has stopped supporting a unique landing page provided in an email promotion.

LINUX: A free operating system derived from UNIX.

LIST: The list of email addresses to which you send a message. This list can be either your house list or a third-party list that sends your message on your behalf.

LIST FATIGUE: A condition that entails diminishing returns from a mailing list whose members are sent too many offers in too short a period of time.

LIST HYGIENE: The act of maintaining a list so that hard bounces and unsubscribed names are removed from mailings.

LIST MANAGEMENT: How a mailing list is set up, administered and maintained. The list manager has daily responsibility over list operations, including processing subscribes and unsubscribes, bounce management, list hygiene, and so on. The list manager can be the same person as the database manager, but is not always the same person as the list owner.

LIST OWNER: The organization or individual who has gathered a list of email addresses. Ownership does not necessarily imply 'with permission'.

LIST RENTAL: The process by which a publisher or advertiser pays a list owner to send its messages to that list. This process usually involves the list owner sending a message on the advertiser's behalf.

LOGFILE: A logfile is any file that tracks and records (logs) activity, typically on a website or server.

MALWARE (MALICIOUS SOFTWARE): A generic term for programs or files such as viruses, Trojan horses and worms that are designed to do harm to a computer or computer system, directly or indirectly.

MASH-UP: A web application that combines data from more than one source into a single integrated tool. For example, merging map information from Google with contact information from the Yellow Pages, or pulling pricing data from multiple vendors into a comparison tool.

MBPS (MEGABITS PER SECOND): 1 million bits per second.

MB (MEGABIT): 1 million bits, that is, one-eighth the size of a megabyte (MB), which is 1 million bytes. There are 8 bits in a byte. In telecommunications, which uses decimal notation, a million is a million. In computer processing a million is two to the 20th power or 1,048,576.

MEGABYTE: Usually thought of as 1 million bytes, a megabyte is technically 1,024 kilobytes.

MERCHANT ACCOUNT: An account a vendor holds with a bank and/or with a credit card company. A credit card vendor account entitles the vendor to accept payments that customers make who use credit cards from the issuing company. A bank merchant account allows the vendor to receive payment into a bank account. Credit cards (e.g. Visa and Master cards) are frequently issued by banks rather than directly by card companies such as American Express. A bank merchant account may not be with the vendor's usual bank, since the scale of operation or perceived risk of the vendor's business may cause its own banks to refuse help.

METASEARCH: A search using more than one search engine, or using a sophisticated methodology that goes beyond simple keywords. Metasearch engines such as Mamma.com automate the process of simultaneously using multiple search engines. (*see also* **search engine, keyword**)

MICROSITE: A page or pages that are supplements to a primary website designed to meet separate objectives. It typically has a separate web address. The marketing purpose of a microsite may include branding, or providing a focal point for a campaign.

MIME (MULTIPURPOSE INTERNET MAIL EXTENSIONS): MIME is an extension of the original internet email protocol SMTP (simple mail transport protocol), which allowed only the exchange of ASCII files. MIME allows people to use SMTP to exchange audio, video, images, application programs and other files on the internet.

MODEM (MODULATOR-DEMODULATOR): A physical device between a computer and a communications line (telephone or cable) that allows the computer to talk to other computers. Analogue modems connect to telephone lines, cable modems connect to cables, digital modems connect to DSL lines.

MOSAIC: The first widely available browser for the world wide web that allowed users to access graphics, text and sound from web servers. Mosaic provided a graphical point-and-click interface that was easy to use. Released by Marc Andreesen at the National Center for Supercomputing Applications (NCSA), Mosaic played a pivotal role in the explosion in web use. Andreesen went on to found Netscape and to become a billionaire at the age of 24.

MP3: A standard technology for compressing a digital audio file to about one-twelfth the size of the original, while still producing a reasonably high-quality sound when played back in its compressed form — though it is not CD quality. Files compressed with the MP3 system have an .mp3 file extension. The MP3 algorithm was developed through the Motion Picture Experts Group (MPEG), and its name is an abbreviation for the 'MPEG-1 Audio Layer-3' project that produced it. MP3 is probably the most frequently used system for compressing whole music tracks for transmission over the internet or for playback on portable digital music players. Anyone can create MP3 files from their CD collection using a free program called a ripper to get a CD track onto their hard disk, and then applying another free program called an encoder to convert the track to an MP3 file. Because it is illegal to copy music from a CD and redistribute it, the mainstream record industry is largely opposed to the MP3 phenomenon — particularly since sites like Napster have made large-scale music distribution popular. (*see also* **MPEG**)

MPEG (MOTION PICTURE EXPERTS GROUP): The Motion Picture Experts Group is a body operating under the International Organization for Standardization, which develops standards for digital video and digital audio compression. MPEG video files have a file extension of .mpg and tend to be large. To view them you can use a freely downloadable MPEG client or a viewer that plays MPEG movies. (*see also* **MP3**)

MULTICHANNEL: A way to describe merchants that use multiple sales channels, as opposed to being strictly one (brick-and-mortar) or the other (web-only or 'pureplay').

MULTIVARIATE TESTING: A statistical model that is used to allow the simultaneous testing of multiple variables, in contrast with A/B testing, which can only effectively examine one variable at a time. It is also known as the Taguchi method.

NAP: *see* **network access point**

NETSCAPE: Navigator is Netscape Communications Corporations' web browser. It is part of a bigger suite of internet communications applications called Netscape Communicator. Netscape evolved from Mosaic and became one of several browsers on the market. The other is Microsoft's browser, Internet Explorer. While Netscape dominated the market for years, Internet Explorer is now the most widely used browser on the web, with Firefox running second.

NETWORK: Consists of any two or more computers connected together to share resources or exchange information. Two or more networks connected together form an internet.

NETWORK ACCESS POINT (NAP): A major connection point on the internet for long-distance transmissions, particularly on very high-speed backbones. All major providers of internet access tend to be connected through NAPs. (*see also* **backbone**)

NODE: Nodes are like the knots in a fishnet or the places where paths cross or terminate. At every node, there is a device such as a computer, router, a bridge, a gateway or a server. The computer you use is a node when connected to a network, as is the server sending you a web page.

NTH NAME: The act of segmenting a list for a test in which names are pulled from the main list for the test cell by number — such as every fifth name on the list. (*see also* **A/B split**)

OFFLINE: Describes any activity that takes place when a computer is not connected to a network. It is the opposite of online, or the real world of bricks-and-mortar.

ONLINE: Describes any activity or resource on the internet, or while connected to a network.

OPEN RATE: The number of HTML message recipients who opened your email, usually as a percentage of the total number of emails sent. The open rate is considered a key metric for judging an email campaign's success, but it has several problems. The rate indicates only the number of emails opened from the total number sent, not those that were actually delivered. Opens also cannot be calculated on text emails. Furthermore, some email clients allow users to scan message content without actually opening the message, which is falsely calculated as an open.

OPEN RELAY: An SMTP email server that allows outsiders to relay email messages that are neither for nor from local users. Often exploited by spammers and hackers. (*see also* **SMTP, spammer, hacker**)

OPT-IN: To give permission for a company to use personal information for marketing purposes. For many sites, such as Yahoo, opting in is the default and users have to explicitly opt out of having their personal information shared with marketing partners.

OPT-OUT: To instruct a company not to use personal information for marketing purposes.

PACKET SNIFFING: The act of intercepting and reading data packets that are in transmission over the internet or an intranet, using software or hardware 'sniffers'. Whatever you send or receive on the internet is broken into small 'packets' that travel across the internet, which are then reassembled at the destination. If not encrypted, these packets are vulnerable in transit. Packet sniffing is a term for inspecting packets of data in transit to see whether they contain anything valuable, and then checking the address of the sender and recipient. It as a sophisticated form of wire tapping, or the virtual equivalent of shoulder surfing. The FBI's Carnivore system, installed in most ISPs in the United States, is allegedly a type of packet sniffer. (*see also* **shoulder surfing**)

PACKET SWITCHING: The technology used to move data around on the internet. In packet switching, the data from the sending computer is broken down into packets. Each packet is addressed with its destination and its origin and then passed from computer to computer on the internet until it reaches its destination. When all the packets arrive, they are reassembled to form the original data. Packets from different sources share the same lines, and are sorted and redirected along the way.

PASS-ALONG: An email recipient who received your message via forwarding from a subscriber. Some emails offer 'forward to a friend' in the creative, but the majority of pass-alongs happen through email clients.

PAYMENT GATEWAY: A service that acts as an electronic intermediary between a vendor and a credit card authorising site. The gateway obtains authorization for accepting the card a purchaser is using and secures payment from the card issuer. Then it passes the payment on to the vendor's merchant account, deducting a percentage of the transaction as a fee.

PAY-PER-CLICK (PPC OR SPONSORED LINKS): In pay-per-click advertising, the advertiser pays a certain amount for each click-through to the advertiser's website.

.PDF: *see* **Acrobat**

PEER-TO-PEER (P2P): Peer-to-peer, in web culture terms, describes applications such as

Napster, Gnutella, Kazaa, Skype, Azureus or Limewire, which allow users to exchange files over the internet with other directly or through a server. Effectively, a P2P application creates a temporary network that allows users to connect with each other and directly access files from each other's computers.

PERMISSION MARKETING: This type of marketing is based on the concept that consumers allow marketers to join their lives, rather than marketers imposing their products or services on the lives of consumers.

PERSONA-BASED DESIGN: Personas are virtual customers; they are useful templates based on common customer types that can guide site design, offer testing, and so on.

PERSONAL FIREWALL: Any software that prevents other users or hacking systems on the internet from gaining unauthorized access to a personal computer. Not as robust as corporate firewalls, personal firewalls typically do not have a hardware component. If a home network is in place, the router may act as a hardware firewall.

PERSONALIZATION: A targeting method in which an email message appears to have been created for a single recipient only. Personalization techniques include adding the recipient's name in the subject line or message body, or the message offer may reflect a purchasing, link clicking or transaction history.

PGP (PRETTY GOOD PRIVACY): Software that is used to encrypt and protect email as it moves from one computer to another; can be used to verify a sender's identity.

PHISHING: A form of identity theft in which a scammer uses an authentic-looking email to trick recipients into impart sensitive personal information, such as credit card or bank account numbers, ID numbers and other data.

PLAIN TEXT: Text in an email message that includes no formatting code (*see also* **HTML**)

PLUG-IN: For web browsers, a plug-in is software — often available free of charge and downloadable from the internet — that is designed to enhance or extend the functionality of the browser. RealPlayer, for example, offers popular plug-ins for adding audio and video capabilities.

PODCAST: A podcast (abbreviation for broadcast to an iPod) is an audio file that is made available for downloading from a website or blog. These files are typically in MP3 format. They are not exclusively for playing on iPods (any media player will do), nor are they intended exclusively for mobile use — you can listen to them at your desktop. Podcasting makes use of RSS technology so that an individual can set up a feed-reader to grab new audio content automatically and load it into a mobile media player.

POP (POST OFFICE PROTOCOL): A protocol used by email clients to send to or receive messages from an email server. Not to be confused with point of presence, an access point for the internet.

POP-UP: A box that appears (pops up) over the content of a web page to deliver information or, more often, to display an advertisement. A pop-under is similar, except that the advertisement appears below the page content, only becoming visible when the visitor closes the page.

PORTAL: A site that is intended to be a major launching point for users when they connect to the web. A portal is analogous to a mall, and may be general or specific, consumer-oriented or business-oriented, content-rich or a simple directory. Examples of consumer portals are Netscape.com (general) and Garden.com (specific). Business portals tend to be specific to markets or industries. TradeCompass.com (international trade) is an example of a business portal. Portals that offer rich content within their field (updated news, advice, white papers, search functionality, promotional services, intraportal commerce functionality) are referred to as vertical markets or vertical portals. (*see also* **directory, vertical market**)

PORT PROBE: A port probe (or port scan) is an attempt to gain access to a computer through a port (a virtual communications address or logical connection place) in the computer system. A port scanner may send a message to each of the more than 65,000 ports on a computer to identify if the port is used, and if so, can be probed for any security weakness. Typically port scans are the tools of unsophisticated hackers using automated hacking scripts to bombard millions of computers at random in the hope of finding an open door. More sophisticated hackers and malware deliberately target known port weaknesses.

PPC: *see* **pay-per-click**

PPP (POINT-TO-POINT PROTOCOL): PPP is used to link a computer through an analogue modem via a phone line to a dial-up ISP or another computer. PPP sends all its data packets on the same line, and requests retransmission of any packets that do not arrive or arrive corrupted. An earlier, less robust version of PPP was known as SLIP (serial line internet protocol).

PREFERENCE CENTRE: In email or website registration, this is the practice of asking the registrant questions that tell the marketer more about them. Typical preference centres will ask about interests and preferences for HTML vs. text emails. They can, however, be more sophisticated and guide frequency and segmentation.

PREVIEW PANE: The window in an email client that allows the user to scan message content without actually clicking on the message.

PRIVACY POLICY: A statement to users of a website that describes what information the site collects and what it will do with the information it collects.

PROFILING: In ecommerce marketing, profiling is the process of collecting data about online customers so that marketers can better anticipate and respond to customers' needs. The data that is collected and the way it is used may result in profiling that benefits the customer or threatens their privacy. Privacy advocates are particularly concerned when different organizations pool the information that they have about individual customers.

PROTOCOL: A standard set of rules and procedures two devices use to allow them to communicate with each other. (*see also* **TCP/IP**)

PROXY SERVER: A common firewall solution acting as a secure post office — requests for access to a server pass through the proxy, and the files requested pass back through the proxy. This conduit is easier to secure than hundreds of individual machines. (*see also* **firewall**)

PUBLIC-KEY CRYPTOGRAPHY: A set of standard protocols, developed by RSA, for securing internet message traffic. Public-key cryptography is used in what is called the public key infrastructure (PKI). Browsers handle all the security as background processes. A vendor provides a public key to make a one-way encryption of the message, it travels in a garbled format, and the vendor decrypts it using its matching private key.

PUREPLAY: In ebusiness, pureplay is a term describing a company that does business exclusively online, without any corresponding physical establishment. Amazon.com is a pureplay — there is no neighbourhood Amazon bookstore into which you can walk. Barnesandnoble.com is not a pureplay — it has a physical business presence.

QUERY: A question that defines a subset of your database. If your database contains sports enthusiasts, then a query might specify, 'males aged 18 or older who play soccer'.

QUEUE: Where an email message goes after you have sent it but before the list owner approves it or the list server gets around to sending it. Some list software allows you to queue a message and then set a time to send it automatically, either during a quiet period on the server or at a time when human approval is not available.

QUICKTIME: A technology from Apple Inc. that allows for the development and playback of multimedia files that combine sound and video with text and animation. The QuickTime player is a standard plug-in to web browsers and is freely downloadable from Apple's site. QuickTime files have .qt, .mov, and .moov. file extensions. (see also **plug-in, browser**)

REAL TIME: Events that happen in real time happen instantly. There are no processing delays, bottlenecks or artificial barriers to progress.

RECENCY: A measure of how recently information was produced. The term usually refers to the age of contacts on a rented or third-party list.

RECORD: A file in a marketer's database. It may contain anything from an anonymous code with preferred site characteristics to an extensive profile of a customer or prospect.

RECREATIONAL SHOPPERS: The segment of the population that reports that it 'likes to shop' and considers shopping a hobby or fun activity.

REGISTRATION: The process whereby someone not only opts in to your email program, website membership program, or other activity, but provides some additional information, such as name, address, demographic data or other relevant information, usually by using a web form.

RELATIONSHIP EMAIL: An email message that refers to a commercial action — a purchase, complaint or customer-support request — based on a business relationship between the sender and the recipient.

REPEATER: Repeaters are similar to amplifiers — they keep a signal strong as it travels along a network. Repeaters simply amplify a signal at stages along the journey. There are different types of repeaters, depending on whether the signal is travelling along cable or fibre-optic lines. But unlike an amplifier, which boosts analogue signals and the noise associated with them, repeaters boost digital signals and are therefore able to clean them at the same time.

RETURN RATE: The percentage of total sales (by item, category or all sales) that are ultimately returned by customers.

RICH MEDIA: Advertising that is more elaborate than conventional banner advertisements. It includes animations, movies or interactions that go beyond the norm.

ROUTER: Routers are located at gateways, where one network meets another. They are the devices throughout the internet that redirect data packets to their destination. Routers assess how busy the lines are and send each data packet to a router closest to its destination, using the route with the least congestion.

RSS (RICH SITE SUMMARY OR REALLY SIMPLE SYNDICATION): An XML format for syndicating web content. A website or blog uses RSS to feed its changing content to RSS-equipped sites that have subscribed to that content. Blogs and newsfeed typically use RSS, which is also being used more and more frequently in business to broadcast corporate PR information or specific data, for example, updates to project plans. RSS allows computers to automatically communicate data without having to be prompted by people. (see also **XML**)

SAFARI: A web browser developed by Apple Inc. and included in Mac OS X. A beta version for Microsoft Windows was released with support for Windows XP and Windows Vista. It was also functioning unofficially on Windows 2000 and on Linux, but web graphics do not render properly. Since its release, usage has climbed. Safari claims to be the fastest web browser on any platform.

SCAM: A fraudulent scheme, or the attempt to defraud someone.

SEARCH ENGINE: A program that is used to find and recommend relevant web pages in response to a search phrase or keywords a user enters. Typically, a search engine uses a 'spider' that crawls around the web collecting information about all the pages it finds. The spider returns this information to the search engine, which compiles a gigantic, dynamic catalogue of available internet pages. This catalogue is what is referenced when a user enters a search. (*see also* **spider**)

SEARCH ENGINE RESULTS PAGE (SERP): The listing of web pages returned by a search engine in response to a keyword query.

SECOND-TIER SEARCH ENGINES: A term that is sometimes used to refer to any search engine beyond Google, Yahoo!, MSN Live, Baidu or AOL. This term is also used to refer to the countless low-priced search engines and networks, as distinct from name-brand search properties, such as Ask, Dogpile, and many others.

SECURE SITE: A site that guarantees that messages that travel between the visitor's browser and the server are encrypted. You can recognize a secure site by https:// instead of http:// appearing in the browser address window, and by one of two icons in the lower browser screen: a padlock or a key. When the key is unbroken or the lock is closed, you are on a secure page.

SEED EMAILS (OR SEED ADDRESSES): Email addresses placed on a list (sometimes secretly) to determine what messages are sent to the list and/or to track delivery rate and/or visible appearance of delivered messages. Seeds may also be placed on websites and elsewhere on the internet to track spammers' harvesting activities.

SEMANTIC WEB: The way users currently search for and interact with data on the web, sophisticated as the background technology may be, is, primitive. The semantic web is both a vision and a major project that aims to build a universal medium for information exchange, by giving a deeper meaning to the content of the web, in a form that machines will be able to understand, interpret and act upon. Web 3.0 is expected to be largely based on the semantic web. The term semantic web was coined by Tim Berners-Lee, inventor of WWW, URIs, HTTP and HTML) and can be thought of as an efficient way of representing data on the web, that is, a globally linked database, where machines can mine the meaning of the data in the same way that humans do. (*see also* **web 3.0**)

SEARCH ENGINE MARKETING (SEM): All the tactics and tools that are used to market a site through search engines.

SEARCH-ENGINE OPTIMIZATION (SEO): The practice of designing and coding web pages to be attractive to search engines. SEO attempts to place pages highly within the 'natural' listings on search engines.

SENDER ID: The informal name for a new anti-spam program that combines two existing protocols: sender policy framework and caller ID. Sender ID authenticates email senders and blocks email forgeries and faked addresses.

SENDER POLICY FRAMEWORK (SPF): A protocol that is used to eliminate email forgeries. A line of code called an SPF record is placed in a sender's domain name server information. The incoming server can verify a sender by SPF record before allowing a message through.

SERVER: A computer or software package that 'serves' data to client software that is running on other computers. The term can refer to a particular piece of software, such as a web server, or to the machine on which the software is running.

SHARE OF WALLET: A measure of how much business a merchant owns in a given category, that is, how much of everything that someone is expected to spend on product X this year will they be spending with merchant Y.

SHOULDER SURFING: The process of acquiring information by stealthy direct observation, such as looking over a person's shoulder or eavesdropping on a conversation. Shoulder surfing is a common and effective technique for acquiring personal information.

SINGLE SCREEN CHECKOUT: An emerging technology that puts the shopping-cart functions of a website onto the shopping page itself. These sites are usually built in Flash or AJAX and may vary in look and feel. They are anticipated to lower the rate of shopping-cart abandonment.

SMS (SHORT MESSAGE SERVICE): Also known as 'texting' SMS is a protocol that allows the exchange of short text messages between mobile devices.

STOCK KEEPING UNIT (SKU): Any product, part or accessory that is numbered. This term is often used to refer to the number of products sold by a merchant.

SMALL TO MEDIUM ENTERPRISE (SME): The definition varies by country, and changes over time, but an SME is any business that is not a major corporation. In the USA it is any business with the lesser of 500 employees or $100 million in annual revenue. In the EU, it is an independent company with fewer than 250 employees and either an annual turnover not exceeding 40 million Euro or a balance sheet not exceeding 27 million Euro. Typically, more than 90 percent of companies in any country fall into the SME classification.

SMTP (SIMPLE MAIL TRANSFER PROTOCOL): The most common protocol for sending email messages between email servers.

SOFT BOUNCE: Email that is sent to an active (live) email address but is turned away before being delivered. Often, the problem is temporary — the server is down or the recipient's mailbox is over quota. The email might be held by the recipient's server and delivered later, or the sender's email program may attempt to deliver it again. Soft-bounce reports are not always accurate because they do not report all soft bounces or the actual reason for the bounce.

SOCIAL ENGINEERING: Social engineering describes an intrusion that uses human rather than technical interaction. It often involves fooling someone into breaking normal security procedures.

SOCIAL MEDIA OPTIMIZATION: The process of tweaking your use of social media (including blogs, web 2.0 sites, communities and word of mouth) to maximize buzz, site traffic and conversions.

SOLO MAILING: A one-time broadcast to an email list, separate from regular newsletters or promotions, and often including a message from an outside advertiser or a special promotion from the list owner.

SOCIAL SEARCH: Web 2.0 tools that allow users to recommend or refer sites, articles, videos or other media to fellow users who have similar interests. Examples include shared bookmarking (del.icio.us), collaborative directories (zimbio), taggregators (Technorati), personalized verticals (Rollyo), social questions and answers (for example, Yahoo! Answers) and collaborative harvesters (Reddit).

SPAM: The popular name for unsolicited commercial email or junk mail.

SPONSORSHIP SWAP: An agreement between email list owners, publishers or advertisers to sponsor each other's mailings or newsletters for free.

SOFTWARE PIRACY: The unauthorized copying or use of digital content.

SPIDER: A program in a search engine that constantly 'crawls' around the internet to gather and update information about websites and pages that it finds. Spiders feed this information back to the search engine's database.

SPLASH PAGE (INTERSTITIAL): A preliminary page that precedes the regular home page of a website and usually promotes a particular site feature or provides advertising; it is frequently annoying to visitors.

SPYWARE: In the context of internet privacy and security, spyware is any program that is installed on a user's computer that secretly collects information about the user and transmits it to another party. The information that is being collected could be as simple as application programs used, or as detailed as passwords, emails sent and received — or the user's every keystroke. Usually, those receiving the information are advertisers, but they could be hackers, employers or government agencies. The FBI's 'Magic Lantern' is allegedly a spyware system.

STATIC IP ADDRESS: *see* **IP address**

STICKINESS: Refers to a site's ability to retain a visitor and to that visitor coming back.

STREAMING: The technology of sending compressed media (video, sound or both) over the internet and displaying the decompressed version in a viewer as the images or sounds arrive. Streaming allows you to see and hear the content while it is arriving, rather than downloading a whole file, decompressing it, and then only playing it. You need a player, client or plug-in to receive and instantly decompress the streaming signal. As with most web media, the client software is freely downloadable. Two major providers of streaming technology are RealNetworks and Microsoft.

STRONG PASSWORD: A strong password always uses combinations of upper-case and lower-case letters, numbers and special characters such as # or %, and is six or more characters long. (*see also* **weak password**)

SUBJECT LINE: Copy that identifies what an email message is about, often designed to entice the recipient into opening the message. The subject line appears first in the recipient's inbox, often next to the sender's name or email address. It is repeated in the email message's header information inside the message.

SUBSCRIBE: The process of joining a mailing list, either through an email command, by filling out a web form, or offline by filling out a form or requesting to be added verbally. (If you accept verbal subscriptions, you should safeguard yourself by recording it and storing recordings along with the time and date, in a retrievable format.)

SUBSCRIBER: A person who has specifically requested to join a mailing list.

SUPPRESSION FILE: A list of email addresses that you have removed from your regular mailing lists, either because they have opted out of your lists or because they have notified other mailers that they do not want to receive mailings from your company.

SYMBIAN: An open-source operating system designed for mobile devices.

SYNCHRONOUS: Literally this term means 'at the same time', and it usually refers to communication among people online. Chat is synchronous, email is asynchronous. (*see also* **chat**, **asynchronous**)

T1, T3: A T1 is the most commonly used digital line in the United States, Canada and Japan. T1 uses copper wire to carry data at a rate of 1.5 million bits per second (Mbps). A T3 line, also copper, provides a rate of 44.7 Mbps.

TAG: A keyword, term or descriptor given to a piece of online information (for example, a web page, an internet bookmark, a video, a photograph), to help it to be found searching or filtering systems.

TCP/IP (TRANSMISSION CONTROL PROTOCOL/INTERNET PROTOCOL): TCP/IP is the protocol (or group of protocols) that allows computers to connect to and interact on the internet. It is the common language in which computers on the internet communicate. (*see also* **internet**)

TEST: A necessary step before sending an email campaign or newsletter. Many email clients permit you to send a test email before sending a regular email newsletter or solo mailing, in which you would send one copy of the message to an in-house email address and then review it for formatting or copy errors or improperly formatted links. Email marketers should also send a test campaign to a list of email addresses that are not in the deployment database to determine likely response rates and how well different elements in the message perform.

TEXT NEWSLETTER: Plain newsletter with words only, no colours, graphics, fonts or pictures; it can be received by anyone who has email.

THANK-YOU PAGE: A web page that appears after user has submitted an order or a form online.

TROJAN HORSE: A well-camouflaged program, imbedded inside, for example, a Word document macro, which can do damage to the computer on which it is executed, is known as a Trojan horse. (If a malicious program does not replicate, it is not a virus.) (*see also* **worm**, **virus**)

TWITTER: A free social networking and micro-blogging service that allows users to post updates (otherwise known as tweets) which are short text-based messages. These messages are forwarded to anyone who has subscribed to the member's tweets, and can be received on a computer or mobile phone.

UNIX: An operating system that is competing with systems such as Windows. It was the first operating system to be written to evolve as a free, open system that could be accessed and modified at will. It was widely adopted by academic institutions and became the basic operating system of many web servers in the early days of the internet. It is still a hugely successful operating system.

UPTIME: Refers to the amount of time that a system is operational.

UNIQUE REFERENCE NUMBER: A unique number assigned to a list member, usually by the email broadcast software, and used to track member behaviour (clicks, subscribes, unsubscribes) or to identify the member to track email delivery.

UNSUBSCRIBE: To remove oneself from an email list, either via an emailed command to the list server or by filling in a web form.

USABILITY: The study of how people interact with their environment. In online marketing, the term refers to a specialized form that focuses on web page and web site design. Usability can be measured in terms of satisfaction, learnability, efficiency, memorability and errors made.

USER-GENERATED CONTENT (UGC): UGC or consumer-generated media (CGM) refers to various kinds of content or media that are produced by end-users. Examples of UGC are discussion boards, blogs, social networking sites, news sites, trip planners, customer reviews, photo and image sharing sites, games, or community based sites that offer people the opportunity to share information about themselves or a common interest. (*see also* **consumer-generated media**)

URL (UNIFORM RESOURCE LOCATOR): A URL is the standard format for addressing any resource on the internet that is part of the world wide web, for example, http://www.britefire.co.za/category.aspx?categoryID=5

UUENCODE: A utility for encoding and decoding files that are exchanged on a network. Originally designed for use on UNIX systems, it is now used on all operating systems, usually for exchanging email attachments if a recipient does not have a MIME-compliant system.

VERTICAL MARKET (OR VERTICAL PORTAL): Portals that offer rich content within their field (updated news, advice, white papers, search functionality, promotional services, intraportal commerce functionality) are referred to as vertical markets or vertical portals.

VIRAL MARKETING: Any form of marketing which seeks to get message recipients to pass the communication on to friends, resulting in exponential growth of exposure to the message.

VIRTUAL: Defined as that which is not real, but displays the full qualities of the real. For example, something that is simulated in a computer, or which exists on-line, such as a virtual world, for example, Second Life.

VIRTUAL PRIVATE NETWORK (VPN): A private network that uses the public internet infrastructure, but augments standard security systems by using a 'tunnelling' protocol. A wide area network (WAN) can be expensive to build and maintain because it uses dedicated private lines. A VPN is a low-cost internet-based version of a WAN. It gives an enterprise the ability to securely share data on public lines. VPNs use encryption, but instead of simply encrypting the message, their tunnelling protocol also encrypts the IP number of the sender and receiver. (*see also* **LAN, WAN**)

VIRUS: A malicious program that invades computers and replicates itself, inflicting temporary or permanent damage of some kind to files, computers or whole networks. A virus is always attached to a legitimate program or data file and usually requires a user to take some action (such as executing the host file) before it can do its work. Viruses can be hidden in documents or other applications, or may be disguised as innocent executable files. They may be transmitted by unknowing users exchanging files by email, FTP, diskette or CD. (*see also* **worm, Trojan horse**)

VIRUS SCANNER: Also known as antivirus software, this is a program that regularly checks a computer's drives or incoming files for any known viruses, alerts users to potential problems and often tries to repair damage done by viruses.

VISUAL BASIC: A Microsoft environment in which programmers use a graphical user interface to put together programs by selecting and modifying pieces of already-written Basic code.

VRML (VIRTUAL REALITY MODELLING LANGUAGE). VRML (pronounced vermal) is a language for creating three-dimensional images and experiences on the internet. Typically, VRML would create a room or a building that appears to be three-dimensional, and a user could 'walk' through it using keyboard commands or a mouse or joystick.

WAN (WIDE AREA NETWORK): Usually an intranet spread out over such distances that the local area networks (LANs) that comprise it are connected by dedicated lines. (*see also* **LAN**)

.WAV: A .wav or WAV file is a common type of audio file in Windows environments.

WEAK PASSWORD: A password that includes your name, or a word that can be found in a dictionary, that is less than six characters long and that does not mix upper- and lower-case letters, special characters and numbers. (*see also* **strong password**)

WEB: *see* **World Wide Web**

WEB 2.0: The term used to describe the evolution of the web from a series of more or less centralized silos of information to a high-speed platform for distributed services, especially social networking and collaboration. User-generated content (UGC) is a key characteristic of web 2.0, which is also known as the read-write web. (*see also* **user-generated content**)

WEB 3.0: There is much debate over what web 3.0 is. Some people say that it refers to the semantic web, others say its all about artificial intelligence, and others define it as an era of web's development (that is, the third decade of the web, from 2010 to 2020). Web 3.0 should be seen in the context of web 1.0 and web 2.0, so web 3.0 will be characterized by semantics, but there will be other important technology developments that accompany it and that upgrade the back-end of the web (as opposed to a front-end user experience focus) to make it an intelligent web. So web 3.0 is web 2.0 with a brain. It is the convergence of the technology, semantics and standards that will drive new applications of the way users interact with information and each other. (*see also* **semantic web, web 2.0**)

WEB BUG: A small graphic on a web page or in an HTML email message that is coded to monitor who is reading the web page or email message. A web bug is typically a colourless (therefore invisible) one-pixel-by-one-pixel graphic. It can collect the IP address of the computer on which it is viewed and other data that is useful to marketers. Web bugs are also known as clear gifs, tracker gifs, 1X1 gifs, invisible gifs or web beacons.

WEBINAR (WEB-BASED SEMINAR): A conference or training session, which geographically remote participants attend by logging on over the internet. Usually in a webinar, the leader shows presentations or software applications on the screens of participants by 'sharing' the contents of his/her own computer screen. Often the leader will remotely take control of a participant's computer to accomplish some task while the participant watches. Webinars use various communication tools for interaction, including chat, instant messaging, audio and video.

WEBMAIL: Any of several web-based email clients. Users have to go to a website to access or download email instead of using a desktop application. Some examples are Gmail, Yahoo! Mail and Hotmail.

WELCOME MESSAGE: A message that is automatically sent to new list members as soon as their email addresses are added successfully.

WEB PAGE: *see* **website**

WEB SPEED: This term essentially means 'much faster than in normal business'. It implies transactions that take place in real time, and business and technology that evolve in internet time.

WEBSITE: A document or collection of linked documents on the world wide web. Each document consists of web pages formatted in HTML. Each web page may contain text, images or multimedia components such as animation, video or sound. The first web page on a website is usually called the homepage. (*see also* **HTML, world wide web**)

WHITELIST: Advance-authorized list of email addresses, held by an ISP, subscriber or other email service provider, which allows email messages to be delivered regardless of spam filters. (*see also* **spam**)

WI-FI: Wireless technology that provides internet access without the need for a cable connection. A Wi-Fi enabled device such as a PC can connect to the internet when within range of a wireless network that is connected to the internet. The area covered by a Wi-Fi access point is called a hotspot. In addition to private use in homes and offices, Wi-Fi is publicly available at Wi-Fi hotspots provided to subscribers either free, or at a fee.

WIKI: Software that allows users to create, edit and link web pages easily. It is often used for collaborative and community websites. Wiki wiki is the Hawaiian expression for 'fast'.

WINDOWS NT: Microsoft's operating system, with a more robust capability than Windows. While Windows is a PC operating system, NT is designed for servers and workstations.

WINZIP: A popular file compression program for Windows systems that saves compressed files with a .zip file extension. (*see also* **compressed file, zipped file**)

WIRELESS WEB: The use of the world wide web through a wireless device, such as a mobile phone or personal digital assistant (PDA).

WISH LISTS: A merchandising technique that allows registered website users to store a list of products they would like, much like a digital version of a wedding registry.

WORD OF MOUTH (WOM): An emerging area in marketing that attempts to measure and/or harness the power of personal recommendations. With the explosion of blog readership, WOM has become a hot topic in virtually every industry.

WORLD WIDE WEB: The part of the internet in which data and multimedia are made available on web servers formatted in HTML. It refers to both the network of web servers and the content of those servers. 'World-Wide Web' was the name of the first software toolset for building web servers and websites. Nowadays 'the web' is typically spelled with a lower-case 'w'.

WORM: Like a virus, but it does not need a disguising host program to travel from one computer to another, nor does it require any action from a human being to do its work. It travels on its own, exploiting chinks in the armour of security systems, operating systems, virus scanners and firewalls. It penetrates computers to replicate and do damage. Worms are designed to disrupt networks rather than individual computers. (*see also* **virus, Trojan horse**)

XML (EXTENSIBLE MARKUP LANGUAGE): XML is a language that allows users to share data and interactive applications on the internet. XML is similar to HTML, but while HTML describes how a document should look, XML describes the nature of the content of the document and how it should function. XML is widely accepted as the language that will enable sophisticated ecommerce to work on the internet. (*see also* **RSS**)

ZIPPED FILE: A file that has been compressed by the WinZip compression program. (*see also* **compressed file, WinZip, zipped file**)

Index